ROUTLEDGE LIBRARY EDITIONS: THE GERMAN ECONOMY

Volume 8

MANAGERS AND MANAGEMENT IN WEST GERMANY

MANAGERS AND MANAGEMENT IN WEST GERMANY

PETER LAWRENCE

LONDON AND NEW YORK

First published in 1980 by Croom Helm Ltd

This edition first published in 2018
by Routledge
2 Park Square, Milton Park, Abingdon, Oxon OX14 4RN

and by Routledge
711 Third Avenue, New York, NY 10017

Routledge is an imprint of the Taylor & Francis Group, an informa business

© 1980 Peter Lawrence

All rights reserved. No part of this book may be reprinted or reproduced or utilised in any form or by any electronic, mechanical, or other means, now known or hereafter invented, including photocopying and recording, or in any information storage or retrieval system, without permission in writing from the publishers.

Trademark notice: Product or corporate names may be trademarks or registered trademarks, and are used only for identification and explanation without intent to infringe.

British Library Cataloguing in Publication Data
A catalogue record for this book is available from the British Library

ISBN: 978-1-138-29360-1 (Set)
ISBN: 978-1-315-18656-6 (Set) (ebk)
ISBN: 978-0-415-78873-1 (Volume 8) (hbk)
ISBN: 978-1-315-22305-6 (Volume 8) (ebk)

Publisher's Note
The publisher has gone to great lengths to ensure the quality of this reprint but points out that some imperfections in the original copies may be apparent.

Disclaimer
The publisher has made every effort to trace copyright holders and would welcome correspondence from those they have been unable to trace.

Managers and Management in West Germany

Peter Lawrence

CROOM HELM LONDON

©1980 Peter Lawrence
Croom Helm Ltd, 2-10 St John's Road, London SW11

British Library Cataloguing in Publication Data

Lawrence, Peter
   Managers and management in West Germany.
   1. Industrial management – Germany, West
   I. Title
   658'. 00943   HD70.G2

   ISBN 0-85664-912-0

TO MY MOTHER

Printed and bound in Great Britain by
Redwood Burn Limited Trowbridge & Esher

CONTENTS

Preface

Acknowledgements

1. Economic Life: Past and Present 1
2. The Structure of German Firms 30
3. The Background of German Management 56
4. The Character of German Management 85
5. The Views of German Managers 101
6. Production Management 124
7. The Foreman 152
8. The Standing of Industry 163
9. Export Potential? 176

Bibliography 191

Index 199

PREFACE

Most books about management have been written by Americans, and with the USA as the empirical reference, implicitly or explicitly. Books in English about management in non-English speaking countries are not very numerous, serious studies of management in such countries usually being the work of their own nationals.

This makes the present book a little unusual. It is about management in West Germany but it is not by a German. What is more, it is probably a different book from the one a German would have written. A German might have chosen, for instance, to emphasise the universalism of management and corporate practice, whereas the present writer has chosen to discuss those features of management in West Germany which appear distinctive and which are interesting from a non-German standpoint. West Germany is a particularly fruitful subject for this kind of exercise since there are many distinctive features for the observer whose base line is American-influenced Britain. The approach and emphasis is different in Germany, where the American business-marketing-corporate-organisational orientation is less in evidence, and where the dominant orientation is (still) technical-production-entrepreneurial-pragmatic.

The treatment here has also been influenced by the author's historical and sociological training as well as his British nationality. This has determined his interest in institutions, the relationship between German companies and their business environment and in the views which German managers themselves express about their work. There are also a number of what one might term sociological sub-plots, or implicit discussions of phenomena which are sociological concerns. These have been deliberately left as part of the latent structure of the book, but they are there nevertheless.

A contribution has been made, for instance, to the study of elites. Industrial managers are members of an elite group, and this claim is particularly valid for West Germany with its national emphasis on economic achievement. The ensuing account of German managers constitutes, *inter alia*, a partial characterisation of an elite group and its relationship to the wider society. In discussing managers and management one is also making an oblique contribution to an understanding of industrial relations. This is not as marked as it would be in a book about British management, since wage negotiations in West Germany are typically between an employers' federation on the one hand and a trade union on the other. Nevertheless, if German management does not constitute one half of the bargaining equation, it is still the major part of one of those 'two sides of industry' and its character has some significance for the quality of industrial relations.

The characterisation of 'the professions', a standard theme in occupational sociology, is also taken up and illustrated with reference to both managers and engineers. The view expressed here is that the issue of whether or not any particular occupation should rank as a profession is not a significant one for an understanding of what work is done, or how it is done. Indeed it is an issue which the Germans, both linguistically and empirically, have largely avoided.

There is also a sociological orientation in the importance attached to the beliefs and convictions of German managers, and these are explored particularly in the three middle chapters. The *point de départ* is that what people believe to be true and primary is an important determinant of action and outcomes. If German managers did not believe in *Technik*, their version of entrepreneurialism, and in the achieving society, the character and practice of German management would be very different.

This exercise of characterising German management tends to expand at various points into a discussion of some institutions and aspects of German society. Most of what emerges, both from the main task and from these discussions, tends to underline the distinctive nature of German society *vis à vis* both Britain and the USA. Indeed the whole book may be regarded as negative evidence for the contentions of convergence theory, which asserts the increasing homogeneity of highly industrialised societies. The more one is able to make comparisons on management and industrial organisation between countries such as Britain, France and West Germany the more suspect even general labels of the 'advanced industrial society' kind become.

The book is also meant to be a reminder that there are other modes of explanation besides the economic. While the main purpose is simply to characterise German management, there are several points at which features of German management and industrial organisation are related to the considerable success enjoyed by West Germany as a national economy. Here a minor paradox exists. Neither management, nor the organisational context in which it operates, is an economic phenomenon in the sense that say a country's monetary policy is. Yet the quality and

Preface

purposefulness of management is an important determinant of a country's economic success.

Finally the discussion of German management also countenances the possibility that other countries may learn from German practice. Although this kind of complex cross-cultural borrowing is fraught with all sorts of difficulties, and these are frankly presented in the last chapter, it is firmly argued in the conclusion that German management does display a number of definite strengths.

ACKNOWLEDGEMENTS

This book is based on a variety of sources. On the one hand I have made use of the literature on management, German industry and institutions, of the research of others, and of handbooks and official publications. On the other hand the book is also, in part, an indirect result of a number of research assignments I have carried out in West Germany, and of considerable direct contact with German companies. In this connection I would like to thank many business firms in West Germany for their hospitality and readiness to help a foreign academic, and many individual managers for giving up time to talk to me about their work.

Several of my friends have read all or part of the manuscript and made helpful comments about it. In this connection I would like to thank Michael Fores, former Senior Economic Adviser at the Department of Industry; Ian Glover, Lecturer in Business Studies at the Dundee College of Technology; Stanley Hutton, Professor of Mechanical Engineering at the University of Southampton; David Jenkinson, Senior Lecturer in German at the University of London, Goldsmiths' College; and Arndt Sorge, Research Fellow at the Internationales Institut für Management und Verwaltung, West Berlin. I have also discussed some of the ideas with Peter Hollowell, Lecturer in Sociology at the University of Southampton. For any errors and inadequacies I alone, of course, am responsible.

Finally I would like to thank my secretary, Mrs Diana Hodgkinson, for a splendid and splendidly fast typing of the manuscript.

Peter Lawrence   Le Grand Pressigny

PREFACE TO THE RE-ISSUE OF 2017

Would-be authors are not always pleased with what publishers say to them. But we writers do get some breaks.

In 1978 I approached a publisher with a proposal for a book that focussed on the training and deployment of engineers in West Germany (as it then was). After hearing about what I had been doing the joint founder of the publishing house came back with a counter proposal: why not go for a general characterisation of German management, underlining what is different and interesting about it, and addressing the issue of whether management itself contributed to the *Wirtschaftswunder* (economic miracle). I bought it. The book was written in four months in the spring of 1979.

What came before was three to four years travelling around Germany to carry out research projects commissioned by the British Department of Industry and later by the Science Research Council. I endlessly visited companies, interviewed managers by the score, had contact with academics, administrators and educators, and carried out a nationwide survey of engineers. The best bit came at the end when I executed what the trade calls observational case studies, that is, spending two or three days shadowing individual managers in manufacturing companies, sitting in on meetings, and being party to all that happened, formal and informal; by then I was a fluent German speaker, and had taught in a German university before this research started.

All this gave me the confidence to say something about what German management is like.

Much has happened since then. Most obviously the opening of the Berlin Wall on 'super-Thursday' (9 November 1989) and the re-unification of Germany the following October. More generally the fall of European Communism left capitalism as the only economic system and this in turn furthering the dominance of neo-liberalism and he dynamic of globalisation. And in all the Western countries the service sector became larger than the manufacturing sector, with (in some countries) much of the latter outsourced to low wage countries.

A lot of this, however, has impacted on Germany as a change of context rather than of substance.

Yes taxes are up and welfare is down, but in the German case this is largely the result of funding the reconstruction of the former East Germany. There have been blips with apprenticeship, but it is still a German institution. Germany is traditionally low on NEETs! The

Preface to the Re-issue of 2017

co-determination system, worker reps and the ubiquitous works council, are largely intact. So is the two tier board system for public companies. Among the personnel of management there are many more managers with Business Economics degrees (this is as close as the German State University system gets to the Western style business school), finance people are more common at the top, and merger and acquisition is no longer the rarity it once was, though Germany still exhibits a reluctance to having it 'done to them'. And the upper tranche of German banks have tended to switch from facilitating the German industrial estate to satisfying shareholder priorities.

But German management is still specialist rather than generalist, has comparatively low inter-company and inter-industry mobility, has an operational focus, benefits from strong training and competence at the lower level enabling larger spans of control and shorter hierarchies. German companies typically expect to sell on quality not price. Marketing is seen as being about the differing needs of individual customers, rather than a generalised promotion of the company offering. Germany still has a robust *Mittelstand* – mid-sized companies, often privately owned – frequently dominating international niche markets. Export is seen as the norm, rather than overseas manufacturing. Germany's boon this century has been selling capital goods to the likes of China and Brazil.

And as befits the last country to cross the 'services trump manufacturing' line, leading German academic Arndt Sorge declares that:

> Germany has remained a dominant industrial economy, in which manufacturing and related services account for more value-added and employment than elsewhere except for its own fringe of alpine countries. This comes out as the singularly important comparative feature in a long-term perspective.

But substantial continuity is not the only issue. We are enriched by knowledge and understanding of that which sustains the social order in which we live, and such a tale is told in my book. A legacy of the Second World War is that eventually it gave rise to a Germany which was prosperous, decent and peaceable.

Let us hope we never lose it.

Peter Lawrence

1 ECONOMIC LIFE: PAST AND PRESENT

Now

The German economy is the context within which management functions. This economic context has been revolutionised since the end of the Second World War, though the revolutionary change itself is already a thing of the past.

West Germany is now a major economic power, and has been for some years. Since the late 1950s West Germany has been the world's second largest trading nation.[1] West Germany also has the fourth largest gross national product in the world:

Country[2]	GNP 1975 (in millions of US $)
USA	1,508,680
USSR	665,910
Japan	495,180
West Germany	408,756

A few comparisons may be of interest:

Country[3]	GNP 1975 (in millions of US $)
France	304,600
UK	214,940
Canada	151,730
Brazil	107,870
Australia	76,190

The richest countries of the world, using the measure of gross national product *per capita*, are no longer to be found in either northwest Europe or North America:

Country[4]	GNP *per capita* 1975 (in US $)
Kuwait	11,510
United Arab Emirates	10,480
Qatar	8,320

2   *Economic Life: Past and Present*

Setting aside these anomalies and concentrating on the industrialised countries West Germany is in sixth place:

Country[5]	GNP *per capita* 1975 (in US $)
Switzerland	8,050
Sweden	7,880
USA	7,060
Denmark	6,920
Canada	6,650
West Germany	6,610

Again some comparisons may be of interest:

Country[6]	GNP *per capita* 1975 (in US $)
Norway	6,540
Belgium	6,070
Luxembourg	6,050
France	5,760
Australia	5,640
Iceland	5,620
Netherlands	5,590
Finland	5,100
Austria	4,720
New Zealand	4,680
Japan	4,460
East Germany	4,230
UK	3,840
Czechoslovakia	3,710
Israel	3,580

West Germany has for years enjoyed a substantial trade surplus:

Year[7]	Imports	Exports (both in millions of DM)
1969	97,320	113,353
1970	109,130	125,144
1971	119,630	135,912
1972	128,146	148,915
1973	144,509	178,228
1974	177,967	230,068
1975	182,521	221,206
1976	220,556	256,303

It will be noted that West Germany continued to enjoy a favourable trade balance throughout the period of the oil crisis and the world recession, indeed 1974 was a record year with a trade surplus of over DM 50,000 million.

The trade surpluses for 1975 and 1976 were not so impressive, but the first nine months of 1977 showed a 10 per cent improvement over the previous year.

All the wealthy industrialised countries fell victim to inflation after the 1973 oil crisis. There were, however, remarkable differences in degree. If we take the change in consumer price indices over 12 months up to May 1978, well after the worst effects of the oil crisis and ensuing world recession, marked differences are still apparent. West Germany is in second place in a list of 25 countries including the major industrialised countries of the free world:

Country[8]	Change in consumer price index over 12 months to May 1978 as a %
Switzerland	1.6
West Germany	2.7
Luxembourg	2.9
Japan	3.5
Netherlands	3.5
Austria	3.8
Belgium	4.4
Ireland	6.2
USA	6.6
Portugal	7.5
Norway	7.7
UK	7.7
Australia	8.2
Canada	9.0
France	9.0
Denmark	10.8
Sweden	11.5
Italy	12.2
Greece	13.5
Yugoslavia	14.0
New Zealand	14.7
Spain	22.0
Iceland	42.8
Turkey	52.3
Average OECD Total	8.1
Average OECD Europe	10.3
Average EEC	7.5

4   *Economic Life: Past and Present*

If one takes the longer term indicator of consumer price indices for 1977 where 1970 = base 100 then West Germany is in first place among the same group of countries. West German, that is, had the smallest rise in consumer prices over this seven year period:

Country[9]	Consumer Price Index 1977 (1970 = 100)
West Germany	146.3
Switzerland	149.2
USA	156.1
Austria	161.0
Canada	165.4
Luxembourg	166.0
Belgium	174.8
Norway	178.0
Sweden	180.2
France	183.2
Denmark	189.0
Japan	203.6
Australia	207.6
New Zealand	217.5
Finland	224.0
Greece	227.0
Italy	236.6
UK	249.0
Ireland	249.9
Spain	258.9
Portugal	302.4
Turkey	307.3
Iceland	519.0

West Germany had, and continues to have, its unemployment difficulties. In comparison with other industrial countries, however, the German record has been quite good. In 1973 Germany was in fourth place on a list of 19 West European countries plus the USA, Canada, and Japan; that is, only three of these countries had lower unemployment figures than West Germany:

Economic Life: Past and Present   5

Country[10]	Unemployed as proportion of civilian working population 1973
Luxembourg	0.0
Switzerland	0.0
Denmark	0.7
West Germany	1.0

By 1977 rather more countries could claim lower unemployment figures than West Germany, but Germany's position was still not unfavourable seen in an international context:

Country[11]	Unemployed as % of civilian working population 1977
Switzerland	0.4
Luxembourg	0.6
Norway	1.5
Sweden	1.8
Japan	2.0
West Germany	4.0
Belgium	4.3
France	4.9
UK	5.8
Denmark	5.9
Finland	6.0
Spain	6.3
USA	6.9
Netherlands	7.0
Canada	8.1
Ireland	9.7

West Germany has a better strike record than most countries. For the period 1966-70 Germany had the best record, that is the fewest working days lost through strikes, of 16 West European countries plus the USA, Canada, Australia, New Zealand and Japan.[12] For the longer period 1966-75, West Germany was in second place:

6   Economic Life: Past and Present

Country[13]	Annual average working days lost per 1000 persons employed 1966-75
Sweden	49
West Germany	52
Norway	61
Netherlands	62
Japan	247
France	303
New Zealand	355
Belgium	368
Denmark	535
UK	775
Finland	833
Ireland	927
Australia	1,036
USA	1,318
Italy	1,766
Canada	1,849

Enough has been said to indicate that West Germany is a rich country, a substantial member of the international economic community, and a country which compares well with most of its neighbours on the evidence of statistics on economic performance and industrial well-being. These facts, other things being equal, give an added interest and salience to the study of German management.

There is an extension to this argument. Not only does German management function in a society that is economically successful now; this same society, only 30 years ago, was just emerging from a period of extreme, if artificial, poverty.

Then

That a country experiences deprivations during wartime is obvious. That Germany, on the losing side in the world's worst war, suffered particularly is well recognised. What is perhaps less readily appreciated is that in several respects Germany suffered more in the period 1945-8 than in the period of her successive military failures, that is, between 1942 and 1945.[14] With the end of the War, death and destruction in combat and through aerial bombardment ended: they were replaced by homelessness, hunger and death by 'natural causes' — malnutrition.

It was, in fact, the purely physical destruction of German cities which most impressed those who wrote eye-witness accounts. Here is a young British lieutenant's account of his entry into Hamburg in an armoured car in May 1945:

> If the damage in Harburg had been startling to our eyes the streets and waterfront of Hamburg were a revelation. None of us had ever seen anything to equal this wholesale destruction. It was Caen all over again, only ten times worse because ten times as big an area was affected. In the half light we could not see the damage in detail, but it was apparent that whole rows of houses, whole blocks, were a mere mass of rubble, sometimes heaped to one side, sometimes blotting out what had been a road.[15]

An American officer, travelling through parts of Germany already liberated by the Allies early in April 1945, still some weeks before the end of the War, made the following comment in his report:

> In every important town the preliminary official estimates of the damage were over 75%. The larger towns are almost completely destroyed, the smaller outlying communities on the other hand are to a large extent unscarred. According to official estimates, for instance, Saarbrucken is more than 90% destroyed, but damage in the area of the town's rural hinterland is very slight. The same applies to Frankfurt and Kassel, where damage is estimated at 80% or more.[16]

Another American officer reported similiarly on a journey through Germany in May 1945:

> The towns offer the well-known picture of destruction, which imposes itself everywhere; only Wiesbaden has been spared serious damage. The centres of the large towns Frankfurt, Cologne, and Essen are completely desolated. In Cologne and Essen even the outer suburbs are badly damaged. The centre of Cologne is completely deserted. In these three towns many streets are still completely blocked, and in some cases it is impossible to recognise them under the rubble. Apart from a few standpipes, the water supply has not yet been reconnected. Nowhere is there any public transport, except in Düsseldorf where one sees the occasional tram.[17]

Germans use two rather vivid phrases to refer to the end of the war and all that it entailed. One is *der Zusammenbruch*, the collapse, break up, disintegration. Used with the definite article it is a standard expression referring to 1945. The other is *die Stunde O*, the hour nought, the absolute zero: the time when there was no government, no index of industrial production, no trams, no water, no bread in the shops. The early occupation period was also characterised by widespread lawlessness. Thousands of foreign workers, the 'slave workers' of the Third Reich, were liberated by the advancing Allies and set about looting. This again was noted in American reports from the April-May 1945 period:

> Without question the foreign workers have plundered on a considerable scale — a universal accompaniment of their holiday mood. The men made for the wine cellars, the women for the clothes shops, taking on the way everything edible they could get their hands on.[18]

And the same source notes that this looting was not confined to the foreign workers:

> In the devastated areas of every town one sees Germans, men and women, with shopping bags stuffed with loot taken from damaged flats and shops belonging to other people.[19]

Another feature of the early *Zusammenbruch* period was the fear of epidemic disease which was noted by an American officer in April 1945:

> The single problem, which really gives cause for concern, is the lack of water, since this poses a threat to public health. In Kassel the officers of the military administration were concerned that the beginnings of a typhoid outbreak might spread rapidly, since the civilian population in Kassel have been taking water from the damaged system and from (flooded) bomb-craters. (At the time of the last heavy air raid on Kassel, hospital patients were dispersed over the town; these included 20 typhus cases, 8 of these have never been brought back to hospital.)[20]

In these American reports dating from April 1945, there is a remark concerning food and health:

Nowhere have I seen signs of acute food shortage or extensive health problems.[21]

This observation, doubtless true when it was written at the beginning of April 1945, was not to apply for long. A month later another American official notes:

> At the moment people in the towns are struggling to solve the simplest problems of human existence: they clear rubble, bring their scattered possessions back into houses, return on foot to their old apartments where these had been evacuated, petition the military authorities for travel permits, and queue for food.[22]

If lawlessness, chaos and rubble were the dominant features of the first few weeks of 'peacetime', these soon gave way to homelessness hunger and illness. The available housing was very poor largely as a result of the Allied bombing. The early eye-witness accounts agree that private housing was the worst victim of the bombing, and some were surprised that even enormous industrial complexes, for instance, the Ford factory in Cologne and the IG Farben chemical works in Frankfurt, had escaped almost unscathed. The housing shortage was made worse by the presence of the occupying forces and military government personnel; to put it bluntly, they requisitioned on a grand scale. As if this was not enough, Germans expelled from Sudetenland, which was acquired by Czechoslovakia, and from the German territory east of the Oder-Neisse line, which was acquired by Poland, poured into the rest of Germany in their millions (see below). The result of all this was two-fold. There was widespread over-crowding, and a large section of the population was forced to live in damaged, inadequate buildings, or quite simply in cellars. A detailed and moving account of the miseries of the housing situation, supported by extensive photographic evidence, is given by Victor Gollancz.[23]

Another British socialist, Fenner Brockway, was quick to observe the effects of malnutrition on a visit to Germany in the spring of 1946:

> As I walk I look at the people. The first glance brings a surprise: they are well-dressed — better, I think, than at home. Then I look again, and notice the frequency of ill-looking faces, grey and yellow, lines running from eyes to mouth, protruding cheek-bones ... Never anywhere else have I seen these gaunt features passing with such regularity.[24]

The explanation is not hard to find. The food allowances in the British Zone at the time of Brockway's visit were as follows[25]:

Basic (i.e. German adults not engaged in heavy or very heavy manual work)	1,048 calories
Heavy Workers	1,753 calories
Very Heavy Workers	2,312 calories
British Civilians	2,800 calories

It should be noted, too, that the 2,800 calorie allowance was for British civilians in post-war food-rationed Britain, not for those working in occupied Germany whose allowance was much higher.

Brockway, or rather his friend Wolf, gives an account of a German family meal, in Berlin, in fact where the calorie allowance was a little higher:

> I've been hearing about calories and proteins: Wolf has seen what they mean in German homes and kitchens. He has been into one home today where there were actually potatoes (not officially distributed for some weeks); the family had bartered their cigarette allocation for them — one meal of potatoes for a month's cigarettes. The potatoes were fried with coffee grouts, kept from the previous day's *Ersatzkaffee*: the woman says that the grouts give the potatoes a 'particular taste'. This main potato dish was preceded by 'soup'. Wolf was present when it was made, and it consisted entirely of bread crumbs and salt dissolved in hot water. The family had 'tea' with the meal, tea made from pine tree needles.[26]

This general food shortage had a number of consequences. Most obviously it encouraged large scale black market operations. It had the effect of depressing the marriage rate, although marriage to members of the Allied Forces was seen as highly desirable by German girls. Similarly, it made employment with the occupying forces, especially employment in their messes, very attractive to Germans since it opened up opportunities for supplementing the small official food ration. And of course undernourishment, over a sustained period, led to a rise in the mortality rate, a rise in the infant mortality rate and in the rates of particular illnesses associated with malnutrition and poor housing. To give one gruesome illustration, in April 1946, the month of Brockway's visit, no less than 3,969 *new* cases of tuberculosis were reported in the British Zone and British Sector of Berlin; this was not an unusually high figure for this post-war period — in the following month the corresponding figure was over 5,000.[27]

There was some easing of conditions as the Occupation period progressed, though these were not dramatic and some of the deprivations detailed in the last few pages lasted into the 1950s. Food allowances were raised from the 1945-6 low (in August 1946 in the British Zone, for instance). The British and Americans set up a relief scheme at an early stage in the Occupation, which was superseded by Marshall Aid (see below). Industrial productivity gradually picked up, though where the availability of consumer goods is concerned the beneficial effects of greater output were not experienced because of hoarding and a devalued currency (see below).

The two pictures of Germany which we have given, Germany now, and Germany at the end of the Second World War, make Germany unique. None of the other very rich nations has experienced this kind of rise from extreme poverty to considerable wealth. Japan, the closest contender, was not laid as low as Germany at the end of the Second World War, and did not suffer from loss of territory as did Germany. Neither have the Japanese reached the same standard of personal wealth as the Germans, and in terms of GNP *per capita* are in fact closer to Britain than to West Germany.

Germany's present economic strength, and the transition from rubble to riches, endow the study of German management with great interest. It is an implicit thesis of this book that German management has made its contribution to this transition and continues to sustain this level of national economic performance. Two qualifications should be made, however, one of which should be developed in some detail. First, there is no suggestion that 'the German way' is the best way, or the only way. It is argued only that West Germany is an economically successful country, that this success is quite overwhelming when seen against the background of the miseries of the Occupation period, that the quality of German management is *a* relevant factor, and that additional interest therefore attaches to understanding the nature and dynamics of German management. Perhaps most of all one wants to know what is *German* about German management, what is particular, distinctive, or unique.

Secondly, there is no suggestion that the German economic achievement is due to the quality of German management *alone*. A lot of factors are relevant to the post-war economic rise of Germany. Some of these factors have nothing to do with management, and in other cases one might argue that German management simply embodied or typified a more general phenomenon. It is not the central purpose of this book to explain Germany's post-war rise, or to offer a comprehensive analysis of that country's economic success. It is, however, worth indicating what some of these other factors are, and for a number of reasons.

First, the recent history of West Germany is unique among European countries. Secondly, although 'what went on' in Germany in the 1933-45 period is well known, the socio-economic features of German life after 1945 are much less familiar. Thirdly, some post-1945 developments, and in particular certain features of the national situation relevant to an understanding of the German post-war recovery, constitute the background and context of German management's performance. And fourthly, this last statement is not only true by definition: there are some very direct connections between features of German management and the way it works on the one hand, and aspects of German society which facilitated the post-war recovery on the other.

How then was the economic recovery of Germany accomplished? By what stages and for what reasons did West Germany become the economic giant of Western Europe? There are many answers, or to put it differently, a range of factors one has to take into account. Paradoxically several of these derive from the War itself, from reactions to Nazism, or from the policies adopted by the Occupying Powers.

Those Lovely New Machines

If one asks Germans to speculate on their economic achievements, and they are quite happy to co-operate in this venture though in a spirit of mature reminiscence rather than boastful pride, the most popular explanation is that wartime destruction and, more particularly, the dismantling of plant and machinery by the Allies meant that Germany was eventually re-equipped with modern plants and technology. This answer is given just as frequently by the man in the street as by the spokesman of industry. It deserves serious consideration, but this should not disguise the fact that it may be an appealing explanation for other reasons. It combines very nicely modesty, impersonality and a touch of irony.

In the discussion of British economic problems in the mid 1970s much play was made with the idea that the basic British problem was too little investment in industry implying too little modernisation of plant and machinery and too little increase in productive output. It is surprising how acceptable this argument has been (whether it is right is another issue). Its charm, also, resides in its impersonality. Lack of investment cannot be blamed on the workers, at any rate it was not their responsibility or that of their organised representatives. Managements may have been accused of lack of foresight, but no more, and they can always blame government policies and wage rises for eating into what would have been retained earnings. Maybe 'the government' should have done something, but it had other things to worry about and anyway 'the facts' did not emerge until after the event. In short, it is an explantion that, while it would be an exaggeration to say it leaves no one responsible, does not make anyone 'a bad manager' or ' a bad worker'; it is safely impersonal.

The 'new technology' explanation has a similar appeal for Germans in that it shifts the praise rather than the blame. It is a modest answer, much better than bragging about hard work and efficiency, and in any case the Germans are tired of being stereotyped in this way. No one can take exception to the humble rejoinder 'well, we just had a head start with new equipment you see'. The answer contains, too, just the right touch of (unspoken) irony. If only USAAF and the RAF had been a little more restrained (with their bombing) and the Occupying Powers a little less zealous over reparations (dismantling factories), the 'economic miracle' might never have happened.

None of this is to say that the argument is not valid, but there are two qualifications. First, the importance of the new equipment has been overplayed by the Germans and sometimes by others writing about them. And secondly, the view that reparations in kind (i.e. the dismantling of plant and machinery by the Allies) was a blessing in disguise because it led to replacements which were modern is meaningless without a consideration of the other vital factor, Marshall Aid.

Dismantling

In settling the reparations arrangements the victorious Allies departed from the tradition established at the end of the Franco-Prussian War (1870–1) and the Great War (1914-18) by providing for 'reparations in kind'. These involved the seizure of German goods, forced levies from current production and the dismantling of German plants and equipment. It is the last which is of central interest here. The dismantled plants and equipment were 'shipped off' not exclusively to the homelands of the Occupying Powers but to these and to various other 'Nazi victim' countries which were regarded as having a right to compensation. The major Allies (with the exception of Russia) did not in fact make massive gains from dismantling. The major work on the French Occupation Zone, for instance, shows that of the 110 factories dismantled in the French Zone between 1945-9, only 22 actually went to France, and France was regarded as the most hard-headed of the three western Occupying Powers.[28]

The whole story of the dismantling of the factories is beset with contradictions. The number of plants and factories designated for dismantling and transfer (by the three Western Zones only[29]) was set high in the first instance and subsequently revised downwards:

	(number designated for transfer)
March 1946	1,800
August 1947	858
February 1949	697
November 1949	680

By the autumn of 1949 all one could say about the dismantling target of 1946 was that 'it seemed a good idea at the time'. The reasons for the downward revision are not hard to find. The western Occupying Powers, at any rate Britain and the USA, were caught in a double contradiction. They were sanctioning the dismantling of factories, and thereby weakening Germany in the short-term, at the same time that they were feeding the Germans at their own expense. Whereas the French, with a largely rural and more nearly self-supporting occupation zone managed to balance the zonal trade balance and only allowed imports to exceed exports when it became clear that the Americans would cover the deficit, the British and the Americans themselves were from the start having to ship in food for the German population. Furthermore, deteriorating relations with the Russians led America and Britain to desire a stable and self-supporting Germany not a weak and economically dependent Germany. The downward revision of the dismantling demands also conceals to some extent the degree of remission granted to Germany in this respect. Each time the list was shortened it tended to be the larger and more important factories which were reprieved.

Even the final list was not strictly adhered to. In the end, the total number of dismantled factories in all three western zones was only 668. These dismantlings represent:

30% of the iron and steel producing industry,
25% of the chemical industry,
13% of the war related mechanical engineering industry,
10% of the aeronautical industry.

This was a serious blow to German industry, but not a crippling one. The dismantling of individual factories could and did cause acute local hardship (and resentment) but we must take an overall view. The principal work on the economics of the occupation period claims that the resulting loss in total industrial capacity in the three western zones combined was only 8 per cent although the corresponding figure for the Russian Zone was 45 per cent.[30]

In fairness to the 'new technology' argument it should be added that the figures on dismantled factories do not do it complete justice. There were also official and unofficial acts of requisitioning which are difficult to quantify. Goods (including industrial plant and rolling stock) taken by Germany from conquered countries during the War were, where they could be identified, returned (the French were particularly zealous in seeking out the fruits of earlier German industrial looting). Berlin was in a special, and disadvantaged, category. The Russians were in control of the whole of Berlin for two months at the end of the War, and practised widespread dismantling in what later became the three western sectors of the City. If we add to the 8 per cent loss in overall productive capacity resulting from dismantling the estimated figure for damage to *industrial plant* resulting from Allied bombing (some 15-20 per cent for Germany as a whole – 25 per cent in the Ruhr in particular), this would give a figure of roughly one-quarter of Germany's industrial capacity destroyed or dismantled, to be advantageously replaced with new equipment subsequently. This rough figure of one-quarter, however, probably exaggerates the issue. When a factory is dismantled or taken away, it is a candidate for *complete* replacement; the effects of Allied bombing on the other hand were more likely to cause serious damage to industrial sites rather than complete obliteration, and several writers on the post-war period in Germany refer precisely to the ingenuity and persistence of German workers in digging through the rubble of factories and piecing together the remains. If, however, all destroyed or dismantled industrial plant and equipment was replaced with modern installations, as no doubt much of it was, this does represent a decided fillip to German industrial capacity.

Marshall Aid

It is sometimes said defensively by Britons that no one should be impressed by the German economic performance because it is all due to Marshall Aid. And it is also sometimes counter-argued that this proposition is invalid since Britain received twice as much under Marshall Aid as Germany.[31] This is partly true. Britain was the principal beneficiary of

Marshall Aid, France was in second place and Germany in third. This leaves out of account the fact that before the introduction of Marshall Aid, or more properly the European Recovery Programme (ERP), Germany benefited from another source of (principally) American aid, namely the Government and Relief in Occupied Areas (GARIOA) scheme. Germany's combined receipts under ERP and GARIOA exceeded those of any other country, amounting to roughly $4.4 billion.

The Western Allies, especially the Americans and the British, found the German population in their zones faced with massive food and fuel supply problems. GARIOA was called into existence to alleviate these problems and the threat of large scale starvation, disease and unrest. It delivered food principally and to a lesser extent fuel, seed and fertilisers, not industrial plant and equipment. In short, it was oriented to relief not reconstruction.

When GARIOA was succeeded by ERP the import emphasis shifted in the direction of industrial raw materials. Even at this stage, however, over half the received aid was in the form of relief rather than industrial supplies. Of over $1,108 million worth of aid received under ERP by the autumn of 1951 food imports accounted for 50.02 per cent, fuel for 4.92 per cent, raw materials and semi-finished goods for 41.50 per cent, machines and vehicles for 3.56 per cent.[32]

It is important to appreciate that the Western Allies did not in any direct sense deliver power plants or steel mills. The supplies delivered under the aid schemes were sold to consumers. The money from these sales constituted 'counterpart funds' which could be used, with the approval of the Occupying Powers and later the Federal Government, for the purposes of reconstruction. The emphasis here is not so much on industrial equipment as on transport and utilities. It served to rebuild the infrastructure of an industrial society rather than the industry itself. Even with these qualifications this foreign and principally American aid is of great importance. It saved Germany from wholesale starvation. It made a massive contribution to the early balance of payments position. And it contributed directly, and more importantly indirectly, to industrial reconstruction. Marshall Aid, commencing in 1948, and coinciding with the currency reform and the freeing of controls (see below) sparked off the economic recovery. Without foreign aid, widespread starvation and a decimation of the population would have been likely.

A limited renewal of plant and equipment and the assistance under the aid programmes were not the only beneficial results of the War. A number of favourable and facilitating circumstances also derive from the War and the traumas of the past. It is readily acknowledged that the West German economy suffered from the division of Germany at the end of the War, the eventual emergence of two sovereign German states and the loss of German territory in 1945 to Poland, Russia, Czechoslovakia and France (Saarland). In particular, the loss of territory to Poland meant the loss of an important agricultural area and some raw material deposits. What is less readily appreciated, however, is that there were some benefits in all this for West Germany.

Ten Million People in Search of a Home

Somewhere between 5,500,000 and 5,700,000 Germans died as a result of the Nazi Regime and the Second World War. These figures include those killed in action, those who died as prisoners of war and those missing believed dead. They also include half a million civilian casualties (principally as a result of Allied bombing), the German Jews who died in the extermination camps and approximately one and a half million who died, were killed, or deported to Russia in the course of the forced evacuations from territory ceded to Poland at the end of the War.[33]

Notwithstanding these gruesome statistics the population census of October 1946 revealed that the total population of the three western zones was five million higher than it had been before the War. The fact is explained by the influx of various categories of refugees. There are four phases or aspects of the refugee phenomenon. First, there is an indeterminate number who fled to the West before the advancing Russian armies. To appreciate the force behind this movement one must recognise the extreme terror inspired by the Russians. As an illustration one may mention a searing account of the early days of Russian occupation offered by a German doctor, Hans von Lehndorf.[34] In the winter of 1945 Lehndorf was working at a hospital in Insterburg, East Prussia (now part of Russia). His hospital was evacuated before the Russian advance and Lehndorf then worked in Königsberg and was there when it was taken by the Russians. The first few days of the Russian occupation proved the most dreadful. In his introduction to Lehndorf's book Constantine Fitzgibbon writes thus of the doctor's experiences:

> Only once does his doctor's courage seem to have deserted him. Trying to run a hospital in Königsberg amidst looting Russians who raped nurses and dying patients alike, who fired into the wards and tossed hand grenades into the blaze when the hospital caught fire, who smashed irreplaceable bottles of medicines and stole his surgical implements, his heart almost broke, and he was glad when he was arrested and the responsibility taken away.

One of the most telling facts in Lehndorf's narrative is that during the seige of Königsberg chemists dispensed cyanide on request to those who preferred suicide to Russian occupation. No one discussed the ethics of this, he noted, only the required dose.

Secondly, and this is by far the most important influx, there were the expellees (*Ausgewiesenen* or *Heimatsvertriebenen*). Some 2.4 million were expelled from Czechoslovakia (the 'Sudeten Germans' of pre-war fame), over half a million from Poland (pre-war boundaries) and a few from Hungary. The largest block however, resulted from territorial changes in the East. East Prussia, the part of Germany that before the War had been separated from the rest of the Reich by the Polish corridor, was divided after the War between Russia and Poland. And Poland advanced her western frontier up to the line of the Oder-Neisse rivers, thus occupying the former German provinces of Pomerania, part of Brandenburg, and Silesia. These territorial changes alone involved the evacuation of more than five million Germans. They did not all come to the western occupation zones but most did.

Thirdly, there were the refugees from the Russian Occupation Zone. From 1946-8 the number ran to an average of 700 per day. By the end of 1949 over a million had crossed to the West and a steady exodus continued, first from the Russian Zone and then from the German Democratic Republic (East Germany), until the erection of the Berlin Wall in 1961.

Finally, there were the returning prisoners of war, the *Heimkehrer*, of whom 1,237,000 were repatriated by 1950. They are not strictly speaking part of the refugee-expellee phenomenon though they serve to swell the ranks even further. By 1953 immigrants from the first three sources totalled ten million. These ten million were, of course, homeless in that they had never possessed homes in the territory of the future Federal Republic. It also goes without saying that they underwent considerable hardship, both in the process of expulsion and in the early years in the West. They constituted a serious problem for the Occupying Powers and later for the government of the Federal Republic itself. They were a drain on its resources, they augmented the ranks of the unemployed and they very seriously exacerbated the housing problem. From an economic point of view they posed the further disadvantage that their ranks contained higher proportions from 'irrelevant' occupational groups — farmers and independent artisans.

In spite of all these factors, their arrival and eventual assimilation constituted, on balance, an economic gain for the Federal Republic.[35] In the first place they more than made good the massive population deficit which would otherwise have resulted from the War. The population structure of the immigrants was also somewhat more favourable from an economic viewpoint than the structure of the indigenous population in the three western zones. Of the expellees, 48 per cent were in the 14-44 age group as opposed to 45 per cent of the indigenous population. The sex ratio was also more favourable to economic activity, i.e. contained a higher proportion of men, especially in the case of refugees from the Russian Zone among whom men predominated. The immigrants further facilitated the regional redistribution of the labour force within the area of the three western zones; they had no local attachments and often no homes, so they were more readily mobile. They were also sometimes able to make a distinctive contribution to economic reconstruction. Some industries which had been lost to Poland or the Russian Zone were largely rebuilt and operated in the West by Germans who had formerly worked in them and even run them in the East.[36] Lastly, the immigrants were the group with the strongest possible economic motivation. They had lost everything by their flight or expulsion. They had one consuming wish: to regain as much as possible of what they had lost and to achieve as quickly as possible an acceptable existence in material terms.

Currency Reform

It was suggested earlier that the darkest days of *der Zusammenbruch* were 1945 and early 1946, and that some improvements were observable in the course of 1946 although malnutrition and its attendant illnesses were very widespread. The first major improvement, however, came with the Currency Reform in June 1948, and was shortly followed by the introduction of Marshall Aid (see above).

The reform of the currency was necessary because, in the words of one commentator, 'the money supply had been inflated to dizzy heights by the system of war finance'.[37] In other words, the Nazis had printed too much money to pay for the War. This was not a serious problem during the War, since the economy was actually functioning, albeit on a war time footing and wage, rent, and price freezes had been in operation since the late 1930s. But when the *Zusammenbruch* came and normal economic life ceased, the problem became acute. Quite simply an over-abundant money supply coincided with a severe shortage of all kinds of goods and services. This did not lead to inflation in the usual sense, since the Allies maintained the various controls on wages and prices. The effect was that the *Reichsmark* was made half obsolete, half irrelevant, as a medium of exchange. Anyone who had anything to sell would not sell it at the official price, which was too low, but on the black market for a much higher price. Or, better still, goods would be bartered, if necessary using cigarettes as an 'intermedium' of exchange. Thus the quite incredible spectacle emerged of an 'advanced industrial country' sliding into a barter economy in the mid-twentieth century, with the *Reichsmark* being replaced by the cigarette.

There were other malfunctions in the pre-currency reform period. Employers, for instance, would deploy workers unproductively: their wages were so low as to be only a negligible 'cost of production'. Or manufacturers would produce fancy goods, for which there was little need, since unlike the necessities of life, these were not subject to price controls.

The currency reform was carried out in June 1948 in the American, British and French Zones. Everyone was given 60 marks, *Deutschmarks* (DM) not *Reichsmarks* (RM), in two stages, to cover their immediate needs. All other currency holdings, bank deposits and savings were reduced to one-fifteenth of their original value (RM 100 = DM 6.5). Debts were reduced on a ten to one basis, that is, any one who owed RM 100 before the currency reform now owed DM 10. And those who would otherwise have benefited from the cancellation of long-term debts were obliged to contribute to a war damage equalisation fund. The reform was also followed by a loosening of the various controls referred to earlier.

The currency reform can only be regarded as an exercise in 'rough justice'. It was unfair to those with savings and to creditors and it benefited debtors and the poor (even the destitute got their DM 60 handout) and those who owned land, property, or industrial shares.

Whatever the merits of the currency reform from the standpoint of social justice, it was undoubtedly an economic success. It put an end to the economic distortions already mentioned. It worked against the black market. It provided a realistic medium of exchange largely ending the barter economy, and it proved a significant stimulus to production. Industrial production, in fact, increased by over 60 per cent in the 12 months after the currency reform. The most noticeable immediate effect was the reappearance in the shops of a range of 'scarce goods' which had simply been hoarded, or bartered, in the absence of a hard currency.

Soziale Marktwirtschaft

The Social Market Economy is the name given to the set of policies and economic assumptions which governed German economic life from the end of the Occupation period until well into the 1960s.[38] The idea of the Social Market Economy was associated with certain neo-liberal economists at the University of Freiburg. Its doctrines were espoused and implemented by Ludwig Erhard, that dominant figure in German economic life. Erhard, after serving on economic advisory councils under the Allies, was Economics Minister in the Adenauer administrations from 1949 to 1963, and then Federal Chancellor himself.

The essence of the Social Market Economy is that it favours an economic order of free enterprise capitalism, limited government control and free play to market forces. This is not quite the truism it may sound since Germany had not actually had such an economic regime since before Hitler came to power early in 1933. Neither was it the economic order desired by the post-war trade unions. The 'social' bit of the formula simply implies that market forces will not be allowed to cause downright hardship and that the less fortunate will be protected by social welfare measures (and indeed West Germany has maintained a high level of social welfare benefits).[39]

The Social Market Economy expressly aims to reduce controls. Many price controls were removed in July 1948, immediately after the currency reform and similar measures followed. It is also part of the policy to reduce the burden of investors and/or entrepreneurs. The rate of income tax was reduced (it had been at a high level during the Occupation), a depreciation allowance was given on equipment whose value had declined before or during the War, and a new accelerated depreciation system was introduced.

In 1951 the Investment Aid Act provided a DM one billion loan to cover initial investment in the coal, iron, and steel producing industries. The loan was raised by a levy on all businesses existing as of January 1951. Apart from the 'counterpart funds' referred to in the earlier discussion of Marshall Aid, much of the investment was financed by a combination of high prices and restrained wages. Towards the end of the decade there was a shift of emphasis towards the encouragement of personal saving. A piece of legislation in 1959 offered a DM 400 bonus to those who bought securities or maintained savings for 6 years. Another measure, the DM 312 law provided that employees who save may receive a tax free donation from their employer (DM 312, subsequently raised to DM 624) to add to their savings, provided these were used for investment not consumption.

How West Germany would have fared under different economic policies can only be a matter of speculation. That the Social Market

Economy worked, however, is beyond dispute and it has had some effect on the attitudes of German managers. It should also be remembered that this growing prosperity occurred in a context of remarkable political stability.

Political Stability

Political stability favours business, especially international business and foreign investment. From the foundation of the Federal Republic in September 1949, Germany has enjoyed that stability so much so that it is now internationally taken for granted. Yet the establishment of a (largely) independent German government in 1949 seemed at the time an adventurous, possibly risky undertaking. Setting aside the horrors of the national socialist period, Germany's previous experiment in democratic republicanism − the Weimar Republic founded after the First World War and ended by the Nazi takeover in 1933 − had been anything but a political success story. Born in the hour of national defeat, it faced open attacks from both the extreme left and the extreme right in its early days, it was bedevilled throughout by the problem of ministerial instability and then confronted by the Great Slump of the early 1930s. Its most impressive achievement was to survive as long as it did.

Yet with the benefit of hindsight we can see that the Federal Republic was likely to succeed. There are three main threats to the stability of a parliamentary democracy, excluding foreign aggression. A democracy may be brought down by economic failure which it is unable to redress, or by serious challenges from the extreme right or extreme left. As we know, far from foundering on the rock of economic difficulties the Federal Republic enjoyed spectacular success, a success which redounded to the credit of the new regime. That the new Republic should have been overthrown by challenges from either right or left in its early years is almost inconceivable. Germany had just emerged from twelve years of fascist rule in circumstances that utterly discredited totalitarian ideology and practices. The unparalleled horrors of the Nazi period made any subsequent appeal from the extreme right very improbable. In this connection one may recall the observation of the post-war socialist leader Kurt Schumacher to the effect that for years *Germans* were rotting in concentration camps while (some) foreign powers made treaties with the government which put them there. It was not necessary for the Germans to be politically virtuous after the War, they did not need to show a 'gift for democracy'; the stability of the Federal Republic was immune to the possibility of totalitarian challenge so long as Germans could not forget the years between 1933 and 1945. And how could they forget them?

For somewhat different reasons a challenge to the nascent republic from the extreme left was also scarcely credible. Whatever the moral and intellectual appeal of Marxism, for post-war Germans it was inseparable from the power of the Russian state. It was the vengeance of Russia that the Germans feared above all at the end of the War; it was Russia which was seen as the cause of a divided Germany and the fact that the eventual territory of the Federal Republic represented only 55 per cent of the territory of pre-war Germany before the annexation of Austria. To this may be added the German experience in areas liberated by Russian troops, the testimonies of the thousands of refugees who came over from the Russian Occupation Zone and later from the German Democratic Republic (East Germany), plus the fact that thousands of German soldiers remained in Russian captivity.

This argument, political stability conditioned by the horrors of the past and the frustrations of the present, should not be treated as an absolute. Some features of the 1949 constitutional arrangements, written into the Basic Law (*Grundgesetz*) are clearly relevant to an explanation of the stability of the Federal Republic. The Basic Law strengthened the Federal Chancellor (*Bundeskanzler*), empowering him to 'determine the guide lines of policy', implying more authority over other cabinet members. At the same time the functions of the Federal President (*Bundespresident*) were rendered largely ceremonial, and the President is not elected by popular vote. These two facts taken together mean that there is *one* central figure in German government and little chance of personal rivalries at this level. It was also made more difficult to bring down the Chancellor and his cabinet; a parliamentary vote of no confidence is only allowed where there is simultaneous agreement as to the Chancellor's successor in the event of the no confidence vote being successful. While the position of the Chancellor was strengthened in these ways, steps were taken to prevent instability deriving from an excessive number of political parties, or from parties basically hostile to the democratic system. Minority parties have difficulty in getting a parliamentary foothold. Unless a party wins 5 per cent of the total vote, or wins a minimum of three constituencies, it is not entitled to any representation at all. The number of parliamentary parties has in fact steadily declined since 1949, thereby removing one of the constitutional nightmares of the Weimar period — a series of unstable coalitions. And the Basic Law also set up the Constitutional Court (*Bundesverfassungsgericht*) which serves to protect the Basic Law itself. The interesting thing about these various features is that they all quite clearly derive from a reaction to the inadequacies of the Weimar Republic, ended by the Nazis.

Another small legacy from the past may be mentioned here. Throughout the history of the Prussian state, and later that of the unified German state, the military establishment enjoyed high prestige. The officer corps attracted not only the socially élite but the ambitious and able too. This traditionally high standing of the military was dramatically reversed at the end of the War. Even today it is noticeable that surveys of the relative prestige of middle-class jobs in Germany generally place army officers at the bottom of the list. The small but tangible gain from the standpoint of economic vitality is that the army could no longer attract the able away from careers in industry. Other factors are involved in the standing of industry in contemporary German society and the issue will be discussed in more detail in Chapter 8.

The German rise to prosperity took place not only against the background of political stability, but also in the context of good industrial relations (see the table of international comparisons presented earlier in this chapter). That German trade unionists, like all Germans, have a mortal fear of inflation is well known, and the restraint and moderation of wage demands in Germany is also a matter of wonder to foreigners. But the German trade union structure, and how it came about, is less readily understood abroad.

The Trade Union Structure

Three basic facts about the structure of the unions are relevant here. There is one, and only one, central umbrella organisation — the *Deutscher Gewerkschaftsbund* (DGB). There are only 16 individual unions federated to the DGB (plus two important white-collar unions). And these are *industrial* unions. That is to say, membership of them is open to all skills, grades and specialisms in the branch of employment covered by the union. These three factors taken together have some important implications. The movement is sufficiently strong and centralised to exercise positive guidance over its members; wage negotiations are structurally simple since they seldom involve more than one union and demarcation disputes are by definition impossible. All this is pure gain for industry.

The movement assumed this form in the post-war years largely thanks to the direction of Hans Böckler and the encouragement he received from the authorities in the British Occupation Zone which was the focal point of post-war union reconstruction. Before the rise of the Nazis the trade union movement had been far from unitary, unions being grouped into blocks according to political and confessional criteria.[40] Before the First World War there had been three such blocks, and by 1933 there were five of them. The number of individual trade unions was also large, and had reached 200 by 1933 when the whole movement was dissolved and replaced by the Nazi Party affiliated *Deutsche Arbeiter Front* (German Worker's Front). The movement had not been able to offer effective opposition to the Nazis, and many of the leaders spent the twelve years of Nazi rule in concentration camps. The lesson that was drawn from this by the architects of the post-war union movement was that German trade unions should in future be unified and centralised. It was a viewpoint shared by the Occupying Powers, especially the British. One of the tasks which the Occupying Powers set themselves was to fashion a society which would be able to resist any future totalitarian bid for national power. A practical implication of this doctrine was to look with favour on the creation of independent institutional power centres which might serve as bulwarks against potential totalitarian challenges. The assumption is that a highly centralised and integrated state is the most susceptible to extremist political takeover. Only 'the Centre' has to be seized, and the state falls into the hands of the successful challenger. It is a paradoxical situation. The German trade unions, since the war, have been inclined to restraint. The standard expression that the Germans use in characterising the unions is *vernünftig* (reasonable, sensible). In fact, German managers often use this as a term of praise. The reasonableness derives in part from the very widespread fear of inflation, from the solidarity induced by the horrors of the early post-war period and also from the fact that the co-determination system gives the unions a measure of participation and control (the co-determination arrangements are discussed in Chapter 2). The paradox is that if there had been no National Socialist past, a unitary centralised trade union structure would in all probability not have been fashioned and the organisational expression of moderation would not have been at hand.

Finally, it is worth remembering that people achieve other things being equal, what they most want to achieve. This simple dictum has a special relevance for the economic rise of West Germany.

The Escape from Deprivation

The hardships experienced by the bulk of the German population, at the very least up to the time of the Currency Reform, were acute. The whole population, not merely the refugees whose plight was discussed earlier, had the strongest possible incentive to contribute to economic reconstruction.

There is, too, an impersonal way of regarding this situation. Germany was in an historically remarkable position at the end of the War. A major European nation had been militarily defeated, morally degraded and was experiencing material hardship. In this situation Germans could not hope to play a part on the world stage. They could not aspire to political influences, in the early days not even to political independence, and still less to military power. Even German culture had become suspect on account of its *Herrenvolk* associations. Only one form of achievement was open to the Germans — at first guardedly permitted and later extolled by the Occupying Powers — economic achievement.

This argument is very relevant to the first ten years or so after the Second World War. But it would be a mistake to think of this as a purely historical phenomenon. It has become ingrained and cumulative. In the first place poverty and deprivation led to an understandable concern with material improvement. When this improvement was achieved it was labelled 'an Economic Miracle'. The German public was conditioned to identify with the national economic performance and this fact sustains that economic performance today. It has become the German banner, and one thing for which Germany is always praised. World recessions come and go, but West Germany is always there with its low inflation rate and huge trade balance.

German Managers and the Recent Past

In exploring some of the factors relevant to understanding Germany's economic success, both the rise from post-war poverty and the sustained performance of more recent years, the economic context of German management and its genesis must be examined. Connections may be perceived between the attitudes and actions of German managers and some of the issues which have already been discussed in this chapter.

German managers, for instance, are fairly benevolent in their attitudes to trade unions. This benevolence is not as pristine now as it was a few years ago, but it is still unusual for German managers to produce unsolicited criticism of trade unions.

A related fact concerns self and image. In talking about themselves and their work German managers are less inclined to emphasise their trouble-shooting, fire-fighting, crisis-handling role than are their British colleagues. And, of course, the British view is conditioned by poorer industrial relations and the pervasive fear that strikes somewhere or other are going to make more problems for the hard-pressed executive. Again, German managers make fewer references to team work and team spirit (see Chapter 5), but it is conceivable that they have more of them. If this surmise is correct it will derive in no small way the fact that the miseries of *die Stunde O* are imprinted on the folk memory.

Another effect derives from the refugee and expellee phenomenon discussed earlier in this chapter. It has produced a kind of regional levelling. Among German managers there is hardly any equivalent of the 'I would want another £1,000 a year to go up there' disposition. If one looks at the informal network in German firms it is difficult to find any German version of the Scots sticking together or the Londoners helping each other out.

This transition from a time when bread-crumb soup and pine-needle tea were delicacies to a very real affluence has positively affected the standing of the German manager (see Chapter 8). The reaction to the controlled economy of both the National Socialist and Occupation periods and the fact that the Social Market Economy became the policy umbrella for success, have coloured the attitudes of German managers towards the free enterprise system (see Chapter 5).

The intention here is not to give an exhaustive list of such interconnections, but rather to sensitise the reader to the manifold relationships between consciousness and the recent past which are a recurrent theme of this book.

Conclusion

It has been argued in this introductory chapter that West Germany is an economically successful country, both relatively and absolutely. Some of the indices of this economic success have been presented, together with comparable data for other countries.

It has also been shown that West Germany has not experienced a gentle and uninterrupted progress to national prosperity, after the manner of, say, Sweden and Switzerland. On the contrary, Germany at the end of the Second World War experienced abject poverty. This fact was documented at some length, with reference particularly to eyewitness accounts. These two facts together, namely the prosperity of Germany now, and its desolation in 1945, endow a study of German management with particular interest.

Germany is a society which, more than most, is conditioned by its recent past. The *leitmotif* of that past is the economic rise of Germany after the War. German management has played its part in this rise, but so have a variety of other factors. In this connection we have considered the impact of aid programmes and technological renewal, of the successfully executed currency reform and the Social Market Economy, of political stability and the structure of the trade union system, the aspirations of the refugees and the involvement of the population in economic achievement. These are all part of the character of modern Germany, and part of the environment in which German management functions.

Notes

1. *The Europa Year Book 1979*, vol. 1 (Europa Publications, London).
2. Ibid.
3. Ibid.
4. Ibid.
5. Ibid.
6. Ibid.
7. Ibid.
8. 'Main Economic Indicators', OECD, June/July 1978.
9. Ibid.
10. *Eurostat: Basic Statistics of the Community* (Office for Official Publications of the European Communities, Luxembourg—Kirchberg, 1978).
11. Ibid.
12. *Department of Employment Gazette*, vol. 86, no. 11 (HMSO, London, November 1978).
13. Ibid.
14. The miseries of post-war Germany are well documented in German: Hans Schlange-Schöningen, *Im Schatten des Hungers: Dokumentarisches zur Ernährungspolitik 1945-9* (P. Parey, Hamburg, 1955); Josef Müller-Marein, *Deutschland im Jahre I: Panorama 1946-8* (Nannen-Verlag, Hamburg, 1960); Hans Dollinger, *Deutschland unter den Besatzungsmächten* (Wissenschaftliche Beratung: Thilo Vögelsang, Munich, 1967). Two valuable British accounts, based on early visits to Germany during the Occupation, are: Fenner Brockway, *German Diary* (Victor Gollancz, London, 1946) and Victor Gollancz, *In Darkest Germany* (Victor Gollancz, London, 1947).
15. Richard Brett Smith, *Berlin '45: The Grey City* (Macmillan, London, 1966).
16. This excerpt is taken from a quite fascinating source. Two Germans have edited and made available in German material from American secret service reports dealing with German conditions at the end of the War. Ulrich Borsdorf and Lutz Niethammer, *Zwischen Befreiung und Besatzung* (Peter Hammer Verlag GmbH, Wuppertal, 1977). The author was given a copy by the Hauni Werke Koerber company of Hamburg-Bergedorf. This, and other excerpts, have been translated into English by the author.
17. Ibid., p. 47.
18. Ibid., p. 31.
19. Ibid., p. 32.
20. Ibid., p. 31.
21. Ibid., p. 30.

22. Ibid., pp. 47-8.
23. Victor Gollancz, *In Darkest Germany* (Victor Gollancz, London, 1947).
24. Fenner Brockway, *German Diary* (Victor Gollancz, London, 1946) p. 9.
25. Ibid., p. 49.
26. Ibid., pp. 73-4.
27. Ibid., p. 146.
28. F. R. Willis, *The French in Germany, 1945-9* (Stanford University Press, Stanford, California, 1962).
29. André Piettre, *L'Economie Allemande Contemporaine (Allemagne Occidentale, 1949-52* (Librairie de Medicis, 1952).
30. Ibid.
31. For instance by Correlli Barnett in his pamphlet 'The Human Factor and British Industrial Decline'.
32. André Piettre, op. cit. 1952.
33. Ibid.
34. Count Hans von Lehndorf, *East Prussian Diary* (Oswald Wolff, London, 1963).
35. For a discussion of the economic significance of the refugees see: Henry C. Wallich, *Mainsprings of the German Revival* (Yale University Press, New Haven, 1955). The major study of the refugee question — Hans W. Schoenberg, *Germans from the East* (Martinus Nijhoff, The Hague, 1970) — concentrates on the refugees as a political force.
36. Henry C. Wallich, *Mainsprings of the German Revival*, 1955.
37. M. E. Streit, 'Germany: Economic Developments, Problems and Policies' in J. P. Payne (ed.), *Germany Today* (Methuen, London, 1971).
38. For a good discussion of the Social Market Economy see Henry C. Wallich, *Mainsprings of the German Revival*, 1955.
39. See in this connection: Siegfried Fassbender, 'Management and its Environment in Germany' in Joseph L. Massie and Jan Luytens (eds.) *Management in an International Context* (Harper & Row, New York, 1972).
40. For a brief and lucid account of trade union history and structure in Germany see E. C. M. Cullingford, *Trade Unions in Western Germany* (Wilton House Publications, London, 1976). For a more detailed discussion see Hans Limmer, *Die deutsche Gewerkschaftsbewegung* (Günter Olzog Verlag, München-Wien, 1973).

2 THE STRUCTURE OF GERMAN FIRMS

The structure of companies is of interest in several ways. First, it constitutes the formal administrative framework within which managers work. The company structure may give expression to a society's values and assumptions. It also has the advantage, from the standpoint of the interested outsider of being a very accessible aspect of management: it can be studied in handbooks. There is a range of structures from the predictable and re-defined to the novel and unusual. German companies, for instance, have some features which, viewed internationally, are or at any rate were, unusual — the two-tier board system and co-determination, for instance. And some features of German companies differ from those of companies in other lands in kind or in degree. In yet other respects German companies are 'just like' those in other countries in the sense that forms and intentions are internationally alike although there may be a little empirical variation. A case in point is the variety of types of company in West Germany, in terms of their legal status. There is a fairly standard pattern. The control of the entrepreneur co-varies with his liability and both vary inversely with the possibility of raising capital on the open market. These liability-control-capital access gradations are common elsewhere though the range may be more complicated in West Germany and requires explanation.

Shapes and Sizes

There are several different legal forms for business enterprises in West Germany:

1. The simplest, and usually smallest, type is the *Einzelfirma*, an enterprise self-financed by an owner-entrepreneur with full liability.

2. The *Offene Handelsgesellschaft* is a collectivised version of the *Einzelfirma*. In the case of the *Offene Handelsgesellschaft* several partners are involved in the venture, also with full liability.

3. The *Kommandit Gesellschaft* is a type of company in which two sorts of partners are involved:
   (a) *Komplementäre* who are like private entrepreneurs with full liability and
   (b) *Kommanditisten* who are liable only to the extent of their commitment and who have a more limited role in running the firm.

This type is usually signified by the abbreviation KG.

4. The *Kommandit Gesellschaft auf Aktien* is like the *Kommandit Gesellschaft* (see 3. above) except that the *Kommanditisten*, type (b) partners, are subject to the rules of the *Aktiengesetz* (Companies Act) which means that they can sell shares on the market.

5. The *Gesellschaft mit beschränkter Haftung* is a limited liability, joint stock company, but it is private and unquoted. It is a legal entity, distinct from its individual members. It is usually signified by the abbreviation GmbH. (N.B. the use of small and capital letters in such abbreviations is not arbitrary: in German all nouns, not just proper nouns, begin with a capital letter.)

6. The *Aktiengesellschaft* is a full public company with limited liability and quoted shares. It is usually designated by the abbreviation AG.

As a footnote it should be added that one sometimes encounters the apparent anomaly 'the xyz company KG, GmbH'. In this case the purpose is probably to have the company treated as a KG for the purpose of corporation tax and as a GmbH for the definition of liability, thus winning both ways. The *Einzelfirma* and the *Offene Handelsgesellschaft* are of little concern in a book about German management. The AG, is of course the most important. This is the category to which all the very big household name companies like Volkswagen and Siemens belong. One should not assume, however, that the AG is the only category that matters, or that the KGs and GmbHs are just corner stores or wooden shed outfits. KGs and GmbHs often have hundreds and thousands of employees respectively, and are certainly big enough to *have* managers.[1]

Not only are professional managers 'spread around' several types of company in West Germany; the companies themselves are 'spread around' geographically. This is not a truism. West Germany is a decentralised country in several ways and these include the dispersal of industry. If France is, or more properly was, the best European example of bureaucratic and cultural centralism ('Paris a vidé France' used to be a folk aphorism) West Germany represents the opposite pole. To start with West Germany is a *federal* republic. There is no principal and central town. The largest town, West Berlin is isolated from 'mainland' Germany; the next two contenders, Hamburg and Munich, are at opposite ends of the country and neither is central. Bonn, the political capital, is in other respects unimportant (it is a little bigger than Southampton) and the commercial capital, Frankfurt, is in the middle. There is no equivalent of the home counties. Federalism is not only a political reality. Most of the *Land* (state) capitals – Berlin, Hamburg, Hanover, Düsseldorf, Frankfurt, Stuttgart and Munich – are regional centres in every respect. And industry is similarly dispersed. If one asks Germans to name 'industrial areas' they name the Ruhr. If one asks, where else, they simply name all the large towns; if one asks, where else again, they name a batch of second-largest towns. If one tries the opposite approach and asks what areas have no industry the result is often disappointing: the Bavarian forest is the only agreed non-industrial area. One of the odd things about Germany is that internationally known companies turn up in places non-Germans have never heard of: Dunlop, for instance, is in Hanau, Volkswagen in Wolfsburg, Opel in Rüsselsheim and Procter and Gamble is in Schwalbach am Tanus.

Some support for this contention is to be found in the literature on industrial concentration, though here one must proceed carefully. First, there are some technical-classificational difficulties in assembling data on industrial concentration – how to deal with wholly and partly-owned subsidiaries, deciding whether some enterprises are primarily manufacturing or distributive, whether or not to include nationalised industries (important when comparing Britain with other countries) and so on. Secondly, statements about the degree of industrial concentration a country has achieved are only of interest when an international comparison is made. These comparisons, however, may be competitive or non-competitive. For instance, if one asks for two countries A and B, what percentage of all workers are employed in companies with more than 10,000 employees, this is a fair if rough indication of the density of big firms in the two countries concerned and it is a non-competitive criterion. If, on the other hand, one asks which of countries A and B has the most firms on the list of the world's 100 largest companies, then one is employing a competitive criterion in the sense that every firm on the list from country A is potentially excluding an entry from country B. This is somewhat more than a definitional quibble: one can obtain different answers to the question 'Does Britain or West Germany have the highest level of industrial concentration?' depending on whether one uses the competitive or non-competitive criterion. The third problem in comparative judgements on industrial concentration, is that it also makes a difference whether, in the language of software testing, one does a 'top down' or 'bottom up' appraisal. It is just as reasonable, that is, to compare proportions of small firms as proportions of big firms.

To examine this third point straight away, it would appear that West Germany has many, that is to say a high proportion of, very small firms compared at any rate with Britain and the USA, although not compared with other EEC countries, according to calculations made by Dr Prais of the National Institute of Economic and Social Research in London in Table 2.1.

Table 2.1: Manufacturing Establishments employing less than 10 persons, Major European Countries, 1963[2]

Country	No. of small establishments (thousands)	No. of small establishments per 100 employed in manufacturing	Proportion of total manufacturing employment in such establishments %
Britain	27	4	2.1
USA	121	6	2.4
France	186	31	10.8
West Germany	157	15	6.2
Italy	245	42	18.5
Benelux	57	23	8.7

This evidence tends to support our claim that in West Germany it is not only the very big companies, the AGs, which matter. It is also loosely consistent with our claim that industry in West Germany is geographically dispersed, since it is not credible that 157,000 such companies are concentrated in the Ruhr, to say nothing of the larger establishments.

At the other end of the scale, Dr Prais suggests that in a comparison between Britain and West Germany, the pattern is consistent. West Germany, that is, has more small companies and Britain has more large companies. Dr Prais argues that as of 1972 the number of manufacturing enterprises in Britain employing more than 40,000 people was 30 and the number in West Germany was 12.[3] It will be noted that the criterion here is non-competitive in our terms. Dr Prais is quite clear that in the matter of industrial concentration Britain belongs with the USA and West Germany with continental Europe:

> In relation to the sizes of the companies concerned, whether measured by their total population or their employment in manufacturing, the calculations in Table 1 (from which we have extracted the Anglo-German figures above) confirm our previous conclusion that Britain and the United States stand close together as generators of employment in large enterprises; but in France and Germany, it appears here that large enterprises occur only about half as frequently as in Britain.[4]

34 The Structure of German Firms

The evidence, however, is not uncontroversial. Alan Hughes, using what we have called a competitive criterion, suggests that at the top of the size scale West Germany has achieved a level of industrial concentration similar to that of Britain, and that in the period from the early 1960s to the early 1970s West Germany's relative position changed (see Table 2.2).

Table 2.2: Number of UK and West German Manufacturing Companies in the 200 largest non-US Petroleum, Mining, and Manufacturing Companies (ranked by sales) 1963-73[5]

	1963		1973	
Rank	UK	WG	UK	WG
1-25	4½	8	2½	8
26-50	4	5	3½	4
51-100	18	6	7	6
101-150	15	5	13	3
151-200	9	5	9	6½
Total	50½	29	35	27½

Note: half of the companies are the result of including 'binationals' such as Agfa-Gevaert (German-Belgian).

Alan Hughes comments:

> This table confirms the impression (refers to an earlier table for all European companies) that by 1973 there was little to choose between the United Kingdom and West Germany in terms of very large companies, with the United Kingdom if anything having a slight edge. It also shows, however, that if we concentrate attention only on the very largest companies (i.e. those ranked 1-50) the West Germans appear to have a decided numerical superiority.[6]

Apart from showing how complicated and controversial the whole issue of concentration is, Alan Hughes' treatment has another interest. It is generally assumed that industrial concentration is, *ceteris paribus*, a competitive advantage for the national economy. Hughes accepts this but refines the assumption. He investigates, that is to say, the particular branches of industry in which Britain and West Germany actually have their very large companies, and some interesting differences emerge (see Table 2.3).

Table 2.3: The Industrial Composition of the Top 95 UK and West German Manufacturing Companies, 1971-2[7]

Industry Group	UK	WG
Food, Drink, Tobacco	22	4
Engineering and Electrical Goods	19	21
Chemicals	11	23
Bricks, Pottery, Glass	9	6
Paper, Printing, Publishing	8	2
Vehicles	6	7
Metal Goods	5	1
Metal Manufacture	5	21
Textiles	4	—
Other Manufacturing	3	5
Leather	2	3
Shipbuilding	—	2
Timber, Furniture, etc.	—	—
Total	95	95

The two key differences are the British superiority in food, drink and tobacco and the German superiority in chemicals. Hughes regards both of these as significant, rightly in our opinion. The British lead in food and drink facilitates the exploitation of a soft domestic market, whereas the German lead in chemicals confers a presumptive advantage in a competitive export sphere. In other words Hughes is asking not just 'How much concentration?' but also 'What end does it serve?'

The present writer has also made a quick independent check on the relative role of chemical firms and food, drink and tobacco firms in Germany and finds some support for Alan Hughes' claim. A check of the top 50 West German firms by turnover for 1975 revealed seven chemical firms and a further four oil companies (it is not clear if Hughes has included oil companies under chemicals), as against six food, drink and tobacco firms.[8] More interesting, however, is the position of these 13 companies within the top 50 league (see Table 2.4).

So far it has been argued that of the six or so types of companies in West Germany, in terms of legal status and obligations, the AG type is generally the largest and the most important as an employer of managers, but the GmbH and KG types also constitute a substantial part of the West German economy. Industrial establishments are not distributed across West Germany in a perfectly even way, but there are few areas which have no industry, and Germans tend not to think in

Table 2.4: Position in Top 50 West German Firms by Turnover, 1975[9]

Chemical firms	1. 4, 5. 8. 27, 43, 44
Food, Drink, and Tobacco firms	14, 19, 27, 37, 40, 50

Note: the double inclusion of number 27 is not an error. It is Deutsche Unilever based in Hamburg, classified under *Lebensmittel, Chemie* — groceries and chemicals.

terms of 'industrial areas' and 'non-industrial areas'; just about everywhere in West Germany is industrialised to a greater or lesser extent, and the two fastest growing *Länder* (federal states) economically are in fact the traditionally rural and scenic states of Bavaria and Baden-Württemberg in the south.[10] While the evidence on industrial concentration is controversial, it is clear that West Germany has a large number of small firms and a larger number than Britain. At the top of the scale it is not clear from the evidence whether Britain or West Germany has the highest level of industrial concentration and the methodological problems of such comparisons are considerable. There is, however, a strong suggestion that West Germany has a higher level of industrial concentration now than used to be the case, and if there is still less concentration there than in Britain the gap has been narrowed.

Two-tier Boards

The shareholders of an AG type of company come together in an annual meeting (*Hauptversammlung*) where they have the right to voice their views on matters relating to the firm's capitalisation — increasing or decreasing the capital, raising credit, even the dissolution of the company. The shareholders at the annual meeting are also charged with the election of the *Aufsichtsrat* (Supervisory Board).

This *Aufsichtsrat* is made up of elected members who are not full-time employees of the company concerned. In this sense the *Aufsichtsrat* members may be equated with the non-executive directors on a British Board of Directors, though there is a possible difference in personnel terms. *Aufsichtsrat* members tend to be exclusively business people — representatives of banks, customers, suppliers, major shareholders, top managers from other companies and so on. The partial difference between *Aufsichtsrat* members and non-executive directors in Britain is that it is unusual to find among the ranks of the former what Vance Packard engagingly called 'status lenders' — hereditary aristocrats, retired generals, ex-ministers or parliamentarians.[11]

The size of the *Aufsichtsrat* may vary considerably from something like three to twenty-one, approximately according to the amount of capital employed. Its functions are definitely supervisory and not executive. The consent of the *Aufsichtsrat* is required for major financial decisions such as credits, investments, raising capital and takeovers. It appoints and in extreme cases dismisses the members of the *Vorstand* (Executive Board). The *Aufsichtsrat* itself does not make decisions, or initiate action, though it has the right to reject the recommendations of the *Vorstand* (see below). Serious differences between the *Aufsichtsrat* and *Vorstand* are unusual, and in the event of a major clash between them, a shareholders' meeting is called to resolve the deadlock. Although the *Aufsichtsrat* has impressive powers on paper, it does not exercise these routinely; it is a high status watchdog exercising a generalised control over the *Vorstand*.

The *Vorstand* (Executive Board) is the real decision-making body, subject only to the need to gain the *Aufsichtsrat's* consent for major financial decisions. The members of the *Vorstand* are, in contrast to members of the *Aufsichtsrat*, full-time salaried executives of the firm; in this respect they may be equated with the executive directors on a British Board of Directors. The size of the *Vorstand* may vary considerably, and there is little agreement in the relevant literature on this subject (the present writer has seen 3-5 and 17-20 variously cited as defining the size range of the *Vorstand*). It is, however, generally agreed that the *Vorstand* is tending to get larger.

The *Vorstand* has a chairman and usually a deputy chairman, the *Vorstand* chairman being the nearest German approach to a chief executive or British style managing director. It is normal for *Vorstand* members to have functional or departmental responsibilities. One or two actual examples may be helpful in this context.

In a firm which the author visited employing some 4,000 people, manufacturing specialist equipment, there is a four man *Vorstand* consisting of the chairman, a member responsible for Sales, another for Finance and Administration and a fourth member responsible for Design, Development and Production – *Vorstand Technik* is the standard term for this member with overall technical responsibilities. Sometimes the technical area is broken down with separate *Vorstand* members for Production on the one hand, and Research and Development and/or Design on the other. This is the case in the next example, a multi-national company in a consumer goods industry employing over 30,000 people. Here there is a nine man *Vorstand*, six of the nine being full members and the other three deputy members, but deputies who regularly attend *Vorstand* meetings, not just go along when a full member is ill or otherwise absent. Here the breakdown of functional responsibilities is: Production, Finance, Industrial Relations, Purchasing, Public Relations, Legal Affairs, Marketing and Product Development, the ninth member being the chairman.

The separate representation on the *Vorstand* of Production and Design or Development, as in the second example just cited, is rather common in West Germany. It reflects the fact that the Manufacturing or Production function in a German company tends to have more standing than in Britain (see Chapter 6). It is also not unusual in Germany to get a proliferation of 'production directors'; several *Vorstand* members, that is, representing different product groups or divisions, but with Design or Development still centrally represented in the *Vorstand*. Consider as an example the following *Vorstand* composition for a very large electrical engineering company. Here there is an eleven man *Vorstand* with a Chairman, four members each representing a product group and a separate member for the overall functions of Finance, Control, Personnel, Major Projects (in effect special development projects), *Technik* (in this case Design) and Production.

Another feature of German industrial life which sometimes finds reflection in the composition of the *Vorstand* is the standing of Design and/or Development. These are quite often regarded as *prima donna* functions, and the reason for this is interesting.[12] Part of it is the idea that people in Design and Development are *schöpferisch* (creative: not used ironically) or have *Erfindergeist* (inventive talent); this is perhaps a variation on the British theme of the academic *élan* of Research and Development and 'boffinism'. The second, and more particularly German consideration in this connection, is the view that Design and Development are the areas in which the company can really distinguish itself, make money, pulverise its rivals and have something everyone wants to buy in five years time. Thus it is again not unusual to come across a 'design weighted' *Vorstand* in Germany; as an example consider the seven man *Vorstand* of a capital goods firm employing 4,000 people, according to one of its personnel managers, the largest company in the world manufacturing this particular kind of equipment and exporting 90 per cent of all produce. According to the company's organisation chart, after the chairman, there are two *Vorstand* members for Design (different aspects of complex equipment), one for Production, another for Design and Production of an experimental and related product, and a member each for Sales and Finance and Administration. To complete the picture, in this case five out of the seven members are engineers, including the *Vorstand* chairman.

All that has been said so far in this section about the *Vorstand* and the distinction between the *Aufsichtsrat* and the *Vorstand* applies to the AG type of company, the largest and most important. Since legislation in 1952, however, the GmbH type of company is also obliged to have an *Aufsichtsrat* if the number of company employees exceeds 500, which it very frequently does. On the other hand the GmbH does not have a *Vorstand* but a *Geschäftsführung*, an executive committee which is usually smaller than the *Vorstand*. Its members are known as *Geschäftsführer*. Probably the typical arrangement with the GmbH company is a three man *Geschäftsführung* comprising the chairman, the *Geschäftsführer Technik* (member for all technical functions) and a *Kaufmännischer Geschäftsführer* (literally, commercial director) responsible for everything else. A variation of this theme which the author has encountered is where the GmbH again has a three man *Geschäftsführung*, where the division of responsibilities is one member for all technical functions, one for Sales and one for everything else, with one of the three additionally acting as chairman.

The small GmbH companies and also most of the KG companies tend to have a single chief executive, usually titled *der Geschäftsführer*. In such cases departmental managers reporting to this *Geschäftsführer* are simply the most senior managers, not members of a collegial or quasi collegial executive committee of the *Vorstand* kind. The point has been expressed tentatively because there are exceptions and one does encounter KG companies with elaborate executive committees. Consider by way of illustration the following ten man executive committee (called in this case a *Geschäftsleitung*) of a KG company employing 2,000 people and manufacturing machinery for a particular branch of the consumer goods industry. The chairman is the owner and founder of the firm, the other nine members being responsible for Production, Design, Patents, Sales, Administration, Finance, Purchasing, Personnel and Projects. Companies of this standing (it has no German competitors though a well-known British firm manufactures the same specialist machinery) and with this structure, are a timely reminder that in West Germany it is not just the AG companies which count.

A general point which emerges from this discussion of the *Vorstand* and *Geschäftsführung* is that there are many phenomena in German industrial life which are not standardised. These things may not be standardised in other countries either, but the point at issue is that Germany does have a reputation abroad for bureaucratic standardisation. It is conceivable that there are some areas of German life in which the reputation is justified but in the author's experience German industry is not such an area. In the present case the distinction with AG type companies between the *Aufsichtsrat* and the *Vorstand* is the only 'cut and dried' feature of the higher executive scene; otherwise there are variations in the size and nomenclature of these executive committees, and in the choice and allocation of functional responsibilities represented.

It is not possible in discussing the *Aufsichtsrat* and *Vorstand* to set up any precise Anglo-German equivalents. A British Board of Directors is not exactly equivalent to either the *Aufsichtsrat* or the *Vorstand*. Since the German company has two boards and the corresponding British company only one, it may be surmised that the German system is more complicated. A possible counter-argument is that in this respect at any rate the German system is more standardised than the British. The variation which one has in Britain where a Board may be composed of executive directors, non-executive directors, or any variable combination of the two, is impossible in Germany. In British directorial terminology a *Vorstand* is always executive and an *Aufsichtsrat* is always non-executive.

There is another minor respect in which the German *Vorstand* arrangements are unambiguous. This is that authority and status distinctions among full-time industrial executives in West German are in the following sense clear-cut. The highest rank a German manager can have is to be a member of the *Vorstand*. Every *Vorstand* member outranks every non-member (the collective name for other managers is *leitende Angestellten*, literally, leading employees). In the British system, on the other hand, it is possible to have minor anomalies where, of several senior managers, having an equal status as full-time executives within the company, some may be invited on to the Board while others may not, and there is then a dual, and inconsistent, definition of organisational status.

Another variable aspect of the *Vorstand* system is the extent to which it is genuinely collegial. The theory is that the *Vorstand* is a collegial institution with collective responsibility. The *Vorstand* chairman is simply *primus inter pares*, not a chief executive in a British or American sense. Some non-German commentators have taken the system at face value and castigated the Germans for institutionalising 'committee management' with all the presumed disadvantages of committee deliberations.[13] Whether or not the system should be taken at face value is an open question. It is not the sort of topic which is researched or made the subject of surveys, since *Vorstand* deliberations are, of course, highly confidential to the company concerned. The author has seized every opportunity to ask *Vorstand* members, and other managers senior enough to be in the know, about the collegial character of *Vorstand* deliberations, and has received a wide variety of answers. First, there is no consensus about the decision-making process, or at any rate no uniformity about it. Decisions of the *Vorstand* may be unanimous, majority, or compromise decisions. Secondly, there is no agreement about the *de facto* role of the *Vorstand* chairman. There is one body of opinion that suggests, obliquely, that the chairman ought to be in command and will be if he is made of the right stuff. This line is often introduced with the remark 'Es gibt gute Vorstände und bequeme Vorstände' ('There are good Vorstands and comfortable Vorstands'; almost a standard expression in this context). If one then asks what a 'comfortable *Vorstand*' is like the answer tends to be that it is an indecisive one where nothing gets done: translated for our purposes this means not sufficiently dominated by the chairman. An alternative, not exactly body of opinion but rather set of testimonies, tends to confirm the collegial nature of the *Vorstand*. The author has also used the more oblique approach of inviting highly placed executives to describe in general terms the character of *Vorstand* meetings. One thing which these accounts have in common is that they mention the presentation of 'decision-relevant' blocks of information, not in the form of *pro forma* handouts before the meeting (to be read by the insecure and filed by the experienced) but actually in the course of *Vorstand* meetings themselves. This does tend to suggest a collegial approach to decision-taking, since where decisions are being directed (stage-managed) the appropriate tactic is to limit the dispersal of information so that only the real boss can claim 'an overall view'.

If we assume that the *Vorstand* sometimes has this genuinely collegial character, or that every *Vorstand* has it to some extent, then it would appear that the Germans are able to make 'committee management' work. This is not as impressive as it sounds since the popular objections to 'rule by committee' — slowness, indecisiveness, desire of members to 'cover their tracks' and not do anything risky or culpable — are based on two assumptions. The first is that the committee members happen to be more interested in procedures than decisions and more concerned with appearances than results. Such orientations, however, do not hold typical for achievement-crazy German managers (the views of German managers are discussed in some detail in Chapter 5). More to the point, the sense of purpose exhibited by German managers is a substantial guarantee against the *Vorstand* degenerating into indecisiveness.

The second assumption is that 'circumstances' allow committees to indulge in prevarication and 'buck-passing'. Now in the case of the

Vorstand there is obviously the general, middle-term constraint of the company's profitability. Put simply, if the *Vorstand* does a bad job it is likely to show. A further relevant consideration is the fact that the *Vorstand* is subject to the general surveillance of the *Aufsichtsrat*, which appoints the *Vorstand* in the first place and can *in extremis* dismiss it. Such an occurrence is unlikely, but the sanction exists and is seen to exist.

Again a conceivable advantage attaches to a collegial system. It means that more people are going to have to convince other people that what they want to do is right. This increases the likelihood that silly ideas get 'screened out' and it implies, *ceteris paribus*, a higher level of a particular kind of rationality. There will be, that is, more emphasis on preparatory staff work: assembling relevant information and interpreting it rationally in so far as this is possible. And then, in discussion, more attempt to convince by argument rather than by 'pulling rank'.

To summarise these last points it is being argued that no one should be to eager to condemn the German *Vorstand* system as 'committee management' because exactly how far the *Vorstand* does in general act as a committee is not easy to ascertain. In so far as it does have a collegial nature, however, one must not assume that it is characterised by the ineffectiveness popularly associated with committees. Furthermore, it is conceivable that a collegial system also confers some advantage in terms of collective rationality.

Industrial Democracy

West Germany, viewed internationally, is not unique in having an institutionalised system of industrial democracy, yet it is fair to regard its various forms as distinctive features of German companies. The German term for industrial democracy is *Mitbestimmung* (literally, co-determination). The German co-determination system was only firmly and finally established in the early 1950s, yet it has a history dating back to the First World War. We will trace the history of the movement briefly, and describe in formal terms the features and operation of the system. Two words of warning are in order. First, the system is complicated; co-determination is a blanket term for several institutions, the present system was not introduced 'at a stroke' but has developed over time and different co-determination arrangements have and do apply in different types and sizes of industry. The second warning is that it is difficult to tell non-German readers all they would like to know about co-determination in West Germany. There is widespread contemporary interest in industrial democracy, and attention naturally focusses on countries such as West Germany which can claim to be pioneers. The problem is that the literature, and especially the research literature, is uneven. One can read up the history of the movement, there are quasi-official publications offering an exegesis of the relevant legislation, procedural handbooks, surveys of the co-determination system in various countries with West Germany included and even a literature on the relationship between co-determination on the one hand and democracy and the political order on the other. What is missing is an empirical literature telling us what the system is like in practice. We will return to this point.

The formal beginning of the co-determination system in Germany may be traced to the later stages of the First World War. In 1917 the Imperial Parliament passed the *Gesetz über den vaterländischen Hilfsdienst*, a measure which set up a modest form of industrial democracy. The Government intention here was to rally industrial workers to the cause of war production by attempting to take them into a limited partnership with employers and the state. This 1917 measure was not far reaching, and it is of interest really because it marks the beginning of co-determination as an industrial fact in Germany.

At the end of the First World War there was considerable industrial unrest in Germany, and some factory occupation. Worker and soldier soviets were established, known as *Arbeiter und Soldatenräte*. This post-war period was not marked by any natural tendency for employers and employees to co-operate; nevertheless, a number of co-determination measures came into existence.

The first of these was the establishment of the *Reichswirtschaftsrat*, provided for by the Constitution of the Weimar Republic (1919-33). This was a joint body containing representatives of both the employers and the trade unions. The intention was that it would be available for consultation by the Government, particularly with reference to proposals for social and economic policy and legislation. This body, the *Reichswirtschaftsrat*, was not very powerful as a policy-making organ, its role being primarily consultative.

The next development came in the early 1920s with the passing of the *Betriebsrätegesetz*. This piece of legislation established Works Councils for most firms; Councils which were empowered, *inter alia*, to negotiate local wage agreements. Also in the early 1920s the *Aktiengesellschaftengesetz* (Companies Act) was changed and in its revised form it required that there should be two representatives of the workers on the *Aufsichtsrat*, one a blue collar worker, the other a white collar worker. These two developments in fact represent in an early form the two principal dimensions of the modern co-determination system.

All these measures were abolished by the National Socialists after their rise to power in January 1933. The National Socialist regime set up the Labour Front and various corporate occupational organisations. The purpose of these moves, of course, was to secure Nazi control of occupations and occupational groups and these measures need not be taken seriously as a contribution to the development of co-determination.

The period after the Second World War saw the spontaneous election of many *Betriebsräte* (Works Councils). This development was followed by administrative decrees in the British and American Occupation Zones requiring the establishment of such Works Councils. During the Occupation Period several forces in fact contributed towards the establishment of a co-determination system. The Allies themselves were keen on a co-determination as a safeguard against any possible totalitarian seizure of power and the rise of an overcentralised government. This attitude was justified in terms of developments before the Nazi seizure of power in 1933. Although it would be an exaggeration to say that Hitler had been 'supported by heavy industry', it would be fair to say that certain sections of heavy industry had contributed to his support and rise to power. Before 1933 Hitler had received a personal introduction to the Düsseldorf Industry Club where he had made several speeches; as a result of this certain iron and steel magnates in the Ruhr area had been won to the National Socialist cause and had made substantial contributions to Nazi Party funds. This is one reason for the post-war Allied view that some (internal) control on the power of industry was desirable. And like the establishment of a strong trade union movement (see Chapter 1) it also relates to the idea that the possibility of any future totalitarian takeover is reduced by interposing secondary collectivities — trade unions or Works Councils, for instance — between the State and the general public.

Again during the Occupation there was some dismantling of industrial plant and equipment (see Chapter 1). One effect of this dismantling was that owners and employers themselves became more favourable to the idea of co-determination. Their hope and expectation was that if they were able to take the workers into partnership via a co-determination system, the workers themselves would have a stronger interest in preventing the dismantling of industrial plants. A practical result, in this situation, was that it was by no means unusual for workers themselves to stand guard at factory gates in order to prevent the dismantling of plant and the removal of equipment.

The trade unions were disappointed by the rise to power of the Christian Democratic Party (CDU) when the German Federal Republic was established in 1949. The unions anticipated that the CDU would not be enthusiastic about the introduction of co-determination, and early in 1950 the unions in fact threatened a general strike if the CDU would not pass a co-determination law. The tactic was successful and the early 1950s saw the establishment of a fairly substantial system of co-determination.

The first measure is the 1950 *Mitbestimmungsgesetz* (Co-determination Law). This law applied only to the *Montanindustrie*, that is to the iron, steel and coal industry. This law enacted that one member of the *Aufsichtsrat* (Supervisory Board) would be elected by both shareholders and workers, and of the remainder half would be elected by the shareholders separately and half by the workers separately. Furthermore an *Arbeitsdirektor* (Labour Director) was to be appointed to the *Vorstand* (Executive Board). As has been noted *Vorstand* members are appointed by the *Aufsichtsrat*; this would also apply to the new *Arbeitsdirektor*, and in addition he would have to be chosen by the majority of the worker representatives on the *Aufsichtsrat*. Thus the *Arbeitsdirektor* is a genuine representative of worker interests in terms of the mechanism of his election.

The 1950 law thus introduced a substantial measure of co-determination, but on a limited industrial front. The *Montanindustrie* in effect means coal mines, iron foundries and steel mills; the formula does not comprise the metal goods industries. This situation altered in 1952 when the Companies Act was changed in its application outside of the *Montanindustrie*. The amended law required that one-third of the members of the *Aufsichtsrat* of all non-*Montanindustrie* companies should be worker representatives, the other two-thirds being, of course, shareholder representatives.

Then in 1952 the *Betriebsverfassungsgesetz* was passed. This established a *Betriebsrat* (Works Council) for all firms or other places of work with more than five employees. As we have seen the Works Councils existed earlier in the 1920s, and also came into existence spontaneously after the Second World War. In the author's view it is the Works Council which is the corner-stone of the system and the institution which is of most practical importance. It is worth outlining its functions.

The 1952 Act in fact endowed the Works Councils with three rights. The first is the *Mitbestimmungsrecht* (Co-determination right) or right of the Works Council to give its consent on certain matters. These include the appointment of workers to new positions, internal transfers of workers, transfers between different wage groups, filling newly created posts (internally), dismissals, setting the beginning and the end of the working day, deciding when breaks should be taken, fixing canteen prices, the prevention and investigation of industrial accidents and holiday arrangements. The second is the *Mitwirkungsrecht* (right to be consulted). This right refers particularly to planning questions such as decisions to close plants, open new plants, or transfer workers from site to site. The third right is the *Informationsrecht* (right to be given information). This right is implemented primarily by means of the *Wirtschaftsausschuss* (Economic Committee) which is composed of members of the Works Council and management representatives. This *Wirtschaftsausschuss* has the right to be given information about the economic performance of the firm, including information about sales, investments and profits.

Members of the Works Council are elected; six weeks' notice of a Works Council election has to be given and election is by secret ballot. Clerical workers and blue collar workers may have separate representation on the Works Council, though it is not unusual for manual workers to elect clerical workers as their representatives and *vice versa*. The Works Council does not however, represent the *leitende Angestellten* (managers below the *Vorstand* level). *Gastarbeiter* (foreign workers) are eligible for election to the Works Councils alongside German nationals. The author once made a practical check on this point at a large car manufacturing company employing thousands of foreign workers, and found that the most numerous national group on the Works Council were Turks.

All members of the Works Council are subject to the confidentiality obligation. This means, among other things, that Works Council members may not divulge information about the economic performance of the firm (except through the *Wirtschaftsausschuss*) even to the workers who elected them. The author has never encountered any complaint on the management side that this confidentiality obligation had been violated.

So far we have described the co-determination system as it has existed from the early 1950s until the late 1970s. A few modifications were made, subsequent to the early 1950s, mainly in the direction of strengthening the Works Councils and enlarging their powers. The most recent development, however, is the new Co-determination Act passed in May 1976 and implemented in 1978. This new Act does not apply to the *Montanindustrie* which is still governed by the 1950 law (see above). It applies to all other firms above a certain size, size being measured in terms of number of employees, capital and turnover. The new law thus refers to the composition of the *Aufsichtsrat* in large *non-Montanindustrie* firms, and it requires that half the *Aufsichtsrat* members should be representatives of the employers and the other half representatives of the employees. There is a qualification, some would say a catch. Among the workers' representatives on the *Aufsichtsrat* there is to be one representative of the *leitende Angestellten* (managers below the *Vorstand* level). The critical assumption is that in the event of a workers *versus* shareholders confrontation (such events are not common in West Germany) the representative of the *leitende Angestellten* will feel that he has more in common with the shareholders. Furthermore, the *Aufsichtsrat* chairman is always an employers' representative and he has a casting vote.

During the 1970s there has been considerable discussion and debate about the co-determination system in West Germany. During the debate which preceded the 1976 law the trade unions and workers have been asking for an extension of the co-determination system as it exists in the *Montanindustrie* to the rest of German industry; managers and shareholders have, on the whole, been trying to resist this development and the struggle has been complicated by the fact that the *leitende Angestellten* (managers below the *Vorstand* level) have been arguing that they should have some representation in the co-determination system. The 1976 Act does establish an *Arbeitsdirektor* (Labour Director) on the *Vorstand* of firms outside the *Montanindustrie*, but he is elected by the *Aufsichtsrat* as a whole, like the other *Vorstand* members, not by a two-thirds majority of the Worker representatives on the *Aufsichtsrat*, as is the case in the *Montanindustrie*. Thus workers and trade unions tend to regard the 1976 Act as something of a compromise. This has been admitted by Federal Chancellor Helmut Schmidt, who has said that those who regard the 1976 Act as imperfect should remember that the SPD-FDP coalition majority was not perfect either.

It may be helpful to summarise the co-determination arrangements now existing in the three types of company distinguished at various times by the co-determination legislation, that is, in the *Montanindustrie*, other large firms and other small firms.

1. *Montanindustrie* (iron, steel and coal). Companies in these industries have a *Betriebsrat* (Works Council); an *Arbeitsdirektor* (Labour Director) on the *Vorstand* (Executive Board), and the *Aufsichtsrat* (Supervisory Board) has one neutral member with half the remaining

members being worker representatives. These worker representatives do not include a representative of the *leitende Angestellten* (managers below the *Vorstand* level).

2. Other large firms. These have a *Betriebsrat* (Works Council); half of the members of the *Aufsichtsrat* (Supervisory Board) represent employers and half are representatives of the workers, or more properly employees, with one of these members representing the *leitende Angestellten* (managers below the *Vorstand* level). The *Arbeitsdirektor* (Labour Director) is not elected by a majority of the worker representatives on the *Aufsichtsrat*.

3. Other small firms. These have a *Betriebsrat* (Works Council); otherwise they are subject to the 1952 change in the Companies Act. That is, one-third of the members of the *Aufsichtsrat* (Supervisory Board) are representatives of the workers, and these do not include a representative of the *leitende Angestellten*; *Arbeitsdirektor* (Labour Director) not elected by majority of worker representatives on the *Aufsichtsrat*.

This is the system in formal terms. There is, as was suggested at the outset, a difficulty about evaluating it because of a lack of systematic knowledge about the way the system works in practice. Even the limited evaluative question, 'Does co-determination lead to better managed or worse managed companies in West Germany?' can only be answered in terms of informed conjecture. To give a practical example, one would like to know what difference the appointment of the *Arbeitsdirektor* (Labour Director) to the *Vorstand* (Executive Board) of companies in the *Montanindustrie* in 1950 made. Was the *Arbeitsdirektor* often in conflict with his fellow *Vorstand* members? What did they argue about? What decisions were affected by his presence on the *Vorstand*? and so on. The people involved in the system know these things, at any rate for their own company, but there is a lack of general and public knowledge about the practical dynamics of the system. Nor is it likely that studies of this kind will be made, because of political and confidentiality considerations. It is not likely that a German company will throw its *Vorstand* meetings open to sociologists from the local university so that they may study the interaction between the Labour Director and his colleagues, fascinating as this would be.

With this qualification about the limits of available evidence, some generalisations are in order. The usual pronouncement by informed Germans, including managers, especially when speaking retrospectively, is that co-determination is 'a good thing' because it has obliged employers and employees to co-operate. This co-operation has actually occurred, and has been, on the whole, successful especially while the economic climate was favourable. It should also be noted that the timing of the (post-war) introduction of this system was rather fortunate. The 1950 Co-determination Act (see above) came two years after the currency reform and the start of Marshall Aid (see Chapter 1), a year after the inauguration of the Federal Republic (September 1949) and during the economic boom engendered by the Korean War. This early 1950s period is one which saw actual improvement and the hope of yet better things to come in West Germany and it was still sufficiently close to the collapse and immediate post-war poverty for a very co-operative attitude to prevail. To extend this perspective it is fair to say that the author has also noticed that German managers have been less enthusiastic in their pronouncements since the 1976 Act came into force. This is not to say that they have expressed clear hostility towards co-determination; it is rather that two subsidiary points have been made. One is the view the 1976 Act should be the end-point of the system; that any further increments of co-determination would not be welcome. The other is the fear that the newly composed *Aufsichtsrat* might appoint inadequately entrepreneurial people to the *Vorstand* (the German entrepreneur tradition is discussed further in Chapters 4 and 5). The author's impression is that these reservations about the system are not 'big issues' among German managers.

It is also noticeable that (managerial) acceptance of the Works Council is just about total. Works Councils have existed in practically every place of employment since 1952, and existed prior to this in the 1920s and late 1940s as has been described. No one can imagine life without the Works Council. The first time the author asked a senior manager about the company's attitude to the Works Council the laconic reply was, 'The Works Council Act is a piece of legislation like any other: we implement it.' That this matter of fact acceptance exists is important because there are grounds for regarding the Works Council as the central institution of the co-determination system, and as one having some positive effects from management's standpoint.

The practical importance of the Works Council, in the context of running companies, is that is provides for the regulation of many issues in an agreed, institutional way, and does so in advance. To put it the other way round, it is unlikely (though not impossible) that there will be strikes or disruptions of normal work about, for instance, canteen prices, appointments, promotions and transfers, because all these issues are regulated by the Works Council. And it is understood on both sides that the Works Council will regulate these affairs, and that it will do so before the event, not after a crisis has become manifest. When one adds to this the fact that demarcation disputes are technically impossible in German firms because of the small number of large industrial unions (see Chapter 1) then it will be clear that the likelihood of small stoppages and disruptions is much less in Germany than in say Britain (this point is elaborated in Chapter 6 in discussing the work of German production managers).

So the effects of co-determination include advance regulation of particular issues, a measure of system induced co-operation between employers and employees, the diffusion of company performance information and a greater constraint on management to explain and justify its decisions.

The Manufacturing Company as Bureaucracy

The word bureaucracy is sometimes used as a generalised term of abuse to stigmatise the character or performance of some organisation. The connotations in this context are slowness, inflexibility, impersonality in the sense of failure to take account of relevant personal (or circumstantial) differences and ritualised inefficiency. Analysts of formal organisation however, regard bureaucracy as a form of organisation marked by certain features. There is no universally agreed version of what these features are, but they are usually held to include specialisation of tasks and personnel to perform them, precise delimitation of authority and responsibility, reliance on written rules and formal procedures, impersonality in the sense of impartiality towards the organisation's clients or customers, graded differences among the organisation's staff and the likelihood that these staff will experience a 'career' — a progression through a number of offices and ranks.

Now on the basis of such a definition it is clear that all business firms are bureaucracies to some extent; they have all or most of the features to some degree. After all, companies do practise division of labour and task specialisation, have hierarchies, job descriptions, operating procedures, communications systems, differences in emoluments and status for employees (especially managerial employees) and so on. But if it is not meaningful to ask whether the business firm is a bureaucracy, it may be meaningful to ask how bureaucratic it is. And this question may be made more meaningful by building in some comparison. So one might raise the question: how bureaucratic are manufacturing companies in West Germany compared with those in other countries?

Thanks to a brilliantly conceived study carried out by a group at a research institute in Aix-en-Provence, France,[14] it is at any rate possible to compare German companies with those in France.[15] The strategy adopted by the research group was to select a small number of companies in France and West Germany and subject them to a detailed comparative analysis. The fact that the sample of companies is small is more than compensated for by their being matched in the two countries for size, product and type of technology. The differences which emerge from this comparative exercise are substantial. If one would summarise in one sentence, the verdict would be first, that German firms do not, in an absolute sense, appear to be very bureaucratic and secondly, they appear less bureaucratic than the matched companies in France. Consider some of the following findings.

The organisational hierarchy was shorter in the German firms than in the French. In the German firms, that is to say, there were simply fewer ranks between the level of the ordinary blue collar worker and the chief executive. In most of the firms the proportion of non-manual workers was lower in Germany (less task specialisation and a smaller administrative component). In the German companies there was less compartmentalisation between the three groups comprising unskilled workers, skilled workers and technicians and non-manual workers, whereas in the French companies these groups were regarded as discrete and as having separate promotion ladders. Similarly the German firms exhibited less compartmentalisation between office staff, junior management and senior management and the German firms had a higher proportion of senior managers who had begun work as junior employees or manual workers. The German companies had fewer supervisory personnel external to the main body of production workers and these supervisory grades were less clearly defined than in the French companies; commercial and administration personnel constituted a lower proportion of the total labour force in the German companies, which also had smaller proportions of ancillary technical staff.

A related study, prefiguring the one just described, also demonstrated that salary differences, not just absolute but in terms of internal relativities, exist between the French and German companies.[16] The most general way to express the difference is to say that the salary hierarchy — the gap between the highest paid person and the lowest paid person — was shorter in the German companies. And several more detailed propositions, consistent with this general fact of a narrower overall salary band in the German companies, are also valid. The gaps between the skilled average wage and the unskilled average, between the manual average wage and the non-manual average, and between the managerial average and other white collar average, were all smaller in the German companies. Finally, it emerged that seniority was less important as a determinant of salary in the German firms than in the French.

It is possible to re-state some of these findings with reference to the characterisation of German firms as more or less bureaucratic. These Franco-German studies suggest that German firms are not very bureaucratic in that they are relatively low on internal divisions, both horizontal and vertical and low on the proliferation of technical and administrative specialisms. Furthermore there is an element of relative egalitarianism with regard to the salary structure in the German case, and seniority, that traditional bureaucratic virtue, turns out to be less important in German firms.

A more recent research development has been the replication of this Franco-German study of structural features of firms in Britain.[17] That is to say, a small number of British firms were chosen which matched those in the original Franco-German sample in terms of product, technology and approximate size. These British companies were then studied with regard to the same features and variables as were compared in the Franco-German study. This British contribution to the now tripartite study is interesting in two further ways. First, streamlining the results somewhat, it emerged that Britain is in an intermediate position with regard to most of the variables investigated. Britain that is, tends to fall between France and Germany, the British firms having, for instance, shorter hierarchies than those in France but longer than those in Germany. In so far as some of these variables are an indication of bureaucracy, then the German companies are also less bureaucratic than the British.

The second point of interest refers to the relationship between specialised knowledge and authority.[18] Or, to express this in more conventional terms, the relationship between staff and line positions. In presenting some of the findings the authors of the British study make an explicit contrast in this connection between the British and the German firms. This is to say that the British companies tend to 'externalise' specialised knowledge at all levels from the shop floor upwards. They tend to create ancillary technical and other posts external to the main body of production workers and to the line management hierarchy. The German tendency, in contrast, is to incorporate such specialist and technical knowledge in the line itself and to expect production workers and their immediate supervisors to do as much as possible for themselves rather than depend on staff specialists and others outside the line. It is an interesting difference and adds to our characterisation of German firms.

This comparative material has been introduced for several reasons. First, it opens up the whole fascinating question of national difference in organisation structure. Perhaps a similar comparative study between say matched firms in Norway and Italy would reveal a range of startling differences on dimensions which no one has yet conceptualised. Secondly, any comparison between German companies and companies elsewhere serves to advance the characterisation of the former. Thus we can say positively on the basis of these Franco-German studies that the German firm tends to be marked by a short hierarchy, large spans of control, relatively few internal divisions, a concentration of workers in Production and a tendency to restrict the proliferation of technical specialisms and ancillary functions by building the relevant knowledge into the line positions, starting at the bottom. Thirdly, in so far as this material suggests that German companies are less, rather than more, bureaucratic, we have a *de facto* characterisation contrary to the national stereotype — a point which was touched on in the earlier discussion of the *Vorstand* and *Geschäftsführung*.

Conclusion

In this chapter several structural aspects of German companies have been examined. The various legal types of company in West Germany were explained and it was indicated that the AG (limited liability) type of company is the most important in the present context of a study of German management. At the same time it was made clear that most GmbH and many KG companies are both large enough to employ professional managers and, taken collectively, make a substantial contribution to German economic life.

The functions of the supervisory *Aufsichtsrat* and the executive *Vorstand* (or *Geschäftsführung* in the case of the GmbH type of company) were described and some comparisons made with a British Board of Directors. Several actual examples of *Vorstand* and *Geschäftsführung* composition were introduced and it was noted that there is in fact a good deal of variation within the German system.

The evidence on industrial concentration in West Germany is not unambiguous especially with regard to a comparison with Britain. There is, however, some evidence that the industrial concentration is increasing in Germany both absolutely, and with reference to Britain. It is also clear that there are differences between Britain and Germany in terms of the branches of industry in which the very large companies are to be found, with West Germany having a relative strength in the chemical industry. At the other end of the spectrum there is also evidence that West Germany has more small firms than Britain, both relatively and absolutely. This finding is consistent with our observation that industry is well distributed throughout West Germany with very few completely non-industrial areas.

The history of the co-determination movement was outlined and the post-war legislation establishing the system in its present form was described in some detail. The system has three elements: the Labour Directors on the *Vorstand* of some firms, the worker representatives on the *Aufsichtsrat* and the almost universal Works Council. It was argued that the last of these, the Works Council, is the most important, and this claim was supported with arguments concerning information dissemination and the institutionalised regulation of a range of issues.

Finally, the question of the extent to which German companies may be described as bureaucratic was raised. It was suggested that in terms of a comparison with French companies German firms are not especially bureaucratic being low on compartmentalisation and hierarchy, tending to keep the purely administrative component of the company 'in its place' and attaching little importance to seniority. In this context it also emerged that German companies, in comparison with French ones, have rather short salary hierarchies, a fact which reflects the affluence of the German worker, not the poverty of the German manager.

Notes

1. See, for instance, the list of the top 500 West German companies by turnover in Dr Ernst Schmacke (ed.), *Die grossen 500: Deutschlands führende Unternehmen und Ihr Management* (Luchterhand Verlag, Neuwied, 1976 edn). It is clear that the 'top 500' include many GmbH and some KGs.

2. Taken from an unpublished paper by Dr S. J. Prais of the National Institute of Economic and Social Research entitled: 'Large and Small Manufacturing Enterprises in Europe and America.' Dr Prais presented a copy of this paper to the author after a personal meeting in 1975.

3. Ibid.

4. Ibid.

5. Alan Hughes, 'Company Concentration, Size of Plant, and Merger Activity' in M. Panic (ed.), *The UK and West German Manufacturing Industry, 1954-72* (NEDO Monograph 5, London, 1976).

6. Ibid.

7. Ibid.

8. Ernst Schmacke, *Die grossen 500*, 1976.

9. Ibid.

10. Michel Beaud, *La Croissance Economique de l'Allemagne de l'Ouest, 1949-62* (Editions Cujas, Paris, 1965).

11. Vance Packard, *The Status Seekers* (Pelican Books, Harmondsworth, 1961).

12. At any rate where Design is concerned there would appear to be a contrast with Britain in this respect. At a Department of Industry seminar in July 1977 Lord Brown argued that Design is typically a low status function in British companies, and is seldom represented on the Board of Directors.

13. In this connection see the discussion of the American consultancy report in Chapter 4.

14. The institute in question is the Laboratoire d'Economie et de Sociologie du Travail, at Aix-en-Provence, France.

15. For a brief overview of the findings and their theoretical implications see Michel Brossard et Marc Maurice, 'Existe-il un modèle Universel des Structures d'Organisation?', *Sociologie du Travail* vol. XVI, no. 4 (1974). For a detailed presentation of findings and interpretations see *Production de la Hiérarchie dans l'Entreprise: Recherche d'un Effet Social – Allemagne-France*, 2 vols. (Laboratoire d'Economie et de Sociologie du Travail, Aix-en-Provence, Autumn 1977).

16. J. J. Sylvestre, 'Industrial Wage Differentials: a Two-way Comparison', *International Labour Review*, vol. 110, no. 6 (December 1974).

17. Arndt Sorge and Malcolm Warner, 'Variety and Determinants of Factory Organisation in Britain, France, and Germany: the United Kingdom National Report', Report submitted to the Social Science Research Council, London, Autumn 1977.

18. See especially Arndt Sorge and Malcolm Warner, 'Manpower Training, Manufacturing Organisation and Work Roles in Great Britain and West Germany', Discussion Paper 78-96, Internationales Institut für Management und Verwaltung, Berlin, December 1978.

3 THE BACKGROUND OF GERMAN MANAGEMENT

Analyses of the social background of managers, the (non-communist) world over, tend to demonstrate that the majority of managers have middle-class origins. Not only are they themselves middle-class in terms of the standing of their occupation, their income, and, certainly in West Germany, their educational level, but many of them have fathers who could also claim all this and the great majority have fathers who were at least non-manual workers. This is not to say that executive work, in West Germany and elsewhere, is not an avenue of upward social mobility. Most of the West German studies show that the executive sons have a higher average occupational standing than their fathers, but in most cases none is measuring transition across intra middle-class boundaries.

This is partly, in the West German case, a function of the samples in such studies of management background. The samples, in the present writer's opinion, tend to be pitched too high. Samples of chairmen and chief executives and of all members of the *Aufsichtsrat, Vorstand* and *Geschäftsführung* abound. There is often concentration on the large or largest companies. Sometimes samples embrace the level (or two) below the *Vorstand* but not often. Only very occasionally does one encounter a study which takes as its sample *all* managers, irrespective of hierarchical position, in a given set of firms.

Another arguable deficiency of much of the management background literature is that it is much stronger on making clear what the facts are than on explaining them. The common finding to emerge from the studies is that most business managers (who actually get into the samples!) have middle-class origins. The higher the executive level, the larger and more illustrious the company, the truer this is. Now this may not seem a very exciting finding. It accords with common sense and common observation. And it is not confined to business managers. Most members of most prestigious occupational groups, from bishops to major-generals, have middle-class origins.[1] But knowing that it is so is not the same as knowing why it is so. If we take the particular case of German business executives we may still inquire as to the nature of the advantage which their mostly middle-class parentage conferred on them. Is it hereditary intelligence, nurtured ambition, the quality of parental advice, connections, organisational *savoir faire*, or something else that no one has thought of yet? Exploring hypotheses of this kind is, of course, not easy. It is a comparatively easy exercise to establish that an executive's father was a clerk and his grandfather a bricklayer and to make statements about social mobility on this basis. It is another matter to decide what would constitute evidence of the quality of parental advice as a determinant of career success and then actually gather such evidence.[2]

One of these studies of executive background, by Hall, de Bettignies and Fischgrund, is in fact an internationally comparative study.[3] The authors sent questionnaires to the chief executives of the 500 largest companies in Britain, France, Germany and Italy and to the chief executives of a smaller number of the largest companies in Holland and Belgium. Unfortunately the response rate was low; 24 per cent for the sample as a whole and 20 per cent for the German part of the sample in particular. With this qualification it is interesting to see that only 72.5 per cent of the Germans had an upper-class background (defined by the authors as having fathers who were business owners, senior executives, or professionals) compared with 85 per cent for France. Britain and Germany emerge from this study as the two countries where the highest proportion of top executives had experienced upward social mobility; in Britain the corresponding figure for top executives with an upper-class background was 69 per cent. To complete the picture for Germany, a further 16.5 per cent came from a middle-class background (in a rather literal sense — fathers who were minor civil servants, school teachers, salesmen and so on). And the final 11 per cent in the German sample had fathers who were manual workers — the highest proportion for any of the countries in the sample.

Now although the sample is small, in fact there are only about a hundred replies from German companies, it is still a very high-powered sample, consisting of chief executives only for companies in the top 500. It is interesting that even at this exalted level one in ten of the German top executives were born into the working-class. The authors' explanation is that this German finding reflects the conditions at the end of the War when there was a premium on drive and ability regardless of social origins. This is an entirely plausible explanation and the study is especially interesting as the only strictly comparative one which we have.

Another interesting point which emerges from several of the German studies of executive background is that a particular kind of middle-class occupational background is over-represented.[4] That is to say, large proportions of the fathers of the executives, in several studies, come from what in German is called the *Beamtenschaft*. *Beamte* in German is usually translated as civil servant, yet the German term embraces more. The *Beamtenschaft* is not just administrative personnel in direct government service but also school teachers, university staff, the police, part of the armed services, the clergy, the judiciary and more senior employees in the post office and railways. It is difficult to interpret this situation where the public service, broadly defined, functions as a parental talent reservoir for higher industrial management, but it is an unusual phenomenon. A lot of different occupations are represented in the *Beamtenschaft*, but if one asks what they have in common it is a devotion to duty-honesty-reliability syndrome: not a bad moral climate for the upbringing of the future senior manager.

Another possible interpretation of the over-representation of *Beamten* as fathers of senior managers is that it certainly used to be the case, and still is to some extent, that being a *Beamte* implied a certain social and occupational standing and also a fair measure of self-esteem. So it is possible that with the over-representation of *Beamte* fathers one is observing a two step model of social and occupational advancement. The father achieves something by becoming a *Beamte* in the first place and the son does better still by becoming a senior manager.

A further distinctive feature of surveyed samples of senior German managers is that Protestants are over-represented and Catholics under-represented.[5] We also know that qualified engineers in West Germany, most of whom are managers in industry, are another group in which Protestants are over-represented and Catholics under-represented.[6] What again we do not really know is why. It is unlikely that it is simply the case that Protestants are somehow or other more ambitious and energetic, since this over-representation of Protestants is much more marked among employed executives than among owner-managers. Unfortunately, there appears to be no evidence on the role of Jews in executive life in West Germany. We know that in the USA, for instance, Jews are under-represented among the ranks of salaried executives even if they abound as entrepreneurs.[7] It would be particularly interesting to know how the Jews fare in Germany in this respect.

Some surveys of the background of German executives inquire as to their place of birth. In fact geographical background, as denoted in the results of such surveys, reveals little that is striking. Small, medium-sized and large towns are all represented; no particular area of West Germany appears to be favoured as 'the cradle of executive talent' after making allowance for population differences from region to region (North Rhine Westphalia is by far the most populous state of the 11

Länder making up the Federal Republic). One line of inquiry, however, which is not generally pursued in surveys, is an attempt to establish the relative proportions of senior managers from within the present territory of the Federal Republic and those born outside. The second category refers not to the tiny numbers of Germans who by chance were born in foreign countries, but to the substantial number born first, in those parts of Germany which were ceded to Poland, the USSR, and Czechoslovakia at the end of the War and secondly, to those born in the area which is now the German Democratic Republic (East Germany) and was formerly the Russian Occupation Zone (see Chapter 1). This point is raised because in personal contacts with German managers the author has noted an apparent marked over-representation of Germans from the east and it would be nice to be able to document this fact. If our observations are correct, this over-representation of, loosely speaking, east Germans, is quite consistent with both 'push' and 'pull' forces of immigration. Those forced out of the ceded territories shortly after the end of the War were those who had lost most and had correspondingly more to gain by their exertions in the West. Refugees from firstly the Russian Zone and after 1949, the German Democratic Republic were, increasingly, those most strongly attracted to the growing prosperity of West Germany and most equipped to do well for themselves occupationally in the context of this general expansion.

A distinctive feature of the background of German executives, at any rate from a British viewpoint, is that this background is not differentiated by any educational experience having a socially prestigious significance. To take the most obvious point, there are in West Germany no public schools in the British sense. In Britain, former pupils of public (i.e private, fee-paying schools) are over-represented in top positions in industry, on Boards of Directors, in insurance and banking and have a near monopoly in stockbroking and merchant banking. There is practically no German equivalent of this. Private schools exist in West Germany but usually with the *raison d'être* of some distinctive educational philosophy; something both stronger and more particularist that the nineteenth-century British ideal of the Christian gentleman or the general idea of educating a ruling class. Furthermore, attendance at a private school in West Germany, although it implies at least middle-class status (since the fees have to be paid!) does not confer any social distinction. And private school is not where most children from upper-middle-class homes are educated; typically they attend a *Gymnasium* (grammar school, educationally selective secondary school). It is a little ironic from a British standpoint, but having attended a private school in Germany tends to provoke raised eyebrows and the silent questions: why did his parents want to get rid of him, why couldn't he get on in the *Gymnasium* like everyone else?

Not only are there effectively no public schools in West Germany, there is also no Oxbridge and practically no Ivy League universities either. There are really two considerations here. First, there are no universities in West Germany which enjoy a particular social cachet, which are especially favoured by the upper class, after the manner of Oxford and Cambridge in England. Secondly, there are no universities which have a high academic reputation *across the board*, such that if one has studied there others are naturally impressed irrespective of what one studied. In Germany it is particular faculties which achieve repute, Business Economics at Cologne for instance or Medicine at Marburg, rather than the university as a whole. Hence there is no 'Oxbridge pattern' in the background of successful executives in West Germany, in terms of either the overall repute of particular universities or their social standing.

A consequence of this situation where all universities have, roughly speaking, parity of esteem both social and academic, is that there is little interest in Germany in where one has studied except in connection with what one studied. If one questions recruitment and training officers of German companies as to their preferences in recruiting graduates they tend to give specific answers about course content or examination standards rather than general answers in terms of prestige categories. This tendency is probably most marked in the recruitment of technical graduates, where one will be told that the mechanical engineering course at such and such a university has some course options particularly relevant to the company's product development programme, or that electrical engineering finals are known to be marked very strictly at some other university so students with good grades from this faculty should be given preference and so on. Another common theme in this context is for personnel officers to say that they are, of course, interested in the (overall) degree grades obtained by applicants but more important are marks obtained in particular courses, forming only part of the degree, where the course content is deemed especially relevant to the company's operations. It is also interesting how widespread this kind of knowledge is. That is to say, it is not only personnel managers at giant multi-nationals hiring hundreds of graduates a year who make this kind of observation: the author has also encountered such testimonies at quite small companies, where it was clear that managers took an interest in course content and standards at (especially technical) universities.

There is one qualification which should be made to the picture given so far of German universities enjoying parity of esteem, free from the distortions of social snobbery, their graduates being evaluated in terms of particularist rational criteria. This qualification is that this state of affairs has been affected somewhat by student radicalism. Those universities, that is, which are regarded as more than usually radical, perhaps the Free University in West Berlin would be the most widely acknowledged example, do not find favour with industrial (and other) employers. This phenomenon dates only from the late 1960s and has not affected the recruitment of those who are senior executives now, but it is presumably affecting current graduate recruitment – certainly there have been disclosures in the German press to this effect in the late 1970s.

That the Germans have in effect no public schools and no Oxbridge and therefore no considerations of social exclusiveness to affect the recruitment and advancement of their managers, is of some interest as part of the German system. It also marks a comparison with Britain and probably some other countries. There is a further point. Quite simply the fewer the number of irrelevant criteria, and social exclusiveness criteria are irrelevant to managerial performance, the more scope there is for the operation of meaningful criteria. This observation is consistent with the German emphasis on *Leistung* (achievement, performance), a phenomenon which is discussed in more detail in Chapter 5.

Before discussing the literature on the educational background and qualifications of German managers it may be helpful to indicate what the range of possible qualifications is and where they are located in the national system of education.

German Education and the Range of Qualifications

Nursery education is neither free nor compulsory in West Germany, except in the state of Bremen. Primary education runs from the ages of six to ten (though it is six to twelve in West Berlin) and secondary education from ten to sixteen (legal minimum). There are a few comprehensive schools, but they are not numerous except in the state of Hessen. Nationally, comprehensive schools probably accommodate about 5 per cent of children in the secondary school age group. What is basically in operation in West Germany is a tripartite system of secondary education roughly similar to that which existed in Britain in precomprehensive school days. There is the *Hauptschule* (secondary modern school), the *Realschule* (technical school) and the *Gymnasium* (grammar school). The proportions attending these three types would be approximately 45:20:25 (with some 5 per cent at comprehensive schools and another 5 per cent at special schools) in marked contrast with Britain where only a tiny proportion attended the technical schools. Since the role of private education is negligible it is fair to say that the overwhelming majority of German managers senior enough to figure in surveys of background and qualifications have attended the *Gymnasium*.

There is an examination known as *mittlere Reife* which is taken at the age of 16 and approximates to GCE 'O' level in England. And there is a further examination, *Abitur*, which is taken at 19 and which corresponds to GCE 'A' level in England. In fact the *Abitur* exam usually consists of a larger number of subjects than the customary three in English 'A' level, some of these being the subject of written examination, others being examined on a continuous assessment basis. Or to put it another way, there is less dropping of subjects in the *Gymnasium* than in the grammar school, though there is some variation from state to state in West Germany and the current trend is towards the more specialised (fewer subjects) exam of the English 'A' level type. *Abitur* admits to university, in principle to any faculty of any university without more ado, though in more recent practice this freedom of student choice has been modified by a *numerus clausus* (limited entry) for overcrowded subjects, usually subjects involving equipment or laboratory facilities – medicine is the notorious example.

The *mittlere Reife* is usually taken by pupils at the *Realschule*, and by pupils leaving the *Gymnasium* early (i.e. not staying on to take *Abitur*). Thus in Germany people tend to have either *mittlere Reife* or *Abitur*, depending on the type of secondary school they attended, or when they left; it is not usual to have both as it is for those who reach university in England. Again managers senior enough to figure in (most of) the background and qualification surveys will generally have *Abitur*.

University courses tend to be somewhat longer in West Germany than in England, the official minimum length being four years and actual average time taken to graduate being longer. Anyone who successfully completes an undergraduate course in the minimum four years can quote this as an achievement in itself in much the same way that one might cite one's double first with pride in England. Degrees, and *Abitur* results for that matter, are also graded in West Germany, the top grade being 1.0.

A general difference between West Germany and Britain is that the relationship between the subject studied at university and subsequent employment and career is much tighter in the German case. Or to put it another way, the German graduate has much less freedom of choice than his British opposite number; the German to a much greater extent chose his career when he decided what to study. To give a practical example, the history graduate in Britian might do research or become a school teacher. He might enter the higher civil service or the liberal professions. Posts in the media are possible and graduate traineeships in industry eminently possible. The German history graduate can become a school teacher and pretty well nothing else. This does not mean that Germany is littered with thousands of unemployed history graduates, since everyone knows 'the way it is' and this is reflected in low enrolments (proportionally) in subjects with limited occupational outlets (this issue is discussed in more detail in Chapter 8).

A subject which does pre-eminently lead somewhere occupationally is engineering. Engineering, however, is not taught at the ordinary universities (except for Bochum and Erlangen) but at the *technische Hochschulen* or *technische Universitäten*. These specialised technical universities were mostly established in the nineteenth century, they enjoy parity of esteem with the ordinary universities and admission to them is also via the *Abitur* examination.

A first degree in Germany is usually called a Diplom, and graduates in particular subjects are designated by a Diplom-plus-subject compound noun. A Diplom Volkswirt, for example, is an economics graduate; a Diplom Kaufmann or Diplom Betriebswirt is a graduate in business economics and a Diplom Ingenieur (standard abbreviation Dipl Ing) is an engineering graduate. The three recurrent subjects, studied by graduate managers who figure in surveys are law, economics, and engineering. Graduates in natural science subjects are not very numerous among the ranks of industrial managers, except in the chemical industry. It is also the case that students of the natural science subjects constitute a relatively small proportion of the total undergraduate population in West Germany compared with Britain (see Chapter 8). Frequently, in the analyses of survey data, scientists are bracketed with engineers; it is important to note that in the German context 'scientists and engineers' means battalions of engineers and a handful of scientists.

Another distinctive feature of the German university scene is that there are no undergraduate courses in management or business studies. Management teaching *per se* is not as developed in West Germany as it is in Britain or the USA. In Germany courses for managers are invariably post-experience, not undergraduate or immediate postgraduate. They also differ from many American and British courses in that they are more specialised as to content and as to the level and more particularly the function of the executives attending them. Germans have also been criticised for not showing as much interest as managers from other countries in the international management education centres such as IMEDE and INSEAD.[8]

There are no master's degrees in West Germany, in the British and American sense of a degree falling between the bachelor's and doctor's degree, though to confuse the issue some German universities (the University of Constance is an example) use MA to designate first degrees. Above the first degree (Diplom) in Germany comes the doctor's degree. Many senior managers in fact have a doctorate, again the most common subjects being law (Dr Jur), business economics (Dr rer pol) and engineering (Dr Ing). Managers with the doctor's degree in chemistry are also very prevalent in the chemical industry. To complete the picture of the hierarchy of university qualifications in West Germany there is yet another called *Habilitation*, a supra and super PhD qualification attained by research and thesis. The *Habilitation* is not a qualification available to anyone who happens to fancy something superior to the doctor's degree: it is a qualification for professional academics, officially a prerequisite for appointment to a full professorship. As such it is not, of course, a qualification that German managers are likely to have, though there are a few managers in West Germany who are ex-professors (in the chemical industry for instance) and who therefore have the *Habilitation*.

This fact does not, unfortunately, come out very clearly in surveys of managers' qualifications in West Germany, but there are also a range of non-school, non-university qualifications. First, there is of course the apprenticeship (apprenticeship is discussed in more detail in Chapter 8). On the craft-technical side there is the *Industrielehre* and the *Handwerkslehre* (industrial apprenticeship and craft apprenticeship). The *Industrielehre* is the dominant one now, though the *Handwerkslehre* carries an added element of prestige. It is not unusual for the engineering graduate (Dipl Ing) to have done an apprenticeship and it is quite normal for the non-graduate engineer (Ing Grad, see below) to start his working life by doing an apprenticeship. In consequence there are many German managers who have done an apprenticeship and who hold the *Facharbeiterbrief* (skilled worker's certificate) obtained by passing the examination at the end of the apprenticeship. The possession of this qualification (the *Facharbeiterbrief*) tends not to show up in the surveys but it is quite common; it is, however, becoming less common both because of increasing academicisation in general and changes in the recruitment to the Ing Grad course (see below) in particular.

There is also the *kaufmännische Lehre* (commercial apprenticeship) which is even more important as an original qualification for at any rate the older generation of German managers. Formal qualifications equivalent to the Ing Grad and Dipl Ing in the technical functions tend to be less common on the commercial side of German companies, so that the *kaufmännische Lehre* is more prominent in the qualification set on the commercial side. Qualification levels are going up all the time, of course, and this applies to the commercial side as well, but there is still a difference. It is unusual to meet a manager on the technical side who has *only* a successfully completed apprenticeship behind him, but it is not unusual to meet quite senior and demonstrably able *Industrie-Kaufmann* (as the ex-commercial apprentice is known) in Finance, Sales, Administration and Personnel.

On the technical side again there are often qualifications which managers may have, not usually in the sense of a terminal qualification such as a university degree, but in the sense of more junior qualifications obtained earlier in their career. There is the *Technikerprüfung* (technician's examination) usually obtained by part-time attendance at a junior technical college. There are certificates in work study, known as *Refa Qualifikationen* and there is a formal qualification for foremen known as the *Meisterbrief* (see Chapter 7 for a discussion of the foreman and his training).

But perhaps the most distinctive feature of the German further education system is the existence of an important sub-university qualification. The courses leading to this qualification are offered in senior technical colleges called *Fachhochschulen*. The qualification is offered in a very wide variety of mostly vocational subjects, of which the two most important as management qualifications are business economics and engineering (all branches). The courses are full-time and last a minimum of three years. Students usually begin these courses at the age of eighteen. Although *Abitur* (the German equivalent of 'A' level) is not required for entry to the *Fachhochschule*, it is normal for *Fachhochschule* entrants to have had twelve years of full-time education and to have obtained an entry qualification known as *Fachhochschulreife* (literally, readiness to attend a *Fachhochschule*) at a junior technical college. The level of this *Fachhochschulreife* examination in British terms would be somewhere between GCE 'O' and 'A' levels, probably closer to 'A' level. All the lecturers at the *Fachhochschule* are themselves university graduates and they are required by law to have a minimum of five years' relevant occupational experience. This, in the case of lecturers in business economics or engineering means, of course, five years' experience in commerce or industry. Students who successfully complete courses at a *Fachhochschule* are described as *graduiert*; so someone who has studied business economics becomes a *graduierter Betriebswirt*, someone who has studied engineering a *graduierter Ingenieur*, or, to use the standard abbreviation, an Ing Grad.

Qualifications at this level are important in West Germany, where vocational education is taken more seriously than in Britain or France. Particularly important is the Ing Grad, a qualification which is very common among German managers. Although there is a general trend towards recruiting and promoting university graduates, the Ing Grad is still to be found at all levels in the German management hierarchy. The Ing Grad is also the dominant qualification in Design and Production (see Chapter 6 for a further discussion of qualifications on the technical side).

It should, however, be added that the Ing Grad qualification, and the younger generation of engineers who are so qualified, will probably figure less in the ranks of German management in the future than is the case at present. This is not only because of a general trend towards the recruitment of graduates; it also reflects changes in the way students are recruited to the Ing Grad course and industry's unfavourable view of the changes. The system of admission to the *Fachhochschule* described above has only existed since about 1970 (the changes were implemented at different times in different federal states). Previously, a three-and-a-half year apprenticeship (as described earlier in this chapter), or two years' supervised practical experience in industry, was the standard route for admission to the Ing Grad course at the *Ingenieurschule* (engineering school, the old name for the present *Fachhochschule*). The point is that under the old system the Ing Grad, the day he left the *Ingenieurschule*, could already claim years of practical experience on the shop floor by virtue of his earlier apprenticeship. The new style Ing Grad does not have this claim to practical prowess and in consequence is not so sought after by industry.[9]

So, if the present situation does not change there are likely to be fewer Ing Grads in the ranks of German management in the future. On the other hand, it is quite likely that the situation will change. The key feature of the new system is the two year full-time course at the junior technical college, after school leaving and leading to the *Fachhochschulreife* (admission requirement for the *Fachhochschule*) in place of the apprenticeship. But two of the states, Bavaria and Baden-Württemberg have in fact compensated for the deficiency in practical experience by instituting two *Industrie-Semester* (industry terms) as part of the Ing Grad course. If other states follow this lead, which is in some cases quite conceivable and would be welcomed by industry, then the decline of the Ing Grad will be arrested.

The Educational Background of German Managers

If we turn next to the educational background and qualifications which German managers actually have as demonstrated by the survey evidence, some introductory remarks may be helpful. As with surveys of managers' social backgrounds there is, in the author's opinion, too much concentration on the higher ranks. When it comes to the educational profile of the *Vorstand* the surveys have achieved overkill, but we know relatively little from this source about the qualifications of the typical salesman and production superintendent. Furthermore, many of the samples tend to be treated in an élitist way as though the only qualification worth mentioning were a university degree. This is a pity for two reasons. First, one of the strengths of the German system is the fact that there are substantial, non-university vocational courses – those leading to the *graduiert* qualifications. Secondly, it is one of German industry's distinctive features that a significant minority of its managers do combine the humbler qualifications listed earlier with the higher *graduiert* and university qualifications.

In discussing some of the extant surveys of the educational background of German managers it becomes clear that the only consistent finding is the primacy of three subjects of study – law, economics and engineering. In one study 70 per cent of the managers will be graduates, in the next only 30 per cent. This does not mean that the whole exercise is a nonsense. It is simply a manifestation of the fact that all surveys are only as good as their samples. In this context it matters a lot whether one surveys *Vorstand* chairmen or *Vorstand* members; owner-managers or employed executives; all managers in North Rhine Westphalia or *Aufsichtsrat* members for the top 100 companies and so on.

In the same connection readers who would like to know how German managers compare with those in other countries have to be satisfied with scientifically second best answers. That is to say, the only wholly satisfactory answer is one based on a simultaneous survey in the two or more countries concerned and one which uses the same sampling frame selecting members of the two or more national samples evenly in terms of company size, executive rank and branch of the economy.

Such studies are very rare, so the best one can usually do is make rough comparisons between unlike samples surveyed at different times.

With this proviso the biggest and newest survey of British managers for comparison is that carried out in 1976 and published by the British Institute of Management in 1978.[10] This is a survey of 10,000 of the BIM's own members, nationwide. The response rate was 45 per cent so that the real sample is 4,525 and all ranks from company chairman to junior manager are included (see Table 3.1).

Table 3.1: Educational Profile of Survey of British Managers, BIM, 1978

Qualification[11]	% of sample
Two or more 'O' levels or equivalent	58
Two or more 'A' levels or equivalent	45
Ordinary National Certificate or Ordinary National Diploma	21
Higher National Certificate or Higher National Diploma	27
First Degree	28
Diploma in Management Studies	36
Other postgraduate diploma	9
Higher Degree (MA, MSc, PhD)	8

Note: The figures do not add up to 100 per cent because many respondents will have several of these qualifications.

It is probably fair to say that this survey overstates the British educational level a little. It is a reasonable guess that those who did not return the questionnaire (over 5,000) were the less well qualified; BIM membership itself probably implies a higher level of professional consciousness and the sample is drawn exclusively from BIM membership. As the author of the BIM report fairly notes the sample also contains minorities of consultants and management teachers.[12] Finally on this question of a British comparison, a very good review of the various British studies and surveys, as a more extended comparative base, has been produced by Ian Glover.[13]

Let us now turn to some of the studies conducted in West Germany.[14] One of the earliest post-war studies was made by Heinz Hartmann using executive registers and address books as the information source.[15] The survey is of senior managers — members of the *Vorstand* and *Geschäftsführung* and of other senior ranks, and the size of the sample was 6,578. Of these some 31 per cent were university graduates, though this figure is probably an under-estimate since academic qualifications were not always given in the sources used. Among the graduates the largest single group were the engineers (36 per cent), with law graduates in second place (19 per cent) and economics graduates third (17 per cent). Hartmann notes that lawyers tended to be promoted at a relatively early age and were favoured for appointments to the *Aufsichtsrat* (supervisory board). Yet engineers were the dominant group; one out of four graduate *Vorstand* chairmen was an engineer and the Dr Ing (PhD in engineering) was the most favoured qualification for the chairmanship of the *Vorstand*.

Moving to the early 1960s the business magazine *Capital*[16] published the results of its own survey of the educational background of some 377 managers. As with Hartmann's survey the sample is very much a top management one — *Vorstand* members, *Geschäftsführer*, and *Prokuristen* (a *Prokurist* is a senior manager empowered to represent the firm legally; this is a legal requirement). Of the sample 62.9 per cent were university graduates. Educational details were not given for the other third, though it is reasonable to suppose that these other managers had some of the non-university qualifications enumerated in the previous section of this chapter. Again engineers constituted the largest proportion of the graduates (42.6 per cent); lawyers were in second place (21.5 per cent) and economics graduates in third (19.8 per cent). Graduates in natural science subjects and arts subjects, taken together, accounted for only a small proportion (9.7 per cent) of the graduate sample.

This *Capital* survey is also of interest in presenting graduate rates for different branches of industry. Taking companies rather than individual managers as the units of analysis the sample is modest, comprising 80 companies. This sample size constraint can lead to distortion, as in the finding that top management in the construction industry is 100 per cent graduate (two companies, represented by five managers, all of them engineering graduates!) Setting aside this chance entity, the order was that 77 per cent of the top managers in the electrical industry were graduates, 76.8 per cent of those in the chemical industry, 72.3 per cent of those in the iron, steel and metal industry, but only 48.8 per cent in the mechanical engineering and motor car industries. In five out of the 80 companies, none of the top managers was a graduate, while in another eleven companies the whole *Vorstand* was graduate.

A similar small sample top manager survey was made in the mid-1960s by Wolfgang Zapf.[17] Zapf's sample, in fact, is even more homogeneous constituting 318 *Vorstand* members drawn from the 50 largest companies by turnover. Of this sample 95 per cent had attended a *Gymnasium* (grammar school) and had *Abitur* ('A' level). Graduates comprised 89 per cent of the sample. Of the 11 per cent of non-graduates, 8 per cent were *Industrie-Kaufmann*, that is, had begun their career by doing a commercial apprenticeship; 1 per cent had served an apprenticeship and gone on to higher (non-graduate) qualifications and the final 2 per cent were (former) skilled workers (with the *Facharbeiterbrief*) — this 2 per cent were probably the Labour Directors in *Montanindustrie* firms (see Chapter 2). A small new finding was that one in ten of the university graduates had done apprenticeships before going to university.

Among the graduates the engineers as usual are in first place; in fact the engineers and scientists together constituted 57 per cent; lawyers and economics graduates both accounted for 21 per cent of the graduate sample. This survey is the most striking illustration of the fact that engineering, law and economics are *the* subjects of study for prospective German managers.

Zapf has also checked the proportion of graduates for different age groups. For those managers in the sample who were over 65 some 88 per cent were graduates; the proportion was lower for the middle age groups (45-65), but for the youngest age group (remember that we are concerned here with *Vorstand* members), those managers under 45 were all university graduates. This is a piece of tangible evidence for the frequently made assertion that German management is becoming increasingly graduate dominated. Incidentally, not only were 89 per cent of the sample graduates, but 61 per cent of these also had PhD's.

A study with a very large sample, dating again from the mid 1960s is that of Hartmann and Wienold.[18] The sample was made up of the 21,707 top managers and owner-managers listed in a directory of leading figures in West German economic life.[19] This enormous sample was a mélange of *Vorstand* members, *Geschäftsführer*, managing partners, and owner-managers.

This time 27 per cent of the sample were university graduates. It will be noted that this is less than the proportion (31 per cent) in Hartmann's earlier 1954 study. This almost certainly represents a difference in sampling since the earlier study concentrated on large joint stock companies whereas this study, with its enormous sample, has sizeable proportions of owner-managers and managing-partners with whom educational standards tend to be lower. Of the graduates 36 per cent had studied engineering and science, 21 per cent economics and 13 per cent law. The employed executives were more likely than the owner-managers to be graduates. For the prize position of chairman of the *Vorstand*, graduates with either a legal training or a PhD seemed to be most favoured. Again law graduates, with or without a PhD, seemed to be favoured for *Vorstand* appointments generally, relative to their numbers and were particularly strong in banking and insurance. The owner-managers, though less likely to be university educated, were most likely to have studied engineering if they had been to university. Like the authors of the *Capital* survey Hartmann and Wienold checked which branches of industry had the highest proportion of graduates and found 'the winners' to be banking and insurance, the power and coal industries and chemicals.

Max Kruk conducted a survey similar to that of Hartmann and Wienold using the same directory of leading figures in the West German economy, though in fact the 1965 edition of the directory (Hartmann and Wienold had used the 1964 edition). This yielded another enormous sample of 31,427,[20] a more heterogeneous sample than that of Hartmann and Wienold including *Aufsichtsrat* (supervisory board) members and non-managing partners as well as the usual categories of senior managers and owner-managers. In fact all types of owner-manager included constituted 59.6 per cent of the whole sample. This again has the effect of depressing the educational profile with 31.6 per cent of the whole sample being graduates, though the graduate proportion rises to 60 per cent for *Vorstand* members. Over half the graduates also held PhD's. The subjects studied were as always engineering, economics and law, in decreasing order of importance, with other subjects playing only a minor role. Kruk concluded that engineering studies were still the best route into higher management, though law studies conferred an advantage for appointments to the *Aufsichtsrat* and to the *Vorstand* of banks.

Moving into the 1970s Pross and Boetticher surveyed a sample of some 538 *Vorstand* members and other senior managers from 13 large joint stock companies.[21] These researchers also found that the majority of managers at this level had attended a selective secondary school, 89 per cent of them having been to a *Gymnasium* (grammar school). The majority were graduates and Pross and Boetticher documented the fact that graduate dominance increases with hierarchic rank. In their sample 58 per cent of the *Prokuristen* (managers with a power of attorney) were graduates and 77 per cent of the *Vorstand* members were. The proportion of *Vorstand* members who were graduates is low compared with the figure which emerges from some other studies; this is probably because Pross and Boetticher chose their companies on the basis of personal connections — the companies do not represent the largest 13 in West Germany nor 13 from among the top 50 as in some other studies already discussed. Incidentally about half the university graduates also had PhD's.

The distribution of graduates among the various subjects was quite consistent with the results of all the other surveys: 60.6 per cent engineering and science, 22.1 per cent economics, 13.5 per cent law. Pross and Boetticher argue that the proportion of lawyers has declined and that the number of engineers in top management has been declining as well, though engineers are still the dominant group. The corresponding gains have been made by graduates in business economics. The authors regard these changes as indicative of a change from production orientation towards a marketing orientation. It should be added that there are other studies which do not show this rise of business economics graduates and a decline in the dominance of engineers. In relation to their overall numbers the engineer's chance of getting to the top (e.g. *Aufsichtsrat* posts, chairman of the *Vorstand*) is not especially good, and not as good as the lawyer's. On the other hand the engineers are the most numerous group and by sheer weight of numbers remain the dominant group at the top (and for that matter in the middle).

Max Kruk conducted a second survey of the background of German managers, to which we referred in a different connection earlier in this chapter.[22] Kruk's later study comprised a sample of 2,053 managers of the 381 largest companies. As in earlier studies it emerged that the great majority, some 88.3 per cent, had attended a *Gymnasium*. Kruk noted here a change over time in that older managers in the sample tended to come from the *humanistisches Gymnasium* with its emphasis on Latin, Greek and Hebrew, while the younger ones were more likely to have been to the *neusprachliches Gymnasium* favouring modern languages and science.

Some 75 per cent of Kruk's sample were graduates, with engineers and scientists, economics graduates and lawyers comprising three approximately equal groups, though engineers were the dominant group in manufacturing industry considered separately. Graduates in other disciplines accounted for a mere 1.6 per cent. Some two-thirds of Kruk's graduate sample also had PhD's. Kruk also characterised the subject groups socially viewing the lawyers as the social elite among top managers (this is consistent with the fact that most surveys show them to be favoured for *Aufsichtsrat* posts), the engineers as lower-middle-class and the business economics graduates as lower-class and also on average younger (c.f. Pross and Boetticher). Kruk noted too that work experience abroad appeared to be significant for a successful career (this point is taken up in Chapter 5 in discussing the German manager's view of career success). It is also claimed by Kruk that although the *Praktiker* (practical man, in this context one lacking university qualifications) is generally losing ground to the graduate manager he is still holding his own in some particular functions including Sales and Purchasing; this claim is entirely consistent with the present writer's experience of German managers.

One of the best studies of the qualifications of West German managers is that of Gerhard Brinkmann.[23] The sample is based on 100 companies, representing several branches of industry and commerce, in North Rhine Westphalia, most of these companies employing over 1,000 people. Brinkmann has included in the sample not just top management but four levels of management. His Level I is the *Vorstand* and *Geschäftsführung* members; Level II the *Direktoren* (not a precise term but usually used to designate major heads of departments coming immediately below the *Vorstand*), and Levels III and IV are the next two levels down. This is about the only survey we have where the sample is so hierarchically all embracing.

There are two general and important findings to emerge from Brinkmann's study. The first is that qualification levels are appreciably higher on the technical side of the firm than on the commercial and administrative side. This difference is already clear at Level I (*Vorstand* and *Geschäftsführung*) but becomes more marked at the lower levels. This finding does not especially contradict the results of other surveys; it is just that Brinkmann has asked what proportion of the technical and non-technical *Vorstand* members are qualified, rather than treating *Vorstand* members as all one and the same at the lower levels. The second and related finding is that on the technical side, not only is the qualification level higher but the managers concerned are *technically* qualified. This is not a truism, as will be clear in a moment. On the technical side, the vast majority of the managers have the Dipl Ing or Ing Grad qualifications, or they are graduates in natural science subjects. People with non-technical and scientific qualifications account for quite negligible proportions of posts on the technical side. 'Non-technical qualifications' here means, in effect, qualifications in business economics: at Level I managers so qualified constitute 2.9 per cent of the total on the technical side of the firms in the sample, 4.2 per cent at level II and less than 1 per cent at Levels III and IV. On the commercial side, however, not only do we find that the largest single group at all four levels are the *Praktiker* (managers without formal qualifications, not managers qualified in business economics as one might have expected), but also the engineers have a significant foothold. At Level I on the commercial side, for instance, economics graduates account for 18.1 per cent of the posts, Dipl Ings for 16.1 per cent and Ing Grads for 4 per cent. At Level II the economics graduates account for 16.8 per cent of the posts, Dipl Ings and Ing Grads together for 13.7 per cent. At Level III it is 10.6 per cent economics graduates and 15.5 per cent engineers (both types) and at Level IV 8.8 per cent economics graduates and 5.4 per cent engineers.

In other words graduates in business economics do not dominate the commercial functions to anything like the extent that engineers dominate the technical functions. And not only are the engineers dominant on the technical side, they have also 'overspilled' into the commercial functions, at all levels, including the highest. This is an interesting finding in view of the observations of Kruk[24] and Pross and Boetticher[25] to the effect that graduates in business economics are gaining strength in top positions, and that such managers (qualified in business economics) tend to be younger than other colleagues qualified in law and engineering. The two sets of findings are not necessarily incompatible. It may well be that there are more graduates in business economics in top posts now than there used to be. It is also conceivable that graduates in business economics have achieved a greater penetration at the top than in the middle: Brinkmann's figures do suggest this where the business economics graduates' best showing is at *Vorstand* level.

A further point about Brinkmann's study remains to be mentioned. If one turns to banking and insurance in the expectation that these, rather than manufacturing industry, will be the stronghold of the business economics graduates, one is disappointed. In these areas Brinkmann found the penetration of the business economics graduate to be even less and the dominance of the *Praktiker* (and at the top the lawyers) even more marked than in the companies discussed earlier. It should be added that in the fifteen years which have elapsed since Brinkmann actually conducted his survey the position of the business economics graduate has probably improved; the present writer has certainly met more managers qualified in business economics in Sales, Purchasing and 'assistant to' posts than a reading of Brinkmann would lead one to expect.

Finally in this connection there is one survey which is in a separate category. In discussing several of the previous studies it has been noted that owner-managers and employed managers have sometimes been 'lumped' together in the same sample. We have in fact one survey devoted exclusively to the entrepreneurs.[26] It was conducted by the *Arbeitsgemeinschaft Selbständiger Unternehmer/Junger Unternehmer* (work association of independent entrepreneurs/young entrepreneurs) on a sample of 1,307 of their own members in the mid 1960s. The respondents to the ASU questionnaire were all owner-managers, mostly of small to medium sized companies: 75 per cent of the sample had companies employing less than 500 people, and only 10 per cent employed more than 1,000.

Less than half of this sample (44.9 per cent) attended a *Gymnasium* (in contrast to the higher proportion in all the other surveys reviewed here). Nearly half (49.7 per cent) went to university though only 35.5 per cent actually graduated. Though to be fair, this figure of over one-third of the sample as university graduates, is not unimpressive. Bear in mind that if these owner-managers founded their own companies they would not have time to go to university and if they inherited them they would not need to! This last jaunty point no doubt explains those who went to university but did not graduate.

Besides the 49.7 per cent who went to university, however, a further 26.2 per cent did more vocational courses at various kinds of technical college. Furthermore some 57.6 per cent served an apprenticeship. This emphasis on vocational training is very German. The author has also noted in contacts with owner-managers of small companies an apprenticeship and/or Ing Grad tradition — for fathers and sons.

If we step back from this mountain of evidence on the qualifications of German managers some general observations are in order. First, the fact that the mountain exists, and the discussion of the evidence here is meant to be illustrative rather than exhaustive, may itself be significant. There are far more studies of this kind in West Germany than there are in Britain, and if we deduce anything from this it would be that managers and entrepreneurs in Germany excite more interest and are more widely considered to be the proper objects of study.

Secondly, it would be fair to say that the educational level of German managers is very respectable. Except for two of the earlier studies discussed here, where in any case there are queries about the sampling frame, surveys of German managers generally show substantial proportions of graduates. And perhaps more important than this is the fact that in all the studies, except that of Brinkmann, those dismissed as 'non-graduates' are very likely to have completed courses at the *Fachhochschule* (or its earlier equivalents) and in this context the Ing Grad qualification is particularly important. Furthermore one can almost take for granted the fact that non-graduates will have completed an apprenticeship, either commercial or technical (with the proviso concerning the changed recruitment to the Ing Grad course).

Thirdly, it is probably fair to say that managers in West Germany are stronger on formal educational qualifications than their colleagues in Britain. Most of the surveys discussed in this chapter suggest that the proportion of graduates is higher in West Germany. This claim is also supported by the INSEAD study of chief executives of the largest companies in six European states which was referred to earlier in connection with the social background of German managers.[27] This study found that 89 per cent of the sample in France were university educated, 78 per cent in West Germany and 40 per cent in Britain. German managers are probably also in the lead at two other points in the qualification spectrum: they are more likely to have PhD's and more likely to have done apprenticeships. The second point is not well documented, but there can be no doubt, for what it is worth, of the greater prevalence of PhD's among the ranks of German managers.

The comparison with Britain will conceivably evoke two other questions: where, in the German studies, are the managers holding the Diploma in Management Studies or its German equivalent and where are the accountants? The answer to both questions is intriguing — there are none.

There are post-experience courses for managers in West Germany but there is no equivalent to the standard widely available British Diploma in Management Studies. With regard to accountants, there is a definite difference between Britain and Germany. In Britain the chartered accountant has some standing, his qualification will often be treated as 'degree equivalent', he is well paid and has good promotion chances in management. There is no equivalent to the accountant in these senses in West Germany. The book-keeping is done by clerks and the higher level functions of financial control, often discharged by qualified accountants in Britain, will these days be in the hands of graduates in business economics in Germany.

Lastly there is, to an outsider, something rather purposeful about the German system. This comes over in two ways. There is the abundance of vocational and especially technical qualifications from the apprenticeship up to the Ing Grad. The fact that all these exist, and, saving our earlier remarks about the changed status of the Ing Grad, are sought and esteemed, tells us something about the standing of German industry. The other aspect is the way university studies are used in relation to industry. There is less going to university for the sake of it and getting a degree to demonstrate general aptitude. The mode is to study subjects perceptibly relevant to a career in industry, most obviously so in the case of engineering, but plausibly so also in the case of law, in a situation where it is accepted that these are the right things to do.

Qualifications at the Top: Some Examples

To round off this discussion of the formal qualifications we will offer a few examples of the manning of particular posts at the top of German companies showing the qualifications of incumbent managers. The qualifications are given in German but with English equivalents or explanations. The set of qualifications which are a little difficult to 'equivalise' are those obtained at the *Fachhochschule* in engineering and in economics (Ing Grad and Betriebswirt Grad respectively). In the sense that these qualifications represent the successful completion of three year full-time courses they might be argued to be equal to an ordinary BSc or BSc (Econ) in Britain, but of course they are not university level qualifications in the German scheme of things. Accordingly they are equated here with the British Higher National Diploma (HND) qualification. The same argument can be advanced with regard to the first degree (the Diplom) in Germany, where the courses are generally longer than the equivalents in Britain. If we take the Dipl Ing as an example, the official (minimum) length of the course is four years (c.f. a standard three in England) but the average length of time taken to complete this course is just under six years. Thus it could be argued that the Dipl Ing should be equated with the MSc rather than the BSc. In the examples which follow we have in fact adopted the Dipl Ing = BSc formula which equates at any rate similar points in the hierarchy of qualifications in the two countries, though the difference mentioned here is of some importance.

In contrast to the majority of German surveys of managers' background and education discussed earlier we are not seeking here to give examples from the very largest and best known AG companies: these are already well documented in the survey literature. Instead the emphasis is on small and medium sized companies including some of the KG and GmbH type. The few examples which follow are all from real life; they represent, that is, various German companies visited by the author. Some of them have already appeared in the previous chapter to illustrate the breakdown of functional or departmental responsibilities in the *Vorstand* or *Geschäftsführung*. Naturally it would be a violation of confidentiality to identify these companies or enable them to be identified.

78 The Background of German Management

Example 1. A small KG firm employing 420 people engaged in the manufacture of sports equipment. The company has a one-man *Geschäftsführung*, a *Geschäftsführer* with a Dipl Ing and Dr Ing (BSc and PhD in engineering).

Example 2. A medium sized KG company employing some 2,000 people making specialist machinery. The firm is headed by a ten man *Geschäftsführung* with the owner of the firm acting as chairman:

Chairman	Dipl Ing	(BSc engineering)
Production	Ing Grad	(HND engineering)
Design	Dipl Ing	(BSc engineering)
Patents	Techniker	(technician's certificate; approx. ONC standard)
Sales	Industrie-Kaufmann	(ex-commercial apprentice)
Administration	Diplom-Betriebswirt & Dr Betriebswirt	(BSc and PhD in business economics)
Finance	Betriebswirt Grad	(HND in business studies)
Purchasing	Industrie-Kaufmann	(ex-commercial apprentice)
Personnel	Staatsexam and Dr Jur	(LLB and PhD in law)
Projects	Ing Grad	(HND in engineering)

Example 3. A medium sized GmbH company employing 2,000 people; electrical engineering industry. The firm is headed by a two man *Geschäftsführung*:

All technical functions and Sales	Dipl Ing & Dr Ing	(BSc and PhD in engineering)
Finance and Administration	Diplom-Kaufmann and Dr rer pol	(BSc and PhD in business economics)

Example 4. Another medium sized GmbH firm employing 2,000 people manufacturing capital equipment. Firm headed by a four man *Geschäftsführung*, with the owner of the company acting as chairman:

Chairman	Dipl Ing & Dr Ing	(BSc and PhD in engineering)
Technical Functions	Ing Grad	(HND in engineering)
Sales	Industrie-Kaufmann	(ex-commercial apprenticeship)
Finance and Administration	Staatsexam & Dr Jur	(LLB and PhD in law)

Example 5. A larger GmbH firm employing some 5,500 people. Two products: industrial gases and specialist equipment. Company headed by a four man *Geschäftsführung:*

Chairman	Dipl Chem & Dr Betriebswirt	(BSc in chemistry and PhD in business economics)
Gases division	Dipl Ing	(BSc in engineering)
Equipment division	Ing Grad	(HND in engineering)
Finance and Purchasing	Diplom-Kaufmann	(BSC in business economics)

Example 6. A very large AG company manufacturing electrical engineering products. Company headed by an eleven man *Vorstand*:

Chairman	Dipl Ing	(BSc in engineering)
Finance	Diplom-Kaufmann & Dr rer pol	(BSc in business economics and PhD in economics)
Control	Dipl Wirt Ing	(BSc in engineering and economics, a joint honours' degree)
Personnel	Diplom-Kaufmann	(BSc in business economics)
Projects	Staatsexam & Dr Jur	(LLB and PhD in law)
R & D	Dipl Phys & Dr Phil	(BSc and PhD in physics)
Production	Dipl Wirt Ing	(BSc in engineering and economics)
Head of Div. A	Diplom-Kaufmann	(BSc in business economics)
Head of Div. B	Dipl Wirt Ing	(BSc in engineering and economics)
Head of Div. C	Dipl Chem & Dr Chem	(BSc and PhD in chemistry)
Head of Div. D	Dipl Ing	(BSc in engineering)

The Dipl Wirt Ing (full title *Diplom Wirtschaftsingenieur*) is a combined engineering and economics course, weighted in favour of engineering, and was first established at the *Technische Hochschule* (technical university) in Berlin in 1921. This joint course is currently available at a number of West Germany's technical universities.

The Standing of Engineers

One general point to emerge from a discussion of the surveys of managers' qualifications in Germany and for that matter from the few examples that have just been offered of the way top positions are staffed, is that engineers are everywhere. More particularly, they are well represented among *Vorstand* chairmen, *Vorstand* members, *Geschäftsführung* members and owner-managers; they dominate all levels of management on the technical side of the firm and appear in sizeable minorities in non-technical functions as well. The only place where they are not well represented is on the *Aufsichtsrat* (Supervisory Board). It may well be that promotion chances for the engineer in German industry, in the sense of the likelihood of his getting to the very top, are not particularly good in relation to the engineer's overall numbers (not as good as the chances of the lawyer, for instance). But the engineers are the most numerous group and if only by sheer weight of numbers, are omnipresent and influential. Their numbers are not entirely revealed by surveys of the kind discussed in this chapter which concentrate particularly on proportions of university educated managers. The fact is that for every Dipl Ing in Germany there are at least three Ing Grads and industry has been traditionally more popular than the public sector with the Ing Grad. West Germany is not unique in this respect[28] but there is some contrast with Britain, where engineers are not so dominant in management, especially top management and where engineers tend not to enjoy the same standing as on the continent of Europe and elsewhere. In view of this qualitative difference some observations on the standing of engineers in West Germany may be helpful.[29]

There are several phenomena which may be viewed as either determinants or manifestations of the engineer's standing in Germany. Their representation in industrial management which has been documented in this chapter, is a case in point. It is also the case that engineers in West Germany are well paid compared with their colleagues in Britain. In March 1976 the journal *Mechanical Engineering News* published the results of a salary survey among British engineers belonging to the Institution of Mechanical Engineers. The median salary which emerged from this was £5,510 p.a. In this same period, early 1976, the author conducted a salary survey among mechanical engineers in West Germany and, in a sample heavily weighted in favour of the nongraduate Ing Grads who earn less on average than the Dipl Ings, established a median salary of £12,119 p.a. According to the United Nations Index for mid-year 1976 the cost of living in West Germany was 36.4 per cent higher than in Britain, so there is a real difference in the disposable income enjoyed by engineers in the two countries.

The Background of German Management   81

Some aspects of the training of engineers in West Germany have already been mentioned in discussing German education earlier in this chapter. The general consideration is that the courses leading to the Dipl Ing and Ing Grad qualifications are generally seen as demanding and worthwhile courses requiring both aptitude and perseverance for their successful completion. Furthermore since there are only these two qualifications (the *Techniker* (technician) does not rank as an engineer in the German scheme of things) their standing is readily understood by both industry and the general public.

The rapport between on the one hand industry and on the other those institutions where engineers are trained appears to be rather good in West Germany. One qualification to this generalisation is industry's critical attitude towards the changes in the system whereby students are recruited to the Ing Grad course, which was described earlier in this chapter. With this exception German industry tends to be satisfied with the engineers produced by the education system. There is also a high level of 'cross fertilisation'. Most professors of engineering have worked for a substantial period in industry; German engineering undergraduates have spent six months in industry as part of their course and the *Fachhochschule* teachers are required by law to have a minimum of five years' industrial experience. And of course one must add to this the complex of research and consultancy contacts.

Some aspects of the German engineer's standing are less tangible than rates of pay and *Vorstand* representation. One relevant factor of this less tangible kind is the fact that there is virtually no concept of 'the professions' in Germany. Germans, that is, do not select some jobs, law and medicine, for instance, label them as professions in the Anglo-Saxon manner and then endow them with an additional element of prestige.

The German word for 'profession', in so far as there is one, is *Beruf*, but this is also the basic word for job or occupation, the word which is used on passports, for instance. The word *Beruf* does have secondary connotations of respectability, but in order to qualify in this secondary way a job does not have to be 'professional' in the Anglo-Saxon sense — a sales manager is as good as a solicitor, a design engineer as good as a country vicar.

The point of these remarks is that at any rate in Britain, the model of 'the professions', based as it is on some notion of an independent but highly educated specialist offering a disinterested service to clients, has provided a phoney standard for measuring the prestige of other jobs. Now engineers can make out some very good claims for being considered as 'a profession', but they do not meet all the criteria. This tends, *ceteris paribus*, to devalue them in a society which has a strong concept of 'the professions'. It has the further undesirable effect that engineers (in Britain) may expend energy in the struggle to be recognised as 'a profession'. The German engineers are spared all this. Furthermore, exactly the same argument applies to managers, and the German manager enjoys the same cultural advantage. It is not possible to express the Anglo-Saxon idea of 'professional management' in German without an elaborate paraphrase.

The chaos and destruction which prevailed at the end of the Second World War is yet another factor relevant to the standing enjoyed by the engineer. The great need for material reconstruction put a premium on engineering abilities. As the need for basic repair and reconstruction was met, industrial expansion blossomed, and the engineer remained the man of the hour, a folk hero of the *Wirtschaftswunder* (economic miracle).

Yet it has to be admitted that none of these explanations, tangible or intangible, captures the totality of the status of engineering in Germany. It is a society in which much interest attaches to making things and this interest is widely diffused. It is a society which has a concept, *Technik*, to encompass the knowledge and skill relevant to making things and making them work, an idea which is explored in more detail in the following chapter. In all this, the engineer is perhaps best understood as the paratypical German.

Conclusion

Some reference has been made at the start of this chapter to the research literature on the social background of German managers. The most general finding is that the majority come from middle-class or even upper-middle-class families. While this is entirely consistent with our common sense appraisal, it is not clear exactly what the relevant advantages of this bourgeois milieu are from the standpoint of the future executive.

Some particular features of the background of managers in West German were also noted. Protestants are over-represented among the ranks of German managers and so are the sons of *Beamten* (civil servants and other public sector occupations). In the experience of the author refugees from the east and their sons are also over-represented. A further distinctive feature of the German scene is that there are effectively no types or institutions of education which have an extrinsic prestige significance of the English public school kind.

Various aspects of the education and vocational education system in West Germany were described as a preliminary to exploring the research literature on the qualifications of German managers. Here the tripartite system of secondary education was outlined, the apprenticeship system, the relevant courses available at the *Fachhochschule* and the existence of a series of technical universities side by side with the conventional universities. It is noticeable that vocational education is a strength in the West German system.

A variety of studies of the educational background and qualifications of German managers have been discussed. In the author's opinion many of these studies suffer from the limitation that qualifications below the university degree are often ignored. With this reservation it emerges from several of these surveys that the majority of German managers attended a *Gymnasium* (grammar school) and obtained *Abitur* ('A' level). Proportions of graduates vary wildly from study to study (from just under 30 per cent to just over 90 per cent) depending on the sampling frame and in particular the inclusion or exclusion of owner-managers who tend to have a lower educational profile than employed executives. In all surveys it was clear that those who had studied engineering, economics and law accounted for the majority of university graduates, with engineers consistently the largest single group.

Finally, in the light of this dominance of the engineers revealed in the surveys of German management's educational credentials some attempt was made to explain the high standing of the engineer and engineering in Germany. Here one can cite certain features of the technical education system, links between the worlds of learning and industry and high remuneration. It is also suggested that certain cultural and historical factors are relevant, not least the widespread German enthusiasm for knowing how things are made and how they work. This last idea is developed in Chapter 4.

Notes

1. For evidence on just how consistently true this is for Britain see Philip Stansworth and Anthony Giddens (eds.), *Elites and Power in British Society* (Cambridge University Press, Cambridge, 1974).

2. A good example of the sort of hypotheses that ought to be tested is to be found in Oppelt's study of the relative promotion chances of graduate and non-graduate engineers in German industry. See Claus Oppelt, *Ingenieure im Beruf* (Max-Planck-Institut für Bildungsforschung, Berlin, 1976).

3. David Hall, H. Cl. de Bettignies and G. Amado Fischgrund, 'The European Business Elite', *European Business* (October 1969).

4. See for instance, Max Kruk, *Die Grossen Unternehmer* (Societätsverlag, Frankfurt, 1972).
5. See for example Helga Pross and Karl Boetticher, *Manager des Kapitalismus* (Suhrkamp, Frankfurt, 1971).
6. Eugon Kogon, *Die Stunde der Ingenieure* (VDI Verlag, Düsseldorf, 1976).
7. Vance Packard, *The Status Seekers* (Pelican Books, Harmondsworth, 1961).
8. See the Booz, Allen and Hamilton Report, English translation, as presented in 'German Management', *International Studies of Management and Organisation*, International Arts and Sciences Press, Inc (Spring/Summer 1973).
9. The disadvantaged position of the new Ing Grad is argued very convincingly in B. Lutz and G. Kammerer, *Das Ende des graduierten Ingenieurs* (Europäische Verlagsanstalt, Frankfurt a.m.-Köln, 1975). For a discussion in English see Peter Lawrence, 'German Lessons for Non-graduate Engineers', *The International Journal of Mechanical Engineering Education*, vol. 5, no. 2 (April 1977).
10. J. Melrose-Woodman, 'Profile of the British Manager', Management Survey Report no. 38, British Institute of Management, 1978.
11. Ibid., p. 16.
12. Ibid., p. 6.
13. Ian Glover, 'The Backgrounds of British Managers: A Review of the Evidence', Report presented to the Department of Industry, London, 1974.
14. A good and detailed discussion of these German studies is offered, in English, in Brigitte May, 'Social, Educational and Professional Background of German Management', Report presented to the Department of Industry, London, Autumn 1974.
15. Heinz Hartmann, 'Der zahlenmässige Beitrag der deutschen Hochschulen zur Gruppe der industriellen Führungskräfte', *Zeitschrift für die gesamte Staatswissenschaft*, vol. 112, no. 1 (1956).
16. 'Jeder Dritte Manager hat nicht Studiert', *Capital*, no. 4 (1964).
17. W. Zapf, 'Die deutschen Manager — Sozialprofil und Karriereweg', in W. Zapf (ed.), *Beiträge zur Analyse der deutschen Oberschicht*, 2nd ed (Piper, Munich, 1965).
18. Heinz Hartmann and Hans Wienold, *Universität und Unternehmer* (Bertelsmann, Gutersloh, 1967).
19. *Leitende Männer der Wirtschaft und der dazugehörigen Verwaltung* (Hoppenstedt, Darmstadt, 1964).
20. See Max Kruk, *Die oberen 30,000* (Betriebswirtschaftlicher Verlag Gabler, Wiesbaden, 1967).
21. Helga Pross and Karl Boetticher, *Manager des Kapitalismus*, 1971.
22. Max Kruk, *Die Grossen Unternehmer*, 1972.
23. Gerhard Brinkmann, *Die Ausbilding von Führungskräften für die Wirtschaft* (Universitätsverlag Wienand, Köln, 1967).
24. Max Kruk, *Die Grossen Unternehmer*, 1972.
25. Helga Pross and Karl Boetticher, *Manager des Kapitalismus*, 1971.
26. 'Selbständige Unternehmer' (Arbeitsgemeinschaft Selbständiger Unternehmer e. V., 1967).
27. David Hall, H.Cl. de Bettignies and G. Amado Fischgrund, 'The European Business Elite', 1969.
28. See Ian Glover 'Executive Career Patterns: Britain, France, Germany and Sweden', *Energy World* (December 1976). One of the general points to emerge from this four country comparison is that engineers are more prevalent among executives in France, Germany and Sweden than they are in Britain.
29. A more detailed account is offered in Peter Lawrence, 'The Engineer and Society', *Energy World* (May 1978).

4 THE CHARACTER OF GERMAN MANAGEMENT

There are many perceptions of reality and this is one reason why we need novelists: there are many aspects of reality and this is one reason why we need academic writers. This is a picturesque way of saying that sometimes one can answer the same question by offering different blocks of information or presenting different sets of ideas. The question: what is German management like? is an example. In Chapter 1 we tried to say something about what it is like by describing the recent historical and economic performance context. In Chapter 2 we described German management in formal organisational terms and in Chapter 3 we 'answered the question' by locating German managers educationally and socially. The aim in the present chapter is to try to give some idea of the character of German management and the ethos of the German company. This is a less precise operation than that attempted in the three previous chapters, and the problem is where to start.

One way of characterising the unfamiliar is to define it in terms of the more familiar. In the case of German management a question which we may profitably ask is: is German management like American management? Or is German management Americanised?

Is German Management Americanised?

There are at least two reasons for regarding this as a fair question. The first is a matter of common observation. Visitors to Germany often comment that it is an Americanised country. American banks, advertisements, companies, radio stations and tourists abound. The number of American troops in West Germany is more than double the number of British and French troops put together,[1] and the American Forces Network operates nearly four times as many transmitters as the British Forces network.[2] It is an affluent, materialistic, achievement-oriented society. There is an apparent emphasis on speed, communications, efficiency and getting things done. English is the foreign language Germans are most likely to speak (with something approaching an American accent) and the language they are most exposed to. There is even a suggestion that Germany may come to emulate America's crime rate.[3]

The second reason relates to Germany's recent history. Not only did Germany experience Allied occupation in the period 1945-9, the Allies were actually there with the express purpose of changing German society, not just holding the country down and extracting reparations — the usual role of the army of occupation. This opens up the question: which of the western Allies had most effect on Germany? This is not a question which can be answered in any definite way, but our speculative choice would be the Americans. The British authorities appear to have been the least crusading; the British administration was regarded as reasonably fair and decent and British troops as more orderly and restrained than American troops. The structure of the reconstituted German trade unions is probably the most important British legacy, though this was also sought by the German unionists themselves. The French made substantial efforts to change and influence Germany in one strategic area: culture and education. They were imaginative and resourceful in presenting the Germans with the best of European (and, of course, especially French) culture as an antidote to the 'cultural' experience of the Third Reich and very energetic in re-opening schools and colleges (the French even re-founded the University of Mainz). The French expenditure on education and school books was much higher *per capita* than that in the British and American Zones.[4] This French forte is important because the French were offering the Germans something which the latter, after twelve years of Nazi propaganda and intellectual impoverishment, actually wanted. On the other hand it is probably fair to say that the French influence was not pervasive. The French were the most hard-hearted of the three western Allies. They insisted that their occupation zone should be self-supporting (which meant in practice no food imports) at any rate until the Americans made it clear that they would cover the deficit, and they regulated trade between France and the French Zone in a way very favourable to France.[5] They were the least sympathetic to the unification of the three western zones, and had to be bullied into it by the Americans. The French administration in Germany was also manifestly overstaffed, with the highest ratio of governors to governed among the three western Allies.[6] Such considerations vitiate the victor's influence over the vanquished.

The American administration differed in several ways. Denazification (trial and punishment of Nazis and their supporters) was pursued with much more vigour than in the French and British Zones, and indeed the Americans sought to change and influence Germany on a wide front. In short, American policy aimed at producing a peaceful, democratic, federal, capitalist society — what, in fact, Germany has become. There is no suggestion of a simple cause and effect relationship here.

American attempts to change the political character of the German populace and to try to call into existence American style grass-roots political participation were clumsy, if well meant.[7] American policy was also inconsistent, changing from punitive to benign as America's relationship with the Soviet Union deteriorated and it is clear that these shifts were viewed with cynicism by the Germans. But with all these qualifications there is a certain congruence between American intentions and German development: West Germany has become what the USA used to be regarded as being — the rather assured, self-conscious and successful exemplar of free enterprise capitalism.

It is also arguable that during the occupation period Americans made some personal impact on the Germans, an impact which had its positive elements transcending the natural resentment of the losers. The American historian John Gimbel, who is sceptical about the results of American democratisation politics, is committed to the view that the Americans exerted influence by example:

> American representatives left what appears to be a lasting impression of their personal characteristics. Marburgers think Americans are energetic.[8] They approached their duties with a zeal that could have been based only upon hope of realizing a high ideal. They provided an example of efficiency and practical know-how by their reconstruction work during the early phase of the occupation, thus verifying for Marburgers the fact that Germany had lost the war and had not been sabotaged from within. American officers and men gave a practical lesson in equality by their familiarity with each other and by their mutual respect. They impressed the Marburgers by their individualism, both in acts of kindness and in crime and corruption. Above all, Americans seemed to get things done. They kept their desks clean. They cleaned up the city. They put public utilities into working order. They provided emergency food supplies when famine and disease threatened. They attacked problems as they arose and solved them without delaying to achieve perfection. Americans, Marburgers think, are practical, energetic, kind, and likeable people.[9]

So it would not be surprising if German management resembles American management, if the German company has something of the ethos of the American company. Are they in fact alike?

There is certainly one difference, implicit in the previous chapter where the training and qualifications of German managers were discussed. German managers usually hold a qualification from a university or from a *Fachhochschule* and that qualification is invariably in engineering, business economics, or law, with the engineers being in the majority. The contrast with the training of (many) American managers is this: the Germans are not trained or qualified in business administration or management studies, at least not at the outset of their careers. Undergraduate courses in business administration, as opposed to business economics, do not exist in West Germany. Business schools do exist, but they differ from British and American business schools in that they do not offer courses to undergraduates or immediate postgraduate students; they are oriented entirely to the needs of post-experience managers. The German courses also differ from the Anglo-American ones in that the course content tends to be more specific; more directly related, that is, to particular management functions, dealing less with the general systemic aspects of management and having less in the way of general social science inputs. Similarly the German courses tend to attract a more homogeneously specialised clientele.[10]

The argument can in fact be taken a good deal further than this comparison in terms of training assumptions and practices; a quite magnificent source is available. The *Bundeswirtschaftsministerium* (Federal Economics Ministry) commissioned a report on German management from the Düsseldorf office of the American consultancy firm Booz, Allen and Hamilton. The Report was presented in German but an English translation has been published accompanied by a critical assessment of the Report by Heinz Hartmann, a sociology professor at the University of Münster.[11] Hartmann is also the author of several books on German management, which have figured in this account. The *Bundeswirtschaftsministerium* chose Booz, Allen and Hamilton precisely because the Ministry were keen to have a non-German (objective) evaluation of German management, and cut through any German tendency towards executive insularity: the Ministry got more than it bargained for.

The Report is highly critical. Its criticisms, however, should not be taken too seriously since the whole operation is vitiated by two quite untenable assumptions:

1. If it happens in the USA it must be good.
2. The American way is the only good way.

What, in fact, the authors do is to work their way through a check list of American executive concerns, assumptions, practices and developments and look to see them reflected or represented in German companies. For the most part they do not find them and to this extent

German management stands condemned in the Report as old-fashioned and unsophisticated. There is another weakness, to which Hartmann in his commentary also draws attention.[12] The Report is not empirically documented; it is never really clear on what the Report's findings are based. There are no references to a sample, to data-gathering methods, to numbers of firms investigated or managers interviewed. Although there are some references to medium sized firms, Hartmann suspects that the Report is based primarily on contact with large firms and condemns this on the grounds that small and medium sized companies constitute a higher proportion of all manufacturing establishments in West Germany than in the USA.[13] This is a fair point and the same difference exists as between West Germany and Great Britain, though to a lesser degree.

Whatever the deficiencies of the Report as a serious critical document it still has interest in the present context. First, it facilitates an answer to the question: is German management like American management? Secondly, it provides a negative characterisation of German management which is a very useful *point de départ*. Consider some of the points raised in the Report.

Booz, Allen and Hamilton Report on German Management

German companies are criticised for being person-oriented rather than system-oriented; that is, being oriented to the practices and predilections of top managers as individuals, rather than to an impersonal management system with its own dynamics. The top managers are not good at formulating company goals and medium sized companies generally lack formal (written) statements of goals. A lot of the top managers are 'operators' first and foremost, that is, they are concerned with the conduct of daily affairs. The Report says of the typical top manager: 'As a rule he does not advance to his top management position from the staff departments of the enterprise. Thus, it is very hard for him to "put his feet on the table" and to consider how the company should develop in the next five to ten years. He tends instead to delegate this assignment to a staff position.'[14] It follows, of course from this contention that corporate planning in German companies is not very satisfactory either. Overall planning is vitiated by 'a strong penchant for details and lack of uniform criteria'.[15] Financial planning tends to be done well in big companies (though not as well as in the USA), but not in medium sized companies. Large firms use the concept of return on investment, but 'on the other hand, there are still many companies of medium size which have hardly heard of return on investment'.[16] And no one appears to use the concept of discounted cash flow.

German thinking on diversification and expansion is also criticised. Research and Development activity, and the acquisition of other existing companies, are just two different forms of diversification, but the Germans tend to treat them as separate activities. But they are, the Report asserts, just alternative routes to higher profit and lower risk. Indeed the Germans are just not aggressive enough. They are lukewarm, it is suggested, in their search for merger partners and takeover victims. Neither has Germany invested enough abroad, certainly much less than the USA has done. Relatively few German firms have subsidiaries abroad and the Germans have even failed to exploit the Common Market countries in this connection.

German firms are held to be weak on delegation, in both personal and organisational ways. Only recently, it is argued in the Report, have big companies started sub-dividing into units. In many medium sized companies 'the principle of delegation of authority has hardly been introduced. A good example for this contention can be found in the large spans of control in many of these companies, and cases are far from rare where top management executives find themselves in charge of ten to fifteen heads of departments'.[17] The Germans are also weak on the 'specification of objectives' as a prerequisite for effective delegation of authority.

The Report assesses German collegial management in the form of the *Vorstand* (see Chapter 2) and manages to say a few 'nice things' about it. The basic orientation, however, is again critical. The *Vorstand* is invested with all the putative ills of committee government: slowness, compromise, reciprocal back-scratching, avoidance of individual responsibility and the emergence of complicated interpersonal relationships. It is fair to add that not a scrap of evidence is offered in the Report for this view and as we argued earlier (Chapter 2) there is not really any evidence available and it is rather difficult to conceive of what would actually constitute evidence.

The Report moves on to some particular American management devices which are held to be neglected in Germany. The Germans make little use of the project team or task force: that is, a group of managers probably drawn from different functions and levels who come together to accomplish some particular major purpose and disband afterwards. The Germans are said to be weak on control (except financial control), not realising that control should correspond to planning and organisation and reveal deviations from the plan. The German conception of Operations Research is primitive and the supply of Operations Research specialists is limited. It is suggested that the Germans are rather vague on simulation, linear programming, decision theory, PERT (Programme Evaluation and Review Technique) and risk analysis. Similarly, the potential of Management Information Systems has not been generally appreciated (apart from its application to accounting systems) but then Management Information Systems require managers schooled in OR with a ready appreciation of what computers can do and the Germans are not in this happy position. German use of the concept of cost benefit analysis is also limited.

The Report claims that Marketing is, or soon will be, the most important management function. By Marketing as opposed to Sales is meant a series of interrelated decisions and activities concerning pricing policy, choice of distribution channels, advertising arrangements, sales promotion and so on. It is suggested that the Germans do not fully appreciate this, tending to emphasise Sales rather than Marketing, with the marketing functions being discharged by a staff group in Sales.

The Germans are praised for their handling of cost control, though the Report makes some criticisms of the way in which overhead and secondary costs are allocated. Cost reduction, however, is another German weakness, in the very basic sense that cost reduction is not regarded as a continuous objective in German companies. Cost reduction programmes tend to be introduced only during recessions, without the real support of top management and with inadequate preparation.

A section of the Report discusses German managers *per se*, and explicitly compares them with American managers. It is argued that the things they have in common are a similar age structure; a similar and rather high proportion of managers of lowly social origin; a high proportion with university education and comparable levels of inter-company mobility.

The differences between German and American managers which the writers of the Report perceive are of more interest. The Germans, it is declared, have been educated: the Americans have been trained (a point argued earlier in this chapter where the absence of university courses in business administration in Germany was noted). The German managers are more specialised; they are willing to change company but do not like to change industry. By American lights the Germans are more conservative, the older German managers having been shaped by economic stagnation between the wars. The Germans, it is argued, are more cautious and more prone to compromise. The German manager feels his achievements are not recognised by the general public and he does not seek the limelight. He has a bad conscience about earning so much. He is industrious, typically working 10-12 hours a day, but 'this industriousness often seems to be compensation for knowledge about modern management'.[18]

The Report ends with some strictures on training. It is maintained that the Germans do not take management training seriously enough, do less of it than the Americans, make insufficient use of the European Business Schools like INSEAD and IMEDE and furthermore do not like having their performance subjected to objective assessment.

It was suggested before this review of the Booz, Allen and Hamilton Report that there are good reasons for not taking it too seriously as a critique. A lot of what is advanced as criticism can be dismissed as a combination of national prejudice and special pleading; the Germans, for instance, are not interested in linear programming and simulation — so what? The present purpose, however, is not to produce a critique of the critique, but to use the Report as a heuristic tool for getting at some of the features of German management and German companies.

The Nature of German Management

Whatever might have been expected in the light of recent German history, or inferred from the observation of general American influence in Germany, it can now be asserted with confidence that German management is not like American management. The Booz, Allen and Hamilton Report reveals a pattern of consistent and far reaching differences — differences in training, in the use of managerial instruments, in organisation, business strategy and in attitudes. We may choose to evaluate these differences in a manner which is not 'all-American', but the differences still exist.

We can go further. In the light of the Report it would also be fair to say that German management appears to be self-sufficient and not easily influenced. The USA has, after all, been the centre of gravity of the business world. It is the USA which has pioneered management training, business education and a disproportionately large share of serious thinking and theorising about the way in which business organisations should or do function. It is surprising that there is so little reflection of all this in West Germany. If Booz, Allen and Hamilton had been commissioned by the British Department of Industry to make a comparable evaluation of British management they would have found more that was familiar to them than they found in West Germany.

A third feature which may be inferred from the Report is that German companies are not doctrinaire. They exhibit what might be termed 'organisational shamelessness'; if it does not suit them to conform to classical management principles they do not do so. Spans of control are characteristically large in German companies (see Chapter 2), hierarchies are relatively short (the corresponding feature) and the textbook line on delegation – individual and organisational – is violated.

Fourthly (and this is in line with the self-contained, non-doctrinaire nature of German management) German companies exhibit some distinctive features – the role of the Works Council, collegial top management, the distinction between *Vorstand* members and the *leitende Angestellten* and so on. These features were described in Chapter 2, but the point to be stressed here is that German companies appear to make collegial top management work. This is distinctive and in so far as German top management is collegial (the point should not be overplayed since the *Vorstand* does have a Chairman who may in fact function as a chief executive) and successful, this is likely to lead, *ceteris paribus*, to a greater integration.

Fifthly, and again in the light of the Report, German companies appear to be relatively uninterested in modern (American) techniques of corporate planning, decision-taking and control. (Readers who are hostile to such techniques may re-define the point and say that German managers are not interested in foreign gimmicks.) This proposition may be developed. German managers take their work seriously, and attach important to it, but they do not see it as so inherently complicated as to involve a body of *secondary* erudition of the kind emphasised by Booz, Allen and Hamilton.

A more general argument which tends to subsume these previous points and is again implicit in the criticisms of Booz, Allen and Hamilton, is to say that Germans simply do not have a very strong concept of management. The status of industry is high in Germany (see Chapter 8), the organisation of production, selling goods and running firms are activities which are taken seriously and well rewarded. But the Germans are much less prone than the Americans (or the British) to think in terms of 'management', in the sense of some phenomenon which can be extrapolated, analysed and talked about in general terms. So our sixth proposition about the character of German management would be to say that it is managerially unselfconscious: German managers think about the functionally specific rather than the managerially general.

A further and related point is that Germans take a comparatively uncomplicated view of the goals of the company. They tend to regard it all as self-evident: the company exists to make and sell something. They are less likely than their British or American counterparts to indulge in corporate soul searching of the 'What business are we in?' kind; less likely to reify corporate goals, and to go in for refinements and redefinitions of objectives. German managers simply put their energies into making something well and delivering it on time. The Report's claim that formal statements of objectives are often conspicuous by their absence is entirely credible.

Similarly, the Report's assertion that German companies do not value Marketing (as distinct from Sales) as much as it is valued in the USA is quite characteristic and consistent with the uncomplicated German approach. German companies expect to sell on the basis of quality, delivery performance and after sales service. And they expect these virtues to speak for themselves, with maybe a little help from a technical brochure. For the most part German goods are not competitive in price terms anyway, so there is little point in agonising over pricing policy and distribution channels. The German approach is to try to make them better than anyone else does in the (generally fulfilled) hope that they will then be purchased. Sales is a tangible and acceptable activity, but Marketing is too indirect to be *as* acceptable to Germans as it is to Americans.

Not only is 'management' in the abstracted sense more of an American concept than a German one, but 'the manager' emerged rather later in Germany and gained acceptance rather more slowly. The word 'manager' in German was first employed to designate people who 'managed' things like circuses and prize fights. They were not wholly respectable people. The respectable person, with status and a legitimated role, was the *Unternehmer* – the entrepreneur. The *Unternehmer* is legitimated not so much by risking his money as by his direct involvement and personal responsibility. Heinz Hartmann, writing in the late 1950s was still able to claim that the hired manager lacked standing,[19] and the same point is argued by David Granick.[20] It is not true any more that the German manager lacks standing, or is regarded as a little bit suspect and of course there are few *Unternehmer* in the strict sense anyway. But it is important to understand that this *Unternehmer* tradition has existed, and has until quite recently exerted some effect on the status dynamics of the German industrial world. If one wishes to praise a German manager for acting responsibly, and in the best interests of his company, one describes his conduct as *unternehmerisch*, not as *managerhaft* (the literal and little used translation of managerial).

This consideration leads to a further feature of German management: German managers are activists ('operators' in the words of the Booz,

Allen and Hamilton Report). They do, even at the top, interest themselves in the day to day running of the company. They do not favour 'arms length' management. Planning can be delegated; what are clever young PhD's for if not to develop planning, innovation and reorganisation proposals and report direct to the *Vorstand*? All this represents the residue of the *Unternehmer* tradition of personal responsibility. Staff positions do not carry high status in the German company and they are not supported in Germany, as in the USA, by a mystique of management erudition. German management is active management, rather than strategically thinking, corporately planning management.

It is argued in the Report that German managers differ from their American counterparts by being more specialised. This is true and is a distinctive feature of German management, though it requires some amplification. The point raised in the Report in this connection, namely that German managers are reluctant to change industry, is true; they tend to move from company to company within the same industry or at least branch of industry and are less likely than American executives to think they can 'manage anything'. But they are also arguably more specialised in the sense of identifying more strongly with a particular function. The German manager is more likely to think of himself, and describe himself, as 'in Design' or 'in Quality Control', rather than to use a general purpose label such as 'middle management'. Only in a context which requires the individual to identify himself in hierarchical or status terms is the German manager likely to describe himself as a *'leitender Angestellte'* (senior manager – see Chapter 2) in preference to a more functionally specific title such as *Konstrukteur* (designer) or *Produktionsleiter* (production manager).

Part of the Booz, Allen and Hamilton critique was to argue that German companies are lukewarm on mergers, takeovers, diversification by acquisition, foreign investment and so on. Whether or not these observations are held to constitute criticism, they are on the whole true. German companies like to make profits, but they expect this to result from making and selling goods. They are much less readily attuned to making profits as a result of business manoeuvres, of the merger-acquisition-investment kind. Of course this happens in Germany too, the USA does not have a monopoly on mergers, but there is a difference of degree, a difference in emphasis. One is much less likely to hear in Germany the phrase 'the business of the company is business'. The German version is: 'the business of the company is making tractors'.

Technik

A further dimension to the consciousness of German managers is the pervasive influence of *Technik*. This is a word and concept which has equivalents in some other languages, for instance, *Teknik* in Swedish and *Techniek* in Dutch, but not in the English language. The starting point is that there are differences in the ways in which societies perceive and evalute skill and knowledge; differences in the way in which they group and label branches of knowledge.

In Britain we distinguish between Arts and Sciences. The distinction is there in common speech and assumptions, is reflected in school timetables and college brochures and is actually thought to connote something. The distinction was formalised, publicised and given a further thrust by Sir Charles Snow's famous 'Two Cultures' lecture at Cambridge over 20 years ago.[21] The key question here is: what is the role of engineering in the two cultures scheme, or the Arts *versus* Sciences distinction? C.P. Snow solved the problem by fitting in engineering as 'applied science',[22] and this is a common, if not invariable convention, in the English speaking world.

This 'applied science' label is, however, rather damaging to engineering. It tends to accord engineering a junior, dependent and subordinate status under the aegis of science. This is unfortunate for the status of engineering in Britain. It is also misleading since it tends to suggest that any advance in engineering is dependent on a prior advance in science and this is simply not true. Sometimes this relationship and dependency exists, sometimes it does not. The 'applied science' label also implies some misconception of engineering work. It suggests, that is, that engineering work consists of the application of knowledge and principles derived from science and again this is only partly and sometimes true. The 'applied science' formula also suggests a similarity between science and engineering, albeit with engineering as the junior partner. This is totally false. The output of science is knowledge; the output of engineering is three dimensional artifacts. Much scientific work takes place in laboratory conditions where the influence of undesirable variables has been controlled: most engineering work is conducted 'on site', and is subject to environmental influences. Scientists who study things, seek ideal solutions and universally valid laws. Engineers who make things, seek workable solutions which do not cost too much. In short the 'applied science' label is damaging and misleading. And it does not exist in Germany.

It is indeed linguistically and culturally difficult to represent the two cultures thesis in German. This is not because the Germans do not make distinctions, but because they make different distinctions. Engagingly, they use the same word for Arts and Sciences. The German term *Wissenschaft* covers all formal knowledge subjects whether arts, natural sciences, or social science in the British scheme of things. And particular subjects are often designated by compound nouns based on *Wissenschaft*; economics, for instance, is *Wirtschaftswissenschaft*; literature, as a university subject, is *Literaturwissenschaft*. The Germans employ a second term *Kunst* to refer to art. Not to 'the Arts' in the British sense of the humanities, but to the end products of art – the paintings and statues and symphonies. And thirdly, the Germans use the term *Technik* to refer to manufacture and the knowledge and skills relevant to it. That is, of course, to engineering knowledge and engineering and craft skills. In Chapter 3 it was noted that more German managers are qualified in engineering than in anything else, that engineers enjoy higher standing in Germany than in Britain, and a lot of reasons for this status difference were advanced. The existence in German culture of the concept of *Technik* not only avoids the demotion and misconception of engineering implicit in 'applied science', it also tends to dignify and even glamorise engineering under its distinctive rubric.

It is important to grasp that *Technik* really does not have any equivalent in English. The English word 'technique' is not a contender. It simply means a way of doing something, and the something is not necessarily technical or related to manufacture. Neither is the English word 'technology' an equivalent of the German concept of *Technik*. There are various objections to 'technology' in this context. First, it is a new-fangled and imposed word, not a culturally rooted concept like *Technik*. Secondly, it again over-stresses the engineering-science link; when examples of 'technology' are offered they are typically from the 'science based' industries such as aerospace and electronics. Thirdly, even if technology connotes some of the relevent knowledge, it does not connote relevant skills – *Technik* does. And fourthly, technology is a rather vague word; there are no agreed definitions of technology, and the word is most often used by politicians wishing to strike a modern pose, politicians who would be hard put to define it. The corresponding word *Technologie* exists in German with the same vague connotations: it tends to be used by journalists, politicians, and social scientists; managers and engineers talk about *Technik*.

It is also fair to add that the word *Technik* is actually used in German, and used in quite homely ways. It is not a term for the exclusive use of those who write books on the philosophy of science. In recent conversations with German managers the present writer has come across such gems as: 'Die Technik ist sauber' ('*Technik* is wholesome' – a manager denouncing the American practice of using pretty girls in machinery advertisements) and 'Ich bin eigentlich Technik Liebhaber' ('Actually I'm a *Technik* lover' – a production manager expounding on his job satisfaction). A standard German phrase is 'technisch gesteuert', meaning technically guided, or directed in terms of *Technik*. One hears of advertising departments which are 'technisch gesteuert', or sales departments, or whole companies.

In short *Technik* exerts a pervasive influence in German firms and on German managerial thinking. We will take up a number of the implications of this in the following chapter, and try to give some further understanding of the nature of German management in terms of the concerns and views actually expressed by German managers. The idea of *Technik*, however, affects the ethos of the typical German company as a whole, as well as the pronouncements of individual managers. The influence of *Technik* tends to account for the uncomplicated view taken by top managers of company goals and the means to achieve them. The goals are in the German view 'technicised'; to the German manager they are self-evident and there is no need to have a seminar on it. *Technik* similarly accounts for the relative lack of interest in techniques of planning, control, and decision-taking extolled by Booz, Allen and Hamilton. The German is more likely to feel that *Technik* is in the foreground and managerial techniques and corporate strategy take second place. The standing of *Technik* again supplies the clue to German apathy on foreign investments, mergers and takeovers. These measures are outside *Technik*; they are not the way in which German firms have traditionally expected to make money.

Technik is also, *ceteris paribus*, a force for integration. The German company is *Technik* in organisational form. The skilled worker, the foreman, the superintendent, the technical director are all participants in *Technik*. Of course there are many things which they do not have in common, but *Technik* is something which transcends hierarchy. It may also transcend particular functions in the company. This is most obviously true for the various technical functions – Research and Development, Design, Production, Production Control, Maintenance and Quality Control. As was argued previously (Chapter 3) the fact of qualificational homogeneity in these functions (nearly everyone has one of two different qualifications and they are all engineers) tends to integrate these functions and *Technik* provides them with a cultural umbrella. It is also conceivable, though we would not press this point, that *Technik* is sufficiently pervasive to have some integrating effect as between technical and commercial functions. The first occasion on which the present writer heard the word *Technik* used by a German manager was in the observation of a Public Relations manager in a commercial vehicle company that 'Die Firma lebt schliesslich von der Technik' ('After all, the firm lives from *Technik*').

Conclusion

In the present chapter we have taken the characterisation of German management beyond the themes explored previously — economic and historical context, the organisational structure of German firms and the social and educational backgrounds of German managers. As a *point de départ*, the question: is German management like American management? was raised since there are *a priori* reasons for supposing that it might be. After a detailed discussion of an American consultancy report on the quality of German management it was concluded that German management is not Americanised.

Again using the German-American comparison it was argued that German management is self-contained, not easily influenced from without, non-doctrinaire, and characterised also by the ability to make collegial top management work. German management was described as relatively uninterested in modern techniques of planning and control (except production control), and in mathematical aids to decision-taking, and indeed it was noted that the Germans in fact lack a strong concept of management as an entity which may be abstracted and made the subject of generalisations and analysis. German managers take a relatively uncomplicated view of company goals and are not particularly prone to either formulating them in writing or reifying them. The idea of the professional manager, as distinct from the entrepreneur, emerged later in Germany and took longer to gain respectability in the face of the German *Unternehmer* tradition. In this context, the continued influence of the *Unternehmer* model, it was noted that German managers, including top managers, do not practise 'arms length management' and tend to see themselves as people running companies rather than as corporate planners and strategists. German managers are also, in certain ways, more specialised (than their American colleagues) and are more likely to argue forward from products rather than backward from profits.

The concept of *Technik* was introduced, and it was argued that there really is no English equivalent to this independent rubric tending in the German scheme of things to dignify engineering knowledge and skills.

Some of the implications of the pervasive influence of *Technik* were discussed, including its integrative function. And some connections were established between the dominance of *Technik* and certain American criticisms of the operations of German companies.

In the following chapter the intention is to stay with the themes of *Technik*, management attitudes and management practices, but to treat these in terms of the testimonies of German managers themselves.

Notes

1. *The World Almanac 1978* (Newspaper Enterprise Association, Inc, New York).
2. *The Europe Year Book 1978*, vol. 1 (Europa Publications, London).
3. West Germany is in the unenviable position of holding some European crime records; see Jorg Nimmergut, *Deutschland in Zahlen* (Wilhelm Heyne Verlag, München, 1974).
4. An informative account of educational policy in the French Occupation Zone is given in F. R. Willis, *The French in Germany, 1945-9* (Stanford University Press, Stanford, California, 1962).
5. Ibid.
6. Ibid.
7. For a fascinating account of the reality of American policy in a particular German community see John Gimbel, *A German Community under American Occupation: Marburg 1945-52* (Stanford University Press, Stanford, California, 1961).
8. Marburg is the community which Gimbel studied; it is a medium sized university town north-east of Frankfurt.
9. F. R. Willis, *The French in Germany*, 1962.
10. Arndt Sorge, 'The Management Tradition: a Continental View', in Michael Fores and Ian Glover (eds.), *Manufacturing and Management* (HMSO, London, 1978).
11. 'German Management', *International Studies of Management and Organisation*, International Arts and Sciences Press, Inc (Spring/Summer 1973).
12. Ibid.
13. Ibid.
14. Ibid.
15. Ibid.
16. Ibid.
17. Ibid.
18. Ibid.
19. Heinz Hartmann, *Authority and Organisation in German Management* (Princeton University Press, Princeton, NJ, 1959).
20. David Granick, *The European Executive* (Doubleday, New York, 1962).
21. C. P. Snow, 'The Two Cultures and the Scientific Revolution', The Rede Lecture, 1959.
22. Ibid.

5 THE VIEWS OF GERMAN MANAGERS

When members of an occupational group give their views they are of interest in at least three ways. Most obviously what is said is of interest, what is not said may be indicative and the words used to express it may be revealing. Discussions with German managers are interesting in all these ways. Their interest is enhanced if one enters them as a non-German (British in the author's case) with a different set of ideas and assumptions.

Vocabulary

If one conducts such discussions in German it soon becomes clear that German is a rich language for talking about work. The vocabulary employed by German managers is not particularly *managerial* in the sense explored in the previous chapter. That is, it does not reflect the language of the business school or the concept of management as a systemic entity which can be analysed in general terms. What does distinguish the German manager's vocabulary is the abundance of words denoting positive attitudes to work and achievement. There is *Arbeitswille*, the will to work, *Arbeitsfreudigkeit*, delight in work, *Arbeitseinsatz*, getting stuck into work, *Arbeitslustigkeit*, love of work — a very common expression, *Einsatzbereitschaft*, a willingness to engage in purposeful action, *Durchsetzungsvermögen*, the ability to get things done, see things through and so on. The word *Termin*, delivery date, deadline, is also very much on the lips of the German manager and there is a block of derived adjectives and compound nouns based on *Termin* (see Chapter 6). Another key word is *Leistung*, performance or achievement, which again gives rise to a set of derivatives: there is *leistungmässig*, compatible with performance, *leistungsfahig*, capable of achievement, *Leistungsorientiert*, oriented to achievement and a cardinal idea is that of the *Leistungsgesellschaft*, the achievement-oriented society or meritocracy. We will return to the idea of *Leistung* later in the chapter.

The second thing which one notices at a linguistic level is that there are a number of key words and concepts in the Anglo-Saxon management vocabulary which are not used much in the original by German speakers, either because they do not have proper German equivalents, or where equivalents exist, they are simply not used very often. The phrase 'human relations', for instance, is usually used in the original when it is used, but this is very seldom. 'Job satisfaction' is not a phrase which is used spontaneously: it will only come up if one asks some specific question. Yet in a wide ranging discussion with British managers job satisfaction (as an expression and topic) will come up quite naturally. The words 'communication' and 'motivation' exist in German; they are used, but they are not key words in the German managers' vocabulary. One notices, in particular, that German managers do not make frequent reference to the importance of communication, although British managers do. The word 'relationship', in the sense of 'relationships at work' is a little difficult to render in German. The German word *Beziehung* does not have the in vogue nuance of 'relationship' in English and tends only to be used in specific and pragmatic ways along the lines of 'There is a good relationship between the foremen and apprentices in the tool room which is good for training'.

These observations are not meant as an indictment of German managers. It is not being suggested that they are monstrous brutes for whom the phrase 'human relations' could have no meaning; nor that they are de-motivated non-communicators whose idea of a relationship is to wreck someone else's job satisfaction. These details have a different kind of interest, especially in the light of the discussion of the American consultancy report in the previous chapter.

First, the fact that such phrases do not figure much in the German manager's vocabulary is a further piece of evidence for our contention that German management is not Americanised and is in fact rather self-sufficient. Secondly, it is again evidence of our earlier claim that German managers have what might be termed low managerial consciousness. They have, that is, a conception of themselves as doing particular jobs in manufacturing companies, rather than a conception of themselves as managers: it is a difference of relative emphasis. Thirdly, it is an indication of the German manager's tendency to think in direct and tangible terms, which was also noted in the previous chapter in the context of discussing the German manager's disinclination to think about 'the company' in abstract terms, or to indulge in soul-searching about 'the goals of the company' or 'the business we are in'. And fourthly, these omissions tell us something about the way industry is experienced in Germany. These ideas – communication, motivation and so on – have in common the fact that they are secondary to what happens in industry (things get made and sold); they all tend to imply society's, or at any rate management's efforts at amelioration. The idea can be clarified by burlesque. What happens in industry is so awful it can only be redeemed by a strong dose of 'human relations'; it is such a jungle that communications are at a premium; it is so intrinsically alienating that motivation (even for the manager) is problematic and the whole repugnant show can only be made bearable if 'relationships at work' are inherently satisfying – as a surrogate. In other words, these omissions tend to suggest that somehow or other industry is more domesticated, less alienating, in Germany than in America where these concepts and shibboleths arose.

There is another omission. In discussing the standing of engineers in German society (Chapter 3) it was argued that the Germans do not really have a conception of 'the profession' – they do not set some occupations aside and view them as having, *ceteris paribus*, an extra increment of prestige. Thus the engineer cannot lose an increment of status through not being a member of a profession (engineering has a claim to be regarded as a profession in the Anglo-Saxon sense but it is not an incontrovertible claim) and the same applies to the manager. What German managers do not say is entirely consistent with this bit of reasoning. They tend not to talk about being 'professional managers'. It is a significant point. British managers do, in the author's experience, use this phrase and talk about the desirability of British management being, becoming, and being recognised as 'professional'. It is easier to spot the difference than to interpret it, but it probably indicates a greater security on the part of the German managers.

The Company and Society

German managers tend to be less defensive than their British colleagues when talking about the role of industry in society. This is not meant as a criticism of British managers: there are objective reasons for their feeling less than properly appreciated. In Germany the phenomenon is noticeable by its absence: German managers tend not to say things like 'After all, it *is* industry which produces the real wealth of the country.' This sort of expression and variations on the theme, are very common among British managers. In the German context it all seems to be taken for granted and no general need to justify industry's existence appears to exist. The author has noticed that German managers occasionally reply to (implicit) specific criticisms, to the idea, for instance, that rationalisation means job impoverishment, but they seldom embark on a generalised defence of industry.

Another Anglo-German difference is that German managers are more likely than their British colleagues to praise free enterprise capitalism openly. We do not mean to suggest that British managers are a lot of crypto Trotskyites; no doubt they believe the free enterprise system to be superior to the state control of communist countries, but they very seldom say so. Germans do say so, without being asked and the tendency used to be more marked than it is today after the demoralising effects of the mid-seventies recession. German managers also make secondary statements implying a belief in the free enterprise system and the virtues of competition. The author has heard British nationalised industries criticised in Germany, not just on the crude grounds that they are not really part of the competitive world of 'real business' but also because government subsidies keep their prices (too) low and this is a violation of the operation of the supply and demand law. Likewise German nationalised firms. Volkswagen, for example, are defended on the grounds that the government is only represented on the *Aufsichtsrat*, not on the *Vorstand* which actually initiates action, so that the free enterprise nature of such companies is relatively untrammelled.

Another German line is to express concern over the equal representation of workers and owners on the *Aufsichtsrat* under the 1976 Co-determination Act. The point is that the *Aufsichtsrat* appoints the members of the *Vorstand* and that 'worker control' could lead to the appointment of the 'wrong type' of *Vorstand* member. Now part of this, of course, is the straightforward reluctance of management (all over the capitalist world) to see (a measure of) power passing to workers or trade unionists. But this expression of concern contains also a specific element – that only the free enterprise system, unadulterated by co-determination laws, will throw up really competitive *Vorstand* members who are properly *leistungsorientiert*.

In this particular comparison, explicitly praising the capitalist system, it may well be the Germans who are exceptional not the British. For the average German hating communism (and loving capitalism) is obviously connected with the German fear of Russia and the division of German after World War Two. This, however, is probably not the whole explanation: it is also simply easier to be vocal about the free enterprise system in Germany since it has been so successful.

A further aspect of this positive attachment to free enterprise is the German manager's attitude to civil servants (*Beamten*). Again there appears to be an Anglo-German contrast. Unless their particular jobs bring them into contact with higher civil servants, British managers are not voluble on this subject. If they want to hit out at anyone it will be the government and politicians rather than civil servants. In contrast, German managers do not have much to say about the government – some criticism of the SPD ('Labour Party') for introducing another dose of co-determination and for some of its educational policies – but that is about all.

There is, however, a tendency to indulge in a kind of ritualistic denunciation of *Beamten*. There is no doubt that in German society managers enjoy higher standing than civil servants (see Chapter 8) though the gap has been closed somewhat in recent years. World recession and unemployment have given the (secure) civil service a new attractiveness and pay increases have been better (at the graduate manpower level) in the public sector, though industrial managers still earn more on average (again see Chapter 8). One also meets in German firms former *Beamten* who have come into industry, saying they were bored before, wanted more action, that industry 'corresponds more to their mentality'. These ex-civil servants in the ranks of German management are not legion and there is mobility the other way round too, but the author's impression is that they are more numerous in West Germany than in Britain where any mobility from civil administration to industrial management is at an exalted level. The phenomenon in Germany is less marked now than in the Economic Miracle period, but the tendency is to see the manager and the civil servant as polar types. The manager is the torch bearer of capitalism – freedom, wealth, competition, success; the civil servant represents the state – control, central planning and the thin end of the East European wedge.

There is one apparent contradiction in the views of the German manager. On the one hand pronouncements in favour of the free enterprise system and a championing of the manager as against the civil servant. On the other, a tendency not to conceptualise the company in a severely economic way. German managers tend to hold what one might term a de-economised view of the company. Some evidence of this was presented in the previous chapter where the contentions of the American consultancy report were discussed: German firms are weak on foreign investments, mergers and acquisitions; they do not regard Research and Development and takeovers as alternative strategies for achieving diversification; they do not bother much about costs except during a recession. In talking to German managers another aspect of this phenomenon comes to light. If one asks them what, as representatives of the company, they are proud of, they tend not to give answers in terms of economic performance.[1] That is, they tend not to mention profits, growth of profits, turnover, market share, assets or acquisitions. They either do not mention them or they are placed third or fourth on a list in which the first places are reserved for product quality type answers (see *Technik*). Now obviously they are not indifferent to profits: 'Gewinn ist kein fremder Begriff' ('Profit is not an unknown concept') as one German manager put it to the author, but it is not what they talk about when asked open ended questions.

The two economic performance features which are mentioned more often are orders (*Aufträge*) especially in capital goods firms where the number of orders is relatively small and their individual importance greater, and exports, though often they even need a bit of prompting to talk about exports. The contradiction is that German managers extol the capitalist system, certainly with more fervour than their British colleagues, but tend to view their companies in technical and quality terms rather than as economic performance units.

Since at least the 1950s the view has been current that in affluent countries class differences are getting less: sociologists find little or no support for this view but this has not stopped many people believing it to be true. Germans are particularly given to the view that their country has become a classless society and German managers especially like to draw the foreigner's attention to this happy state of affairs. Now in a formal sociological sense of course the notion is rubbish. There are as many differences of educational level, income and occupational standing in German society as elsewhere.

On the other hand, one can see why the claim is made in West Germany; it does have some verisimilitude. Working-class affluence is rather more striking in West Germany than in battling Britain. The American dictum of 'If you can pay you're equal' has more currency in Germany than in Britain, though probably the strict German version would be 'If you are *leistungsfähig* (capable of achievement) you're equal'. It is genuinely more difficult to classify Germans in social class terms. There are fewer differences of dress. Accents tend to have a primarily regional significance: diction may give a clue to class, or at any rate educational level, but not accent alone. There appear, at any rate to the foreign observer, to be fewer class associated differences of deportment, manner and style than in Britain. A German writer on the industrial scene has noted the strong external resemblance in West Germany between industry bosses and trade union bosses in this vein:

> The boss of IG Metall (West Germany's largest trade union) and his associates roll up at meetings with the employers in the same large discreet cars, they wear the same well cut suits (often from the same tailor) and are not embarrassed if someone asks them at dinner if they prefer Chablis or a Beaujolais.[2]

A further consideration is that if one compares West Germany and Britain there are less ascriptive, that is non-achievement based, criteria of social prestige in Germany. West Germany has no monarchy, no military caste (any more), no public schools — at any rate in the English sense — and no Oxbridge.[3] Neither does coming from, or living in, any part of the country confer any element of prestige. There is a general residential preference for the area around Munich — a big city surrounded by lakes and forests — and some disinclination to live in the heart of the Ruhr, but these preferences do not have any class significance. Germany does not have any equivalent of 'the home counties', or of 'county families', or even of 'the gin and Jaguar belt' — every sizeable German town has one, though it is difficult to find a cultural equivalent of the gin and Jaguar as symbols.

All this has some reflection inside the factory. Everyone arrives with a briefcase, in the case of the workers usually containing salami sandwiches and at 'knocking off' time, German managers tell you proudly, you cannot tell the difference between the lathe operator and the personnel manager as they cruise past the gatehouse in their BMWs. German firms, especially the medium sized ones, are more likely than is the case in Britain to have integrated eating facilities and where a separate facility exists it is often for entertaining purposes; when not entertaining the managers will eat in the general canteen. This is also something which German managers are often consciously proud of.

Meetings in German firms also have a strong dash of egalitarianism. They tend to be attended by a wide variety of ranks: one gets clerks and chargehands alongside managers immediately below the *Vorstand* or *Geschäftsführung*. And although meetings in German companies tend to be well chaired and purposeful, they are not sedately respectful. People attend as needed, say their bit and go, start side discussions and make phone calls at the host's desk while the meeting proceeds at the conference table. Chargehands and skilled workers take part in meetings on machinery purchase and are listened to with respect by PhD's from Engineering. There is a lot of speaking your mind and answering back and the use of titles ('Herr Direktor' and so on) is not at all widespread in the author's experience. The interesting thing about all this is that the classless society idea is particularly espoused by managers and industry is seen as an exemplary scenario of classless German life. This German claim is not to be taken at its face value but, particularly if one compares West Germany with Britain, it can be seen to have some substance.

Being a Manager

It is a reasonable inference that German managers are ambitious, but it is noticeable that they do not have very much to say about their ambitions. They make few references to their aspirations and where they expect to be in four years' time. Also the word 'career' is not used much.

Interestingly enough in this context, another writer has noted a similar difference between British and Swedish managers.[4] Alistair Mant has interviewed Swedish managers in multinational companies having British based operations and tried to build up a picture of the Swedish view of Britain. Part of this Swedish view is that British managers have a higher consciousness of themselves as managers (like the Americans but unlike the Germans as we have argued), less interest in the technology of their companies and more overt ambition which is more readily voiced. Incidentally, this Swedish view is not all critical of the British who are praised for being more creative and handling sales operations better.

Parallel to this German disinclination to discuss personal career ambitions goes what might be termed a diminished consciousness of status. This is paradoxical in the sense that German managers certainly enjoy higher standing in German society than their British colleagues do in Britain and the status of industry itself is higher in Germany (see Chapter 8). So to put it bluntly, where status is concerned German managers, from a British standpoint, have more of it but talk less about it. In Britain, status differences are a part of everyday life. If one talks to British managers one can ask questions like: is Marketing a *prima donna* function in your company? Is it true that the modern foreman has lost status compared with the pre-war foreman? Do you think the prestige of the Civil Service in Britain has a negative effect on the status of industry? and so on. In Britain such questions are meaningful, comprehensible and get straight answers. Britons in general have no difficulty in thinking in these terms.

Not so the Germans. There is less awareness of status differences and less willingness to discuss them. If one puts this sort of question to German managers the reaction tends to be a little apathetic. Sometimes such questions are seen as being in rather poor taste. On one occasion the author asked a German manager whether there were perceptible prestige differences as between different functions in the company, perhaps reflected in salary differences and received the answer, 'When I get paid at the end of the month I don't ask whether my colleagues in

Sales and Finance have earned their pay: I ask myself if I have earned mine.' When questions about status differences do elicit interest among German managers, on the other hand, it may well be because the questions are thought to have novelty appeal. The author, for instance, once asked a German personnel manager whether the foreman's loss of function implied a loss of status too (see Chapter 7 for a full discussion of the issue). The basic response was no, but the personnel manager was so intrigued by the question he immediately telephoned colleagues at other companies in the group to get their views as well.

In this context of low status consciousness and non-vocalised ambition one may well ask: what determines the German manager's success in climbing the corporate hierarchy? Or rather, what do German managers *think* determines career success? This is something they will discuss — in a way.

The author felt it would not be productive to ask individual German managers how they hoped to claw their way to the top and instead adopted a more indirect approach. Imagine you had an ambitious and capable son, who wanted to go into industry and get on quickly, what advice would you give him? This formula produced a lot of interested discussion, at any rate on the preparation for a career in industry. There is almost universal agreement that it is desirable to go to university first. Recommendations about what one should study at university reflect what most German managers actually have studied. In other words, the only subjects discussed and recommended are engineering, economics and law. The rival merits of engineering and economics are often discussed in this connection, with a small majority in favour of engineering. On the subject of engineering it is sometimes suggested that an Ing Grad course at a *Fachhochschule* should be followed by a Dipl Ing course at university (see Chapter 3); the point here is that the Ing Grad is thought of as a good practical course, which is what is needed and the Dipl Ing gives the aspirant the advantage of being a university graduate as well. Running through these prescriptions is the *leitmotif* that the two kinds of knowledge required are engineering knowledge and knowledge of business economics. Sometimes the joint economics and engineering course of *Diplom Wirtschaftsingenieur* is recommended as giving the candidate both advantages. This course is is not a recent development; it was started at the technical university in Berlin in 1921 and is currently 'on offer' at several technical universities. There is, however, a substantial body of opinion among German managers which argues that this course is spread too thinly, that it is not an adequate education in either engineering or economics, considered singly. But it is also often argued that advantage would accrue from doing two first degrees – one in engineering and one in economics. And it is sometimes suggested that an ideal qualification set would be a first degree in engineering followed by a doctorate in economics.

The other dimension which is stressed in discussing the preparation for a career in industry is the importance of practical grasp and experience (a consideration which sometimes leads managers not to urge double degrees and doctorates on the grounds that the aspirant will be 30 before he sees the factory floor!) The most frequently recommended measure is that the aspiraant should do an apprenticeship in industry before actually going to university. An apprenticeship usually lasts three-and-a-half years but this will be reduced to about three years if the candidate has *mittlere Reife* (German equivalent of GCE 'O' level), and to two years for a candidate with *Abitur* ('A' level). These reductions in the length of the apprenticeship make the advice quite feasible and there are certainly plenty of graduate managers in Germany who have done apprenticeships. In connection with the importance of practical experience, taking ordinary jobs in industry during university vacations is recommended, and that students should make the most of the *Praktikum* (the six month practical in industry for engineering undergraduates; the undergraduate course in business economics also includes a *Praktikum*).

This very reasoned and interested discussion as to how the lad of parts should prepare himself for a career in industry which German managers offer makes the listener eager to hear about the career itself. This, unfortunately, is an anti-climax. They wind up by saying the aspirant for executive greatness should simply pick a first job in a function and area that interests and suits him and work hard – the rest will follow. One presses for more: well, a year or two spent abroad, early in the career, can be an advantage it is conceded and if one could get a personal assistant job to a *Vorstand* member this would bring one into contact with top managers and maybe it is good to avoid taking a first post in which one is alongside fifty similarly placed and qualified colleagues. And these few observations are really the sum total of positive suggestions as to what the young hopeful should do when he actually reaches industry.

Drawing on American textbooks and British experience the author has put lead questions to his numerous interlocutors. Does the professor's son have an advantage over the welder's son? The answer is no. It is sometimes conceded that to have a father who is an industrialist or banker would be an advantage, but simply having a middle-class or even upper-middle-class background has no significance. Does it help to be a graduate of any particular university (say Heidelberg) one asks hopefully? No, universities as such do not have different prestige levels; only particular faculties or departments. Here one may be told that to have read business economics at the University of Cologne would be well thought of, or that the *Fachhochschulen* (engineering schools) in the Stuttgart area have a good reputation for *Feinmechanik* (precision engineering). Is it a good idea to start in some prestige function? No, one should do that for which one has most talent and interest (sometimes this question is answered affirmatively but there is no consensus about what the *prima donna* functions are). Is it desirable to get experience in a number of different functions? No, at any rate there is no managerial folk wisdom on this point. Should one alternate between line and staff posts? No and staff posts do not have much standing anyway (see Chapter 4). So what do you have to do to get on, one demands in desperation? Just have *Fachkompetenz* (ability in your field), work hard and show *Leistung* (achievement). Yes, they say (repeatedly), 'Es geht um persönliche Leistung' (It is a matter of personal achievement).

This view is, in the author's experience, expressed consistently by German managers and it is expressed without cynicism or jocularity. It is interesting in a number of ways. It is old-fashioned, in the sense of not being slick or devious, reflecting the moral assumptions of the *Unternehmer* (entrepreneur) rather than those of the 'operators'. It is unselfconscious in its lack of tactical thinking, career folk wisdom, and manipulation. It is un-American in the relative indifference to further training and/or management training (mentioned only occasionally). And again in the American sense it is *un-managerial* in that if management can be systematically analysed then it should be equally possible to construe ideal executive career types. It is also a view which is free from stereotyping and prejudice: if little is actually said about how to get on in industry apart from knowledge, work and achievement, neither are any exclusion clauses introduced. That is, German managers do not tell one in this context that it is better not to be a Jew, that there is no place for intellectuals, or that 'creatives' should go and work on television. It is likely that a wider issue is involved here.

German thinking about work in industry, who should do what and how, is remarkably free from stereotyping. The sort of antitheses which are often felt to exist between theory and practice, thought and action, specialist knowledge and generalist judgement, commercial and technical aptitude, even line and staff, do not seem to bother the Germans. They do not show much zeal for putting people into boxes. One is less likely to hear remarks like 'He has a good honours degree in engineering – put him in Research and Development' or 'What we really want our Sales people to have is personality'. The Germans do not seem to see any incompatibility between intellectual ability and educational attainment on the one hand and working in industry on the other, in line positions or even in 'sharp end' functions like Maintenance and Production. They do not seem to fear that clever people will be bad at 'action'. If one looks at advertisements for executive posts in German newspapers it is again quite clear that there is no perceived incompatibility between technical knowledge and commercial aptitude.[5]

In this connection, the relative absence of 'placement sterotypes', one encounters some quite magnificent anomalies in German companies, which would give the Anglo-Saxon organisational planner or management developer a feeling of surrealist unease. First, there is qualificational heterogeneity. Members of a *Vorstand* (top executive committee of the AG type of company) are usually graduates and often PhD's). The *Geschäftsführung* (top executive committee of the GmbH type of company) where the companies tend to be smaller, often has a membership where the range of qualifications is considerable. In fact, an actual example was given in Chapter 2 of a *Geschäftsführung* of a medium sized company where qualifications of individual members ranged from technicians' certificates to PhD. One finds similar variations at lower levels in the management hierarchy, even though the *average* qualification level is high. In Britain, although the proportion of graduates is smaller and the number of PhD's fewer, the same phenomenon is to be observed: a heterogeneity of qualifications at any particular level. We make this point about qualificational heterogeneity in Germany, however, not because the contrast with Britain is sharp, but because it may be at variance with what people would *expect* in Germany.

A second feature is that qualificational differences seem to inspire relatively little envy among German managers. In a survey of German engineers the majority of whom were working in industry, conducted by the author, the Ing Grads (non-graduate engineers) were asked how they would explain the higher average pay of the Dipl Ing (graduate engineer). The majority answered in a 'straight', un-hostile way: that the Dipl Ing underwent longer training, had a higher level qualification and so on.[6] One also encounters examples of this harmonious heterogeneity. In a company the author visited there were eight production superintendents (the rank immediately above the foreman). Seven were Ing Grads (non-graduate engineers), the usual qualification at this level, but the eighth was a Dipl Ing (graduate engineer), was working for a PhD and had an impressive record of patented inventions and technical papers given at conferences. Just the sort of egg-head the non-graduates ought to love to hate. But no, he was in fact picked out for praise by colleagues, not on account of his academic prowess but because 'he sets the highest standards, and drives himself the hardest'. These eight superintendents reported directly to a production manager who was a graduate and a PhD, and again one might have anticipated some hostile stereotyping by the non-graduates, closer to the workshop. But once again, the production manager is popular with his juniors, one of whom describes him as 'absolut tadellos' ('pretty well perfect').

The only occasions on which the author has heard criticisms (of a stereotyping kind) of the better qualified by the less well qualified, the criticisms have also been made across the staff-line boundary and even so have not been numerous. Examples of this phenomenon include remarks like 'typical of Engineering' (line manager), 'Dr X (head of a staff bureau) is a bit naive' (line manager), 'Es ist fein was sie sagen, aber . . .' ('It is fine what they – staff specialists – say, *but* . . .') as a general comment by a divisional manager.

A third point of interest is that one also encounters anomalies of function and control. A firm will have some decentralised production facilities, for instance, a few kilometres from the main works, and one will find one such site is run by a production manager, the next by a foreman. There is a kind of rationale for such variations. German managers are usually able to offer a clear prescription as to what qualifications a job incumbent should have and tend to do so more precisely than their British colleagues. But they also say, without hesitation, that they won't necessarily stick to the formula if they find a good candidate without the designated qualifications – *Leistung*, proven or presumptive, comes first.

Another good example concerns the scholarly production superintendent referred to earlier. He is in charge of a workshop, his immediate subordinates are two foremen, then come production workers. This is not all. He also runs a Development and Quality Control laboratory, which is, *inter alia*, responsible for the quality control of the output of his workshop. The workshop, incidentally, is primarily a production unit but also handles repair and maintenance of the company's capital equipment goods periodically returned by customers. And he has a sales activity, since he is the expert on part of the manufacturing process (handled by his workshop) and gives technical sales addresses to potential industrial customers — on these occasions he is accompanied by someone from Sales who will hand round the cognac and lay out the brochures. So here we have a junior manager with a stake in Production, Maintenance, Development, Quality Control and Sales. It is not suggested that such cases are legion in West Germany, but they are probably more common there than in Britain. Perhaps more interesting is the fact that so long as the incumbent is *leistungsfähig*, no one is likely to object with reference to some dictum about discrete spheres of responsibility or with some shibboleth to the effect that 'Development and Sales are functions requiring a different type of person'.

Notwithstanding the general lack of stereotyping among German managers, and its implications for job placements, there is one stereotype which is generally subscribed to. Ironically, the Germans know that they have a reputation for being authoritarian and bureaucratic and they have come to believe it themselves. The question as to whether German firms are bureaucratic was discussed earlier (Chapter 2) and firmly rejected. The idea that German managers are authoritarian, or to make the proposition meaningful, more authoritarian than managers (in other countries) usually are, has a certain plausibility. To put it bluntly, orders are more likely to be carried out in a German company than in a British one. The key question is why? Here one would have to take into account the higher standing of industry in Germany, the national identification with economic achievement, fear of inflation, fear of foreign competition, better industrial relations, the more integrated nature of the German company and the influence of *Technik*. These factors serve to explain 'obedience', though the term is too strong, at least as well as the imputation of a *Befehl ist Befehl* (orders are orders) mentality, which assumes the German manager is a more forceful power figure and his subordinates more submissive. All one can say is that authoritarianism cannot logically be excluded, but it is not an inevitable explanation and the author has seen little evidence of it.

Whatever the truth, many Germans think that their country's management is authoritarian, though the individual manager who tells you this usually represents himself as a shining exception to the dreary national rule. Time and again the author has been told by German managers that they like to conduct meetings democratically and let everyone have their say (even if it is irrelevant). But, they darkly suggest, 'others' do not see it this way. Another line is that individual managers stress their 'open door' policy — allowing everyone access without appointments — while suggesting that this puts them in the vanguard of European liberalism. Again it is often suggested that authoritarianism varies regionally in Germany. A manager will tell you that here in the Ruhr democratic management is the norm but heaven help you in Baden-Württemberg. It is difficult for a foreigner to decide if there is any truth in this last proposition but its credibility has been weakened for the author by the fact that he has heard every region denounced by every other region so that the testimonies tend to cancel each other out. On the general charge of authoritarianism the author has seen little evidence of the stance vaguely attributed by individual German managers to others.

Another thing that German managers agree about, and this time without any international prompting, is the primacy of the practical. There is a little jingle (it rhymes in the original) in German:

What is theory?
Something that should work
And never does.
What is practice?
Don't be silly,
Something that works and no one knows why.

It is an engineers' saying, but it catches the spirit of German managers. They make frequent references to the practical, to working solutions, realism and experience. Their emphasis on practical experience in connection with a successful career in management was discussed earlier in this chapter and in Chapter 3 it was noted that the criticism of the changed route to the *Fachhochschulen* (engineering schools) focussed on the neglect, under the new system, of practical experience in industry. The few criticisms which managers make of the undergraduate engineering courses are also to the effect that they are not practical enough, there is too much higher maths which is not used in subsequent work in industry, that the *Praktikum* (six month period in industry as part of the undergraduate course) should be longer and so on. These are not frequent criticisms, but they are just about the only criticisms ever offered.

Another dimension of this cult of the practical is the apprenticeship system. Apprenticeship is a revered institution in Germany. There are 467 occupations which are classed as *Lernberufe*, for which, that is, an official apprenticeship exists. Being a *Facharbeiter* (skilled worker) means having successfully completed an apprenticeship and it is a legally protected status. As we have seen German managers are keen to recommend doing an apprenticeship as a career investment for the ambitious manager. It is also clear that there are people around who have taken this advice. In a survey of German engineers[7] it emerged that a quarter of the university graduates had actually done an apprenticeship and until the recent changes in the technical education system (described in Chapter 3) an apprenticeship or near equivalent was a mandatory requirement for admission to the Ing Grad course anyway. German managers are agreed on this emphasis on the practical. As a 30-year-old head of Research and Development put it to the author, 'Experience is the decisive thing, not qualifications' (the speaker, of course, had a PhD); or in the words of a rather scholarly looking training manager at Head Office, 'Wir wollen Könner haben' ('We're looking for people who can *do* things').

These anecdotes perhaps express the difference between Britain and West Germany. This practical emphasis is also common among British managers, though apprenticeship in particular is not so salient in the British system. The difference is that those in Britain who press the claims of experience and practical aptitude are often arguing that these commodities satisfactorily replace further and higher education: in West Germany those arguing the case usually have formal qualifications, take this for granted, but plead for the practical as well.

It is only a small point but judging by their pronouncements, German managers appear to place less emphasis on teamwork and/or group integration. German managers make some references to teamwork, all pulling together and so on, but they do so less frequently than either their British colleagues or the exhortatory Anglo-Saxon management literature. Incidentally, in this context the Germans use the word 'team', though they could use the German word *Mannschaft*. One also encounters, albeit occasionally, remarks to the effect that people who cause *Unruhe* (disturbance, friction, 'aggro') in the company are a positive force. The phrase 'constructive opposition' is quite often employed by German managers, and is a standard expression. Looking at it the other way round it is interesting to note that there is no idiomatic phrase in German for 'rocking the boat'.

If we are right in inferring less emphasis on harmony among German managers this would be quite consistent with other considerations. First, they do not need to emphasise it so much because, paradoxically, they have more of it anyway: compare, for instance, German strike figures with those of *any* English speaking country (see Chapter 1). Secondly, it is a further small piece of evidence of Germany's relative isolation from Anglo-Saxon influence. Thirdly, it is also consistent with the *Unternehmer* tradition: a bit more self-reliant inner-direction, a little less adaptation and conformity.

Another minor manifestation of this *Unternehmer* legacy is the pattern of reprimanding in a German company: that is, who gets 'told off' by whom and why. This is a phenomenon the author has observed in action rather than inferred from the comments of German managers. Now German managers are, of course, more likely to tell their subordinates off than be told off by them. The interesting thing, however, is the frequency with which people reprimand their equals and superiors. This is not to be done lightly. One has to have a good case for imputing dereliction of duty to the victim, but if one has, then it is possible to ignore status and hierarchy and open fire. This again is the moral legacy of the *Unternehmer* – the purpose is too serious to be compromised, a touch of righteousness is preferred to a plentitude of discretion.

Punctuality provides a neat, minor example of this norm in action. Things tend to happen on time in a Germany company. If a manager has scheduled a meeting for 8 a.m., dead on 8 a.m. his door will open and the delegates will troop in. Punctuality is expected rather than exhorted and it is no respecter of rank. The manager who summons his subordinates to a meeting, and is then ten minutes late himself will not find them waiting. If you catch out your boss in an act of unpunctuality you can denounce him to his face, or his secretary. And the higher the manager's rank, the more serious is the offence because he has a greater obligation to set an example. They are not usually articulated, but these seem to be the unspoken assumptions – those of the entrepreneurial rather than managerial age.

The German manager's approach to the articulation of problems is interesting: to put it very simply, they do not seem to have many. That is, if one asks German managers to enumerate recurrent operational problems in their *particular* sphere they will do so, undramatically. If one asks senior managers to speculate on problems confronting the company as a whole there are in the author's experience three reactions, not mutually exclusive. The first is to try to think of something, just to be obliging. In this context increasing foreign (Japanese) competition may be mentioned with some conviction, likewise a fall off in orders since the great days of 1973-4. Thereafter the tendency is to mention problems which might confront other firms – 'Competition from other German suppliers, but this does not really apply to us', 'Raising capital for expansion may sometimes be a problem' and so on. The most obvious interpretation is that this low profile on company problems reflects the overall success of the German economy with its favourable trade balance and successes. It is probably also a reflection of the uncomplicated nature of German managerial thought. In the German scheme of things, if there is some difficulty about making the product, selling it, or designing a better one than you had before, that is a problem. But German managers do not go looking for problems in the management system or in secondary analyses of its performance.

This direct orientation finds expression in the second reaction. This is that where problems *are* indicated with interest and conviction they tend to be technical or product-related concerns. Here statements made to the author include:

'Maintaining technical creativity while expanding',
'Consolidating after rapid expansion' (of productive capacity),
'Deciding what we need to be producing in five years time',
'How to mass produce a *variety* of products',
'Effecting the changeover from unit production to mass production — but without losing our reputation for quality' and
'Improving the quality of our after sales service: that's the way to get the edge over our competitors'.

The third reaction to an open ended question about problems is also consistent. The most frequent reply is to say that there is a shortage of *Facharbeiter* (skilled workers) or of particular kinds of skilled worker (welders were often given as an example). This again is illustrative of the down to earth German approach: not having sufficient staff specialists skilled in Operations Research is not a problem (see Chapter 4). But a shortage of welders is a problem: it means delays, bottlenecks, permanent overtime, shift-working which has to be negotiated with the Works Council and inter-firm poaching. The shortage is usually explained in terms of the 'educational explosion' of the 1960s which means that some people who would, earlier, have done an apprenticeship, instead entered the further education system and emerged with a superior academic qualification.

There is an interesting corollary to this German shortage of skilled workers. In Britain it is often alleged that a lot of jobs which used to be skilled are not skilled any more, or not as skilled. The reasons usually cited are dilution at some earlier stage, de-skilling as a consequence of the increasing subdivision of tasks and de-skilling as a result of technical change. The point of interest is that there is very little reference to these issues in West Germany. Although the middle aged German tradesman may feel that 'Apprentices are not what they used to be ', one does not encounter the idea of structural change having a de-skilling effect. This idea was also explored in a preliminary way in Chapter 2 where it was shown that German firms, compared with similar firms in France, have a higher proportion of production workers and a lower proportion of ancillary technical workers. These facts tend to imply, *ceteris paribus*, that German production workers are required to be both more autonomous and more versatile.

Technik Again

Conversations with German managers afford many instances of the influence of *Technik*, described in the previous chapter. We also discussed in Chapter 3 the status of engineering in Germany and the fact that some studies of the qualifications of German managers suggest that the overall qualification level is higher on the technical side of the typical firm than on the commercial side. Apart from references to the firm 'living from *Technik*' (very common) mentioned in the previous chapter, one also notes that 'engineer' is a term of praise. The author has encountered, for instance, such comments as: 'Ich bin mit Leib und Seele Ingenieur' ('I'm an engineer, body and soul' — a technical director of a large company), and 'Er ist Vollblutingenieur' ('He is a full-blooded engineer' — a young personnel officer praising the founder of his medium sized company). On another occasion a German manager passed on to the author the observation of a Greek purchasing agent who had visited the company the previous day: 'We always buy German; we know the Germans live with the idea of making things from childhood on.'

Another manifestation of this *Technik* stance is the fact that German firms tend to take the view that if they are really proud of what they make they ought to make all of it. One encounters firms which maintain specialised facilities for the manufacture of some component, although this could be 'bought out'. Consider, for example, a medical equipment firm running its own paper mill, because paper is used in breathing masks and air filters, though these were only one of several product lines. Or a fork lift truck factory which made its own electric motors: it is not as though there is a shortage of reputable electrical engineering companies in West Germany. It is also noticeable that foundries proliferate in Germany: one often comes across companies which are not primarily foundries but which run one on the side. Another example is inspection equipment. German managers will frequently tell the visitor when he is being shown round that the company 'has to' make its own inspection devices and/or equipment. Now the claim will often be realistic; sometimes the reference is to specialised electronic testing devices for the company's advanced products. But on other occasions what one is shown is not so much technically sophisticated as practically clever – an expression of local ingenuity not a technical revolution. In other words, they do it this way because they like to.

The most forceful expression of the dominance of *Technik*, however, relates to the products. It was noted earlier that German managers, if asked what as senior representatives of their companies they are proud of, tend not to emphasise economic indicators of the profit-turnover-market share-growth kind. What they do mention is the products, either in general terms or by naming some particular product achievement. One receives answers like:

'I am proud when I see our vehicles on the streets of Munich',
'The largest continuous casting mill in Europe',
'Our original marine engine was world famous' and
'We have built the biggest bulldozer in the world'.

Or one is given product related answers in response to an open ended question as to sources of executive pride: our products reflect the quality of management, satisfied customers, the quality of our products, our after sales service, our capacity to introduce modifications at the request of customers, a reputation for products of even higher quality and so on. These are all actual examples and none of them are quotations from *production* managers.

The German View of Britain

It may be of interest to round off this tour of the German managers' opinions and preoccupations by presenting their image of Britain, particularly in so far as this relates to the British economic performance. As might be expected, Britain comes in for a fair amount of criticism. But it is fair to say that neither Germans in general, nor German managers in particular, are in any overall sense anti-British. The criticisms are precisely of British industrial life and economic performance, not global criticisms, and the critics do not generally impute negative characteristics to the British as a nation.

There is another qualification. Germans are not especially well informed about Britain. The typical German manager, in the author's experience, does not know that Britain has a comprehensive school system, for instance, or that the proportion of university students in Britain whose fathers are manual workers is more than twice the proportion in Germany. Nor, unless he has been to Britain recently, does the average German manager realise that Britain introduced decimal currency at the beginning of the 1970s and most Germans are unaware of the fact that there was a *post factum* referendum in Britain on Common Market Membership and it produced a majority in favour. In short, Germans are not better informed about the realities of British life than Britons are about West Germany.

It is a sad fact but the phrase *die englische Krankheit* (the English disease) is now a standard expression in German. It is invoked when Germans feel things are going badly for the West German economy and they want to frighten themselves; the newspaper headline 'The English Disease: Can Germany catch it?' is representative of this usage. The phrase may also be used as a reprimand. The author recently attended a production progress meeting at a German plant; a foreman at the meeting maintained that some mishap 'was not my fault', and the Chairman caustically remarked that this was the way *die englische Krankheit* began!

In German eyes this possibly contagious ailment has three dimensions. The first is indicated by the above anecdote. It is thought that British managers do not try hard enough or take their responsibilities seriously enough (occasionally the criticism is in the form of 'do not work hard enough'). Personal unpunctuality, poor delivery performance, slow responses, weak prosecution of export openings and failure to learn foreign languages for business purposes are the usual sins cited by Germans in this context. The relatively low pay of British managers, together with high rates of personal taxation (58 per cent is the highest rate of income tax in West Germany), are also sometimes mentioned in this context, as tending to explain poor management motivation.

The second dimension concerns the British system of industrial relations and it is both the structure and the performance which are criticised. The Germans, with their 16 industrial trade unions, can afford to be critical (see Chapter 1). The particular things which are attacked are the number of unions in Britain, the presumed unreasonableness of some strikes and most of all, demarcation disputes. German managers who have experience of installing or assembling in Britain are particularly hot on the demarcation phenomenon.

The third dimension (and this is the only attempt at explanation which is made) lies in attacks on the English class system. These tend to be a little dated and picturesque, with references to Lords in top hats strolling down Piccadilly, but they do encompass a basic point — that class differences in Britain are more numerous, more obvious and people are more conscious of them. Germans tend to ascribe lack of industrial harmony and a sense of common purpose at least in part to this consideration.

Conclusion

We have attempted to enrich the characterisation of German management by citing the managers' own views, with interpretative comment, on a range of issues. The raw material for this chapter is the author's own experience in terms of much informal discussion with German managers, formal interviews with them and some time spent as a guest observer in a number of German companies.

It has been argued that the German managerial vocabulary both underlines German management's distinctiveness *vis à vis* the USA and gives evidence of the cultural emphasis on work and achievement.

German managers tend not to be defensive and sometimes exhibit a bouncy enthusiasm for free enterprise capitalism while at the same time taking a less economistic view of the company than their Anglo-American colleagues. They are often committed to the view that West Germany is a classless society.

German managers are less overtly concerned with ambition and status. They take seriously preparation for a career in management, but have little folk-lore on 'how to get to the top' — the standard view is that promotion is all a matter of personal achievement (*Leistung*). They emphasise the practical, are less given to stereotyping than the British, are more punctual, less insistent on group harmony and have an uncomplicated view of what constitutes a problem for management. They are not markedly authoritarian, though the individual German manager is inclined to think that he is an exception to the national rule in this matter.

A consideration of the views of German management gives further evidence of their low management consciousness in the American sense discussed in the previous chapter and illustrates the rival German *Unternehmer* tradition.

The preoccupations of German managers are also evidence of the pervasive influence of *Technik*: pride in the company's products is particularly marked.

Notes

1. This idea is also developed in Peter Lawrence, 'It's the Product that Counts', *CBI Review* (Winter 1977/8).
2. Bernt Engelmann, *Meine Freunde die Manager* (Franz Schneekluth Verlag KG, München, 1966). Excerpt translated from the German by Peter Lawrence.

3. This phenomenon is discussed at greater length in Peter Lawrence, 'Engineering Education and Meritocracy', *Higher Education Review* (Summer 1979).

4. Alistair Mant, 'Authority and Task in Manufacturing Operations of Multinational Firms' in Michael Fores and Ian Glover (eds.), *Manufacturing and Management* (HMSO, London, 1978).

5. The same holds true for Swiss executive advertisements; in this connection see: Peter Lawrence, 'Executive Head Hunting', *New Society* (May 1978).

6. S. P. Hutton, P. A. Lawrence and J. H. Smith, 'The Recruitment, Deployment and Status of the Mechanical Engineer in the German Federal Republic', 2 vols., Report to the Department of Industry, London, 1977.

7. Ibid.

6 PRODUCTION MANAGEMENT

The Production function deserves some separate discussion for two reasons, or groups of reasons. First, it is by definition the central activity of any manufacturing company. It provides the tangible, measurable output of the company; it is what most of the plant, equipment, and machinery is for. And it is what the majority of those employed by the company are engaged in, even if the relative proportion of direct production workers appears to vary between different countries as was demonstrated in Chapter 2. Production is also the *logically* central function, even if the temporal sequence of activities may vary.[1] The logical order of operations, that is to say, is that commodities are designed and/or developed, then produced and finally sold and distributed.

These generalisations about Production apply to manufacturing companies throughout the world, but the basic fact of the centrality of Production is particularly true for Germany. This will already be clear from various ideas discussed in the two previous chapters: the relative strength of the line as opposed to the staff, the *Unternehmer* tradition and the rejection of 'arms-length' management, the down to earth approach to management problems, the relative German immunity to American style analyses of management as an abstracted entity and the pervasive influence of *Technik* are all conducive to a positive valuation of the Production function. This is not an exhaustive statement; we will endeavour to elaborate and substantiate this thesis in the next few pages, but it should be clear that what we have to say about Production in particular is consistent with various other propositions about German management in general which have been developed in this book.

The second reason is that a book in English about German management is bound to be concerned with aspects of German management which are distinctive or interesting from a non-German point of view, to be concerned at some points with comparisons and contrasts. The nature of production management is a case where this comparative interest may be exploited with profit. There are, in short, some interesting differences between production management in Britain and Germany. To appreciate this it is worth spending some time on the British half of the equation; this is again a fruitful exercise since there have been a number of recent studies of production management and production managers in Britain.[2]

Production Management in Britain

There are two *Leitmotifs* in these British studies. One is that Production is not something we British are particularly good at. The second is that Production, relative to other executive functions, is neglected and lacks standing. That it is, in short, a 'Cinderella function'; no manager who had any realistic choice would make a career in Production. The tone of this series of studies, for the Production function has been an object of consistent interest in Britain in the second half of the 1970s, is set by the first sentence of Colin New's report on his study of British production management published in 1976:[3]

> There has been considerable debate in recent years on the relatively low status accorded to the manufacturing function in industry and also on the calibre of those recruited into manufacturing management.[4]

Colin New's study took in 186 British companies and his findings make depressing reading. He is concerned that the educational qualifications of British production and production control managers are too one-sidedly technical and that there is too little managerial mobility in to and out of the Production function. He feels that the salaries of production managers are low and found wide variations in salary level between different branches of industry.

His report is also critical of performance: poor showing on meeting delivery dates (and a high proportion of these deadlines fixed by Sales rather than Production), a poor record on product innovation, too little attention paid to purcashing policy and stock control and poor co-ordination of the various phases of production with component batches lying idle on the shop floor for long periods. An interesting twist to Colin New's account, however, is that he is not primarily critical of production managers themselves, but of the neglect or misapprehension of the manufacturing function by others.

This idea of the slighting of Production is a dominant theme in a highly critical report published by the Business Graduates Association in 1977.[5] The Association in fact commissioned a study of production managers which was carried by O. W. Roskill Industrial Consultants, in the form of extended interviews with a sample of 38 production or ex-production managers. The ensuing report has a positive aspect. It claims a high level of intrinsic interest for production management work, and characterises it in terms of inherent complexity, a substantial planning component, need for qualities of leadership, an important 'dealing with people' component and a range of satisfactions including those associated with a tangible output — the finished goods.

On the other hand, this report argues, production management work is also characterised by pressure, frustration deriving from industrial relations problems and a general lack of investment resulting in old plant and equipment and poorly laid out factories. Production management tends to be neglected by top management and to be staffed by 'old faithfuls' with poor career prospects. It is relatively disadvantaged with regard to pay, the allocation of company cars, fringe benefits, general promotion prospects, access to the Board of Directors and general status. Working conditions may be poor in certain tangible ways; small offices, noisy and dirty environment, long hours, difficulty in taking time off (to go on management training courses, for instance) and with little contact with the outside world compared with managers in other functions such as Sales, Finance and Personnel. The image of production management work is poor and Production is above all the function which the ambitious executive will avoid.

A third British study was commissioned by the joint Confederation of British Industry/British Institute of Management Advisory Panel on Management Education and conducted by Roger Gill and Keith Lockyer of the Bradford University Management School. Their report appeared in 1979.[6] It tends to substantiate certain points in the Business Graduates Association Report above in that some evidence emerged for the thesis that Production is an underprivileged function. More than a quarter of the senior production managers in the companies surveyed complained about the status of Production in the company and sizeable minorities thought that pay and fringe benefits were inequitable, expected no promotion in Production, or expected to have to transfer to other functions.

Some new themes also emerge from the Gill and Lockyer study. There are some systematic differences between British owned and foreign owned firms in Britain, including the fact that the proportion of graduates (among senior production managers) is substantially higher in foreign owned firms and the level of reported frustrations due to labour relations problems is significantly higher in British owned companies.

Gill and Lockyer also investigated the relationship between Production and other functions. In most cases the respondents were so senior that they controlled Maintenance and Production Control as well as Production itself (the survey was aimed at the highest person in the companies with responsibility for Production; typically, that is, a Director). Where they did not also control Maintenance and Production Control an overwhelming majority thought that such control would serve the end of efficient output. With regard to the relationship between Production and other (non-controlled) functions those most frequently criticised as unsatisfactory were with Maintenance, Research and Development and Design, in that order. Only a small minority criticised the relationship with Purchasing, though another interesting finding was that senior production managers in American owned companies in Britain were significantly more likely to have Purchasing under their control than were their colleagues in British owned companies.

The Gill and Lockyer Report is also enlivened by some direct quotations from production managers who were interviewed in the course of the study. One or two of these may 'give the flavour' of the British situation, especially its deficiencies:

> There isn't a single member of our Board who's had direct production experience. How on earth can they realise what's going on if they've never been there? (Factory Manager, large paint manufacturing company.)

> We don't need our production managers to have any education . . . so long as they have a bit of experience elsewhere we're quite happy. (Managing Director, small textile company.)

> My status is as good as anybody's in the company . . . of course the Sales Director gets about £5,000 a year more than I do. (Production Director, car accessory manufacturer.)

> The beauty of this job is that there's enormous variety . . . no two days are the same. (Production Manager, medium sized engineering company.)

Some of the Lockyer and Gill findings are echoed by another study carried out by Mrs M. K. McQuillan, the results of which were published by the Cranfield Institute of Technology in 1978.[7] The McQuillan study is more specialised than the three other studies we have discussed so far; it focusses on the potential employment of graduate engineers in Production in small and medium sized companies in the British engineering industry. In a different way the McQuillan report also takes up the question of the relationship between Production and other technical functions, taking an organisational rather than experiental view:

> Although it is normal practice for engineering and other technical functions to be separated organisationally from production line management, a price is often paid for this arrangement in terms of lack of understanding and differing objectives.[8]

A new theme in the McQuillan Report is what with a little overstatement one might call 'graduate aversion'. There are two aspects to this. First, a feeling on the part of companies that an infusion of technically well educated managerial manpower, symbolised by the graduate, may be mildly desirable but will not make any decisive difference:

> The major problems faced by the sample of companies examined are not such that an infusion of graduate engineers into production could have solved directly.[9]

The second aspect centres round some rather critical attitudes in the companies studied towards graduates:

> Management at all levels was critical of the new graduate turned out by the academic institutions, both as to the training received and to the personal quality and attitudes of the individual. The training was seen as too theoretical and providing no practical experience of engineering problems. The graduates themselves were described as 'too gentlemanly', 'thinking themselves superior', 'unwilling to get their hands dirty', 'unable to talk to ordinary people', 'expecting too much too soon', 'not knowing how to handle people', 'thinking paperwork beneath them', 'expecting to be doing high powered engineering' and 'being unwilling to learn'.[10]

These what we might politely term 'doubts about graduates' are particularly interesting for an Anglo-German comparison.

Finally, in this content of a brief review of the British situation as seen in the reports of the researchers we should mention the work of a research group at the Newcastle upon Tyne Polytechnic.[11] They have surveyed some 300 manufacturing companies of all sizes in northeast England. A particular point of interest which this study has is that it gives some factual foundation to one of the claims of the Business

Graduates Association report which we discussed earlier, namely that Production tends to be staffed by 'old faithfuls', or at any rate by 'home grown' talent. Of the firms surveyed 80 per cent acknowledged that they recruit their junior and middle production managers (above the foreman, below the Board of Directors) internally and 64 per cent of the companies even recruited their senior production managers internally – this tendency being strongest for the larger companies. The same finding emerged in a different form in response to a multiple choice question inviting respondents to indicate their weighing of different factors in the recruitment of production managers – the relative merit of experience and qualifications, and so on. Here only 7 per cent of the companies gave a high preference to production management experience in a different industry.

Furthermore, this Newcastle study breaks new ground by inviting senior production managers to give *their* views on factors affecting the efficiency of Production. The response includes two surprises. The respondents do not put industrial relations problems top, only second in a list of six named factors. First place was awarded to 'lack of a market for our goods'. Now this is a biased view of course (blame Sales, that will teach them) but there may still be something in it. The other surprise is that these senior managers did not attach much importance to the lack of investment argument, although this has figured prominently in debates about Britain's lack of international competitiveness. These managers placed lack of modern equipment at the bottom of the list, after market problems, industrial relations problems, planning difficulties, scarcity of managerial talent and technical difficulties. We do not, of course, wish to recommend lack of investment in plant and equipment, but again there may be some substance to the production managers' views. A series of studies conducted by Professor N. A. Dudley in the period 1970-4 in the West Midlands, concluded that increases in production of up to 100 per cent could be achieved by a more efficient use of existing resources.[12]

Now this is not a book, or even a chapter, about *British* production management. The British situation has been reviewed because it is a useful *entrée* to a discussion of some aspects of German production management. There are some interesting differences and fortunately production management in Britain is well documented as a result of recent research. Before confronting the question: what is characteristic and distinctive about production management in Germany? a comment on the British studies which have been briefly discussed here is in order.

The simple point is that if one based one's estimate of British production management *only* on research reports of the kind discussed here one would conclude it to be a good deal worse than it is. This is not because the reports are in any simple sense 'wrong'. In fact their findings tend to be mutually reinforcing and the present writer has also found some support for their conclusions.[13] It is rather that these studies do not tell the whole story, and that some of the phenomena they investigate, while real and important, are not decisive for performance.

Take, for instance, the central idea that Production is a low status executive function, with a poor image and relatively poor remuneration and slow promotion. There is not much doubt that this characterisation is true, but it does not mean that British production managers are demoralised and their will to act paralysed by depression over relative status. They may well have, and in the author's experience some certainly do have, a degree of personal integrity and a sense of purpose which transcends status deprivations. Again, the studies we have referred to have been conceived and conducted in a particular climate, one of concern about Britain's economic performance. They naturally highlight what is wrong and do so with a view to stimulating constructive change. But this orientation is not equally likely to highlight the 'corresponding strengths'. British production managers are not mobile between functions (unless or until they leave Production for some area of managerial work offering better promotion chances) and even less mobile between companies. Their corresponding strength is that they have a thorough understanding of the work of their companies, technically and organisationally. The context in which they operate is less favourable than that of their German colleagues both in general and particular terms, but this is not the end of the story. If British production managers cannot get what they want (or need) for the asking, they will know how to do it by manoeuvre, special pleading and 'working the informal system'. In short, their effectiveness cannot be fully estimated by questionnaire surveys or interviews because these do not capture the totality of what managers do and the way they do it.

German Production Management: the General Context

One of the most striking and probably decisive differences between the British and the German production manager is that the German operates in a much more favourable context. This is true in respect of some finite circumstances and it is true of less tangible, general considerations. Apart from the obvious contrast in the matter of industrial relations and strike record (see Chapter 1) this contextual difference may not be generally appreciated.

Some of the dimensions of this difference have been, at any rate one-sidedly explored in the two previous chapters. The somewhat 'de-economised' view which German managers have of the business enterprise is central. The idea that the firm is not 'a money-making machine' but a place where products get designed, made and eventually sold, with profits ensuing, tends in Germany to restrict the allure of accountants and financial controllers and to dignify the makers and those associated with them. So the way the industrial enterprise is conceptualised in Germany, those links in the chain of activities and purposes which are strongest, tend to give Production more standing than it enjoys in Britain.

One should add to this the fact that the status of industry itself is higher in Germany than in Britain, a theme which will be developed more systematically in Chapter 8. This has the effect of raising managerial morale generally and production managers are among the beneficiaries.

In the earlier discussion of the background and qualifications of German managers generally (Chapter 3) it was shown that more German managers are qualified in engineering than in anything else. We also argued in this context that engineering and engineers enjoy a higher standing in Germany than in Britain and examined the reasons for this. The fact of the relatively higher standing of engineers in Germany is again relevant for production managers in particular. The vast majority of production managers, at all levels in the hierarchy above that of the foreman, do hold formal qualifications and these qualifications are invariably in engineering. The chemical industry is an exception to this generalisation, but the only exception. Here the majority of production managers are graduates and frequently hold doctorates in chemistry. Otherwise, the production management function in German enterprises is dominated by qualified engineers, in a society which accords considerable esteem to engineering. So in terms of attitudes towards the nature and purpose of the manufacturing company, towards the role of industry in society and the standing accorded to engineers, German production managers may be said to function in a more favourable context than their British colleagues.

There is a further general consideration which is relevant here. This is the fact that work, if not always a popular activity, is at least an activity which is taken seriously. This idea is introduced hesitantly first, because it does smack of the national stereotype and national stereotypes deserve to be examined critically, and secondly, because it is not a contention which is easy to prove (or disprove) in a formal scientific way. What can be reasonably argued is that foreigners who live or work in Germany, or even travel extensively in that country, do encounter instances and evidence of a general identification with work.

One notes that people doing quite ordinary jobs are concerned that they should be done well. There is a tendency for the worker not just to do the job but also to internalise its purpose. Postmen worry if the letters they are to deliver have unclear or incomplete addresses, bus drivers worry if they fall behind schedule, repair men worry if they cannot effect a repair quickly. If we might offer one picturesque example of this pervasive attitude, German speaking readers might be exhorted to listen in to the late night phone in musical request programme *Von Telefon zu Mikrofon* (from telephone to microphone) broadcast on a Thursday evening. Members of the general public simply phone in, have a five minute chat with the compère and then request a record. The interesting thing is what they chat about. Now the compère has to play this by ear and follows obvious lines like asking his or her interlocutors about their families, holidays and hobbies (football has pride of place here). But a standard theme in these informal discussions is work. The caller is always asked what his job is and if there should be any doubt about its skill status a regular question is: "Ist das ein Lernberuf' ('Is your job one which requires an apprenticeship?' since apprenticeship is a revered institution). Those whose work involves the operation of machinery or equipment are also generally asked about the qualities of the machines as well. The engaging thing is that the people concerned do not usually have jobs which would generally be regarded as exotic or exciting; they tend to be factory workers and public employees rather than film stars or mountaineers, but it is assumed that they will want to talk about their jobs and the listeners will find this interesting too. Sometimes the accounts will be quite impassioned. On one occasion a post office worker who rode the mail van on the Direct Orient Express held forth for some minutes on the importance of stacking mail and parcels in such a way that they can be unloaded fast at Kehl (the French-German border town near Strasbourg) ending with the punch line: 'If you don't get it all out in four minutes, the train will be late at the next station.'

This leads to another of these intangible facts of German life — the cult of punctuality. It is equally noticeable in industry and in the public services. If one takes as an indication the classic question: are German trains punctual (say, more punctual than trains in other countries)? the author, having travelled regularly in Germany by public transport for several years, would say they probably are, but this is not the most interesting thing about the contrast. What strikes a foreigner travelling in Germany is the importance attached to the idea of punctuality, whether or not the standard is realised. Punctuality, not the weather, is the standard topic of conversation for strangers in railway compartments. Long distance trains in Germany have a pamphlet laid out in each compartment called a *Zugbegleiter* (literally, 'train accompanier') which lists all the stops with arrival and departure times and all the possible connections *en route*. It is almost a national sport in Germany, as a train pulls into a station, for hands to reach out for the *Zugbegleiter* so that the train's progress may be checked against the digital watch. When trains are late and it happens, the loudspeaker announcements relay this fact in a tone which falls between the stoic and the tragic. The worst category of lateness which figures in these announcements is *unbestimmte Verspätung* (indeterminable lateness: we don't know how late it is going to be!) and this is pronounced as a funeral oration.

The importance of these two impressionistic points, the concern with work and punctuality, is that they are also part of the more favourable context of the German production manager. The production manager is, *par excellence*, concerned with the organisation of work. And it is work in which punctuality, in the sense of medial and final deadlines, is of vital importance. It is simply noted here that, *ceteris paribus*, the production manager who operates in a society which emphasises work and punctuality, has an easier job. We will take up the question of punctuality (deadlines) later in this chapter. With regard to the work and sense of purpose ethic it may be noted that this is very noticeable in German companies. To take one quite straightforward indicator, if one listens to German managers on the telephone, when they are telling someone what they want, or want done, it is noticeable that they neither plead nor command. There is no suggestion of the exercise of military authority; nor is there any trace of the idea that the speaker will get his way as a special favour, because he is 'a regular guy' and has asked nicely. Requests are made and/or instructions given in a rather matter of fact way, suggesting that the speaker regards it as quite reasonable, the listener is going to regard it as quite reasonable and it will happen.

So far we have referred to rather intangible phenomena in construing the work context of the German production manager — questions of attitude, ethos and evaluation. There are also some quite specific and tangible advantages enjoyed by production managers in German companies. If we use the term production manager comprehensively, to refer to all ranks in the line production hierarchy above that of foreman or general foreman, then it may also be argued that the foremen themselves are on average better qualified, more secure and have higher standing, than their British colleagues. This point will be developed in more detail in Chapter 7. The simple fact is that the German foreman can undertake more, give more support to his boss and his boss can delegate more to him.

Another specific consideration concerns the organisation of industrial relations in Germany (see Chapter 1). The fact that the number of trade unions in Germany is small and that they are *industrial* unions, offering membership to all types and grades of employee in a given industry, means that demarcation disputes in a formal sense are impossible by definition. There is, in fact, no phrase in German for demarcation dispute and the idea has to be elaborately paraphrased. One manifestation of this is the less rigid division between Production and Maintenance as functions and activities, which has been noted at several points. Another practical implication is that the German production manager has more freedom to move workers around to satisfy immediate manning needs. That is, it is that much easier in a German factory to cover manpower gaps due to sickness and holiday absenteeism and to deal with changes in short-term manning needs deriving from changed output priorities, re-scheduling of jobs and additional assignments.

This freedom enjoyed by German production managers (to re-deploy workers) is not absolute. But so long as the worker is neither de-skilled nor financially disadvantaged by the move, short-to middle-term redeployment is easy to arrange. A worker who is frequently re-deployed in this way and does not like it, may complain to the *Betriebsrat* (Works Council) but that is, from the manager's point of view, the worst thing that can happen. And German managers attach positive importance to the individual worker's readiness and ability to be so redeployed. There is a standard term for this redeployment capability, *Einsatzbreite*, which is used both formally and informally in evaluating individual workers for merit rises and possible promotion. The author has specifically asked a number of production managers about their freedom in this respect. Some of the replies are instructive:

> A worker might object (to a job change) if some safety issues were involved.

> A skilled machinist might not be able to do electrical repairs.

Naturally the carpenters help to dig the foundations. (Production manager: building firm.)

Everyone can do fitters' work. (Superintendent, iron foundry.)

For long-term or permanent transfers, the *Betriebsrat* (Works Council) has to be consulted and give its consent. On more than one occasion the author has sat in on discussions between production managers and *Betriebsrat* representatives on such issues. On these occasions it can only be said that the *Betriebsrat* acted in an accommodating way from the point of view of management: no unreasonable difficulties were made. On one of these occasions the production manager's wish was to end overtime working on a particular section and substitute shift-work. After he had given a very lucid and convincing account of his reasons the *Betriebsrat* chairman replied: 'I know we (the Works Council) are supposed to oppose shift-working, but if it is in the interest of the firm . . .' It was all wrapped up in ten minutes.

Perhaps the most tangible difference in the context in which production managers operate in Britain and Germany is in the matter of strikes. German industry is not actually strike-free; but from a British standpont it looks like it. In all the time the author has spent in German factories, interviewing, collecting data and spending periods as an observer, a strike has never been witnessed, nor the threat of a strike mentioned. Indeed the only time the word 'strike' has ever been used in the author's presence was in the context of a senior manager in a very large mass production consumer goods plant explaining that they not only double and treble banked on suppliers but distributed their orders around the various 'tariff areas' (wage negotiations occur at state, i.e. *Land* level, so the 11 *Bundesländer* which make up the *Federal* Republic are 'tariff areas') so that a strike in one 'area' would not prejudice supplies from another.

That the individual German production manager is virtually free from strikes in his own company is the most obvious outcome, but not necessarily the most important. The advantage is cumulative. The German production manager also benefits from the fact that in all probability no one else is striking either. Raw materials and 'bought out' parts are supplied, co-operative projects or multi-phase operations involving several companies are not jeopardised, industrial customers are ready to take delivery of finished goods and it is less likely that transport services will be disrupted or communications fail. The cumulative importance of all this can be highlighted by contrast. In Britain it is eminently possible to find good, well-run, harmonious companies where they cannot remember when the last strike occurred. But if you spend some time in such companies it is also pre-eminently possible that one will hear of the production efforts being hamstrung by failures elsewhere. Some vital raw material consignment is stuck in a railway yard because of a local transport dispute, finished goods are being stockpiled because the 'customer' is on strike, mail posted first class at a subsidiary on Friday has not arrived by the following Tuesday at the Main Works (even without a strike), there is a shortage of oxygen cylinders because of 'some trouble at the docks' and the production manager is chasing compressors and mobile generators as power-cuts are threatened.

This last example, power-cuts, is yet another instance where the German production manager is more favourably placed. If one quizzes British and German managers on the thoughtful provision of emergency supplies and generators, the British win. This does not mean that the Germans are reckless in this respect: they are just less likely to need such provisions. Power-cuts are not unknown in Germany but they are generally the result of short-term technical failure or freak weather conditions. They are infrequent and taken very seriously. In December 1978, for example, freezing rain fell across the northern half of Germany. It caused widespread traffic chaos and closed Frankfurt airport, the biggest in Germany and the third biggest in Europe, for seven hours. The freezing rain affected a power station near Bonn with the result that the capital city suffered a four minute power-cut. This made front page news.

Finally, the weather itself might be cited in this litany of contextual advantages enjoyed by the German production manager. The German winter tends to be colder than the British and there is more snow. These mundane considerations are important for the production manager. If the work force does not turn up until 10 a.m. because they are stuck in snow drifts, or there is 50 per cent weather determined absenteeism, this is as crippling as a strike. The author once visited a number of German companies just after there had been a heavy snow fall in southern England (but not in Germany) and took the opportunity to ask a sample of German managers if a heavy snow fall would have disruptive effects on *their* operations: nearly all these companies were in fact in Schleswig-Holstein, the most northerly state. The managers made very light of this issue; the most damaging testimony was: 'If we had a meter of snow overnight we would have to reckon with some of the workers coming a couple of hours late; our catchment area has a thirty kilometer radius.'

A year later the author had a chance to see if this debonair attitude was justified, spending two days at a medium sized company in a town on the Baltic coast. In fact a blizzard raged for two days. Schools closed, the town was completely cut off by road, all but one of the railway links were cut and on the second day the authorities announced a DM 500 fine for anyone attempting to leave the town by road. The factory carried on working. There was 10 per cent absenteeism on the first day and 30 per cent on the second, when most of the absentees were the victims of the driving prohibition in force outside the city limits. The firm had its own snow plough and hired a second one. Snow clearing teams at the factory began at 4 a.m.; the factory salted and sanded its own roads and the maintenance engineer announced that the firm had sufficient supplies of heating oil to last until May (the blizzard was in February) even if there were no further deliveries.

The weather conditions in this instance were extreme. Hamburg, the largest town in Germany after Berlin, was also cut off by road and on the second day of the blizzard tanks were sent down the Bremen-Bremerhaven Autobahn to rescue stranded motorists. Within the city itself the snow clearing was very effective: it was possible to drive, taxis were available, public transport ran all the time, refuse was collected, mail delivered at the normal hour and there were no power-cuts.

Blizzards and power-cuts are not the most important contingencies in the production manager's life, but the story is instructive. To a foreigner, it appears that in Germany all agencies conspire to make his job easier and less vulnerable to unpredictable disruption.

German Production Management: Qualifications

German Production Managers tend to be relatively better qualified than their opposite numbers in Britain, a little better qualified than their German colleagues in Sales and Finance and not as well qualified as their colleagues in Research and Development, Quality Control and Engineering. It should be noted that we are using the term 'production manager' in a functionally narrow sense to indicate those managers whose direct or indirect subordinates are production workers, not people who 'help' production workers. Thus we are excluding from 'Production' not only Research and Development and Design, but also Quality Control, Engineering, Production Control and Maintenance. This in fact runs counter to German usage. Germans tend to treat Production as connoting the whole company minus Sales and Finance. German production managers if asked if they have always worked in Production will often tell you that they have and then regale you with an account of their five years in Design after leaving engineering school before reaching Production (in our sense) via Quality Control, or Maintenance. We are adopting a functionally narrow conception of 'production manager' here for two reasons. First, it is necessary if one wishes to make some intra-organisational comparisons and we will attempt this later in the chapter. Secondly, it is necessary for a proper estimate of the qualificational levels in the technical areas of German companies, one which does not exaggerate in the Germans' favour. This can be approached, level by level, up the hierarchy.

German companies often have a working semi-supervisor equivalent to the British chargehand. In Germany this worker supervisor is called a *Vorarbeiter* and there are probably more *Vorarbeiter* in German companies than chargehands in British ones, since in Britain trade unions have tended to be hostile to this ambiguous rank. The German *Vorarbeiter* does not usually hold any formal qualifications, except that he is rather more likely than his British opposite number to be a skilled worker and being 'a skilled worker' in Germany implies the possession of a formal qualification (see Chapter 7).

The first fully supervisory rank in the German production hierarchy is that of foreman, the German foreman being called a *Meister*. According to the regulations the German foreman should have satisfied a number of requirements relating to age, experience, skill level, courses and examinations and the majority have done so. The system will be explained in more detail in the following chapter, but by way of preview it would be fair to say that the German foreman is typically better qualified than his opposite number in Britain and there is less variation in skill and qualificational levels among German foremen than among British foremen.

Sometimes there is a senior foreman or general foreman rank in German companies, the incumbent being called an *Obermeister*. The *Obermeister* is simply a *Meister* with experience and greater, presumed, organisational talent: no additional qualification is required. This rank is not very common in the author's experience and is found most often in large mass production mechanical engineering firms.

The next rank above the *Meister* or *Obermeister*, the first unequivocally managerial rank, has no standard name in Germany. It is the rank which, in the British production hierarchy, is usually denoted by the title superintendent. In Germany the 'superintendent' is usually an Ing Grad (three year full-time course in engineering beginning at the age of 18: see Chapter 3 for details of the educational system). There are also a minority of Dipl Ing (university graduates in engineering: again see Chapter 3 for details) at this superintendent level, and occasionally one comes across a Dr Ing (PhD in engineering). The author has made it a practice to ask German managers what qualifications are usual in particular jobs at specified levels: in the case of the production superintendent he has been told that there are a minority with qualifications inferior to that of the Ing Grad. These will be promoted foremen, *Techniker* (holders of the technician's certificate) and possibly people with REFA (work study) qualifications. This fact is presented a little obliquely because although the author has been told that the minority exists he has never actually met a representative of it in spite of spending a lot of time in German companies including some quite small ones.

For the next level in the production hierarchy, two ranks above the foreman or general foreman, there is again no standard title, though that of *Produktionsleiter* is common. At this level the Ing Grad is still probably the dominant qualification, though the Dipl Ing minority is substantial. There is no talk of incumbents with lesser (than the Ing Grad) qualifications. PhD's, while not exactly common at this level are not sufficiently uncommon to excite any comment either.

Where further levels exist in the production hierarchy, above the *Produktionsleiter* and below the 'Board', they will typically be staffed by Dipl Ings; PhD's are more common at these levels and one will still find some Ing Grads. At the Board level, the way in which the production function is represented varies with the type and size of the company concerned. In the GmbH type of company (see Chapter 2) typically having a three man *Geschäftsführung*, Production is usually represented by the *Geschäftsführer Technik* (technical director) along with the other technical functions – Research and Development, Design, Quality Assurance, Engineering, Maintenance and so on.

This is also a common arrangement in the AG type of company (see Chapter 2) where the *Vorstand Technik* (technical director) is responsible for all technical functions including Production. Where the company and its *Vorstand* are larger however, there may be a *Vorstand Produktion* (production director) who is distinct from the *Vorstand Technik*. And occasionally one finds companies with, in effect, more than one production director, their areas of responsibility being demarcated according to product groups or geographical areas of operation. In all these cases – *Geschäftsführer Technik*, *Vorstand Technik* and *Vorstand Produktion* – the incumbents are generally graduates, Dipl Ings in fact, and frequently hold the Dr Ing (PhD) in engineering, as well. It should be added that the ubiquitous Ing Grad is also occasionally found at the *Vorstand* level too. The Ing Grad at this level will be very much outnumbered by the Dipl Ing and the Dr Ing but one does sometimes meet *Vorstand* members who have the Ing Grad qualification and Ing Grads abound in the top positions of small, privately owned, or KG type companies (see Chapter 2). The relevant consideration with regard to the ubiquity and mobility of the Ing Grad is that although it is a non-graduate qualification it is nonetheless a substantial one. If one thinks of it as a three year full-time course beginning at the age of 18 then it is, thus far, comparable with a British first degree course. Add to this the fact that, before the recent changes in the educational system described in Chapter 3, the Ing Grad could also claim considerable practical prowess, having typically started by doing an apprenticeship and his potential becomes clear.

It may be useful to broaden the picture by looking, briefly, at qualifications in the other technical functions. Research and Development is dominated by graduates and a PhD in whatever branch of engineering is relevant to the company's products. Design is pretty well dominated by Ing Grads. That is to say, the designers tend to be Ing Grads and those who 'manage' them may be either Ing Grads or Dipl Ings. Production Control and Maintenance tend to have short (managerial) hierarchies being subsumed at a low level under production managers. In these two functions Ing Grads again predominate and in the case of Production Control the author has actually met one or two managers with lesser qualifications. Engineering and Quality Control tend to be graduate dominated and PhD's are quite common one or two levels above the foreman, even in smallish companies.

This qualification profile of production managers is interesting in a number of ways. First, the level of qualification is fairly high. In Production in the narrow sense and in the allied technical functions, there are few managers with anything less than the Ing Grad qualification and many with graduate and post-graduate qualifications. Secondly, there is no abrupt disparity between the related functions. Research and Development is 'better educated' than any other function — a universal phenomenon — and in the German case there are more graduates and PhD's in Engineering and Quality Control than in Production or Maintenance, but that is as far as the discrepancies go. And perhaps the key fact is that the Ing Grad threshold (almost everyone is at or above this level) is sufficiently high for no one to be seriously disadvantaged educationally in dealing with anyone else. It is noticeable that in Britain it is not unusual for managers to make mildly self-deprecatory remarks about their education, along the line of 'Of course, I can't claim any kind of superior education' and 'Afraid I left school at 14 and anything I've learned I've learned here'. In Germany, on the other hand, remarks of this kind are rather unusual and the difference is probably 'threshold determined'. Thirdly, there is an obvious element of homogeneity: just about everyone is qualified at one of the levels and what they are qualified in is engineering. The three points raised here taken collectively, are all to Production's advantage and to that of the company. In short, production managers are well qualified, there are no sharp qualificational discrepancies between Production and related functions and engineering knowledge is widely shared — or to put it in German terms they are all part of *Technik*.

There are at least two other manifestations of this loose unity between Production and the related functions. The first relates to the career backgrounds of German production managers. The author once had cause to interview some thirty production managers in Germany: one point of interest which emerged from this operation was that only two of these managers had always worked in Production in the narrow sense. If one compares this finding with the figures for a much larger sample in Britain[14] it would appear that German production managers are more mobile functionally than their British colleagues. The rest of this small German sample, taken together, had experience of every management function from Sales to Research and Development, with concentrations, of course, in Design and Engineering.

Any difference between British and German production managers in terms of breadth of functional experience is, in fact, probably larger than is suggested in the previous paragraph. Or at any rate, another qualitative difference intrudes. Most British production managers have probably worked their way up the production hierarchy from fairly lowly beginnings. Where they have worked outside Production in the strict sense, in say Inspection, Production Control, or Maintenance, it may often be the case that this was in the early days of their career and their experience there was as worker, clerk, or technician. In Germany, on the other hand, since the vast majority of the production managers are qualified and the qualifications are all obtained on full-time courses lasting at least three years, the German production manager who claims experience in other functions is in fact claiming *managerial* experience in these functions. When a German company hires a Dipl Ing or an Ing Grad they are hiring a middle manager or a staff specialist and the first appointment (after College) will definitely be above the clerk-technician level.

142   Production Management

The second manifestation of this loose unity we are attributing to the technical functions in German companies is that there does not seem to be much inter-functional criticism, at any rate among those functions coming under the *Technik* umbrella. One of the themes explored in the British studies is the relationship between Production and other functions.[15] Where the British production managers did not themselves control the function in question, sizeable numbers tended to criticise it, to suggest, that is, that the quality of support and service left something to be desired. In conversations with British production managers the author has also found some support for this attitude, encountering remarks like:

> The best I can say is that it is a sort of friendly context. (Production superintendent referring to Production Control.)

> Not a complete sinecure I suppose. (Production superintendent referring to Sales.)

> I suppose they think of themselves as doing their best. (Production manager referring to Purchasing.)

> This is Work? (Production manager referring to Financial Control.)

These kinds of dissatisfaction are very easy to understand. In the first place Production is impinged upon by practically every function and sub-function. The production manager is not only affected by the decisions of higher management and the company's investment policy, but also by what is, in effect, demanded of him by Sales and presented to him by Design. He depends on Engineering, especially in Britain, for help on methods, rates, improvements and problem solving and on Production Control for an orderly and feasible work schedule. If Maintenance do not do their bit he cannot run the plant, if Purchasing fall down on the job he lacks raw materials and 'bought out' parts and if Quality Control are critical he cannot dispose of the goods he has produced. And in case he hasn't enough to do orchestrating these disparate functions the financial controller will bombard him with regular computer print-outs showing to what extent he failed to achieve overhead cost recovery in the previous month. In the second place, if the production manager is operating in Britain he may be the victim of disdain as well as complexity. If, that is, the research literature is right and Production is regarded as a low status function and felt by top management to be an irksome constraint on the pure administration of profit, then it will not be surprising if the British production managers have something to complain about when their dealings with other functions are concerned. Now all these possibilities of frustration and irritation are not unknown in Germany but there is a difference in degree and the pattern is different as well.

If one pursues these issues with German production managers, a dominant impression is that there is simply less criticism, or one has to probe more to find it. The Germans have a term *reibungslos* (literally, frictionless) which is almost a standard expression for voicing satisfaction at the relationship between different departments or entities: this word does actually figure in discussions with German production managers! When criticism is voiced it tends to be more residual than in Britain, for instance: 'There's bound to be some friction between Production and Engineering' (production manager, shipyard). Or, expressed in a more conditional way, for instance: 'Most of the time the relationship between Production and Production Control is fine (*reibungslos*); it is only when there are major changes in product mix that friction occurs' (production controller, medical equipment firm).

The other interesting difference in Germany is that not only is there less criticism but a difference in department emphases. The department or function most likely to be criticised by German production managers is Purchasing and with a greater frequency than is the case in Britain according to the Gill and Lockyer study mentioned at the beginning of this chapter.[16] This is intriguing as an Anglo-German contrast, but it fits the German pattern. Purchasing is the only non-technical function in a close dependency relationship with Production: as such it is relatively immune to the homogenising influence of engineering qualifications and diversity of technical experience.

Again in German companies the 'down' on Purchasing is counterbalanced by the favourable attitude of production managers to other functions. Maintenance, a favourite whipping boy in Britain, is virtually never criticised in Germany. And one hears very little complaint in German companies about Quality Control. The author has pursued this last point particularly with German production managers, feeling they would not be human if the decisions of Quality Control did not sometimes get on their nerves. The result of the 'pursuit' was a lot of statements about how important quality is, why inspectors are highly respected in this particular company, how helpful Quality Control is in solving production problems, what a splendid fellow the Quality

Control boss is and so on. One was obliged to conclude that friction between Production and Quality Control was not a major feature of the German executive landscape.

It has been suggested that this apparently higher level of integration between the various technical functions derives from a loose homogeneity of qualification, technical knowledge and experience. This is a reasonable hypothesis but, especially if one is surveying the company scene from the production manager's cockpit, an incomplete explanation: some organisational factors are also involved.

German Production Management: the Organisational Dimension

It has been suggested at various points in this book (see for instance Chapters 2, 4 and 5) that in Gemany 'the line', as opposed to 'the staff' is stronger than is the case in Britain or the USA. Now 'the line' *par excellence* is the series of ranks from foreman upwards in Production and this production management hierarchy is noticeably strong in the typical German company. Part of this strength is organisational in a formal sense. That is there appears to be a stronger tendency in Germany for other (sometimes subsidiary) technical functions to be integrated into the production management hierarchy, or integrated at a lower level than is the case in Britain. Quite simply one tends in Germany to find that managers responsible for other functions related to Production actually report to a production manager, rather than to 'an appropriate' Board member or chief on site executive. The point is an important one; it has been introduced guardedly in terms of appearance and tendency because the evidence is not conclusive. To prove that this organisational feature is more marked in Germany than in Britain would require a very tight comparative study of company structures. What the author can assert is that he has encountered evidence of this integration more often in German companies than in British ones.

This is what it looks like in practice. Two key support or subsidiary functions from the standpoint of Production, are Maintenance and Production Control. In the typical German company they are integrated two levels above the foreman. That is the Maintenance and Production Control bosses report to a manager two levels above the foreman. This manager is a production manager, usually having the word 'production' in his title, whose most numerous subordinates are production superintendents. This is the most noticeable feature but there are two others.

The first is that the Purchasing function is more frequently made subordinate to Production. The author has noticed two variations on this theme. One is where Purchasing is made responsible to a technical or production director instead of having its own representation at Board level or reporting to a Finance and Administration director. The other, more common variation is that particular production managers, say two or three ranks above the foreman, will have control of some sub-unit of Purchasing which serves the particular needs of his production unit. And where neither of these arrangements exists, one may still encounter some evidence of the assumption that Purchasing is there for Production's benefit. For instance, there may be 'pairing'; a linking that is, of each production manager at a given level with a particular person in Purchasing, specialising in the requirements of that production manager's department. On visiting the administrative block of German companies the author has also noticed several times that the Purchasing Department is located on the same floor as *Technik*: one of the many uses of *Technik* in German is to indicate in buildings the floor or area where the senior technical managers − Design, Production, Quality Control and so on − have their offices. Finally, in this connection, the author has also seen some cases in German companies where a production manager controlled Quality Control. To put it more modestly, what was happening in these cases was that a production manager was controlling the personnel and process of inspection at an 'executive' level, to use constitutional language. The Quality Control 'legislature', setting of standards that is, was still independent with its own hierarchy and Board representation.

None of these organisational arrangements relating to the integration of Maintenance, Production Control, Purchasing and Quality Control are unknown in Britain. It is simply asserted that their incidence seems to be higher in Germany. In so far as this is the case it is a manifestation of the greater strength of the line and the higher standing of Production. And arrangements such as these tend to strengthen the production manager's hand in his daily dealings and facilitate the achievement of his objectives.

It is also fair to say that there is a less formal aspect. If managers of one function report to higher managers of another this must be because someone who designed that part of the organisation wished and intended it. Whether 'someone' also wished and intended German production managers to be great expressionists is more problematic, but they are.

Production managers in any country will interest themselves in a lot of different things, because a lot of different things impinge on Production. And in Germany in particular boundaries tend not to be rigorously defined. So if a German production manager wants to expand he has scope. There are particular things which German production managers are often, or sometimes, 'into'; things which go beyond the formal organisational arrangements. One example is action in accordance with legislation designed to protect the environment. Germany in the 1970s has seen the same public concern about the environment as has Britain and the USA. From the standpoint of the busy production manager instituting analyses of the firm's polluted water and changing arrangements for dumping the firm's waste, are unenviable extra chores. It would not be very difficult to push them sideways onto a staff department, but in the author's experience German production managers handle these issues themselves and do so with surprisingly good grace.

Again it is surprising how often German production managers are involved in Sales. It is more likely in Germany that potential customers will want to know how and where a product is made; this is the production manager's territory, and it is only a short step from here to preliminary discussions and wining and dining customers. In the capital goods industry, in particular, another way in which production managers become, indirectly, involved in sales is by giving lectures on the company's products, lectures of a serious technical kind to industrial customers on invitation or at trade fairs.

The purchase of machinery is another example. There is no doubt about who decides in German companies whether new machinery and equipment should be purchased: it is line production managers, not staff specialists or people from Engineering or its German equivalent. Meetings are not held to decide *whether* to buy: this the production manager decides according to his technical conscience. But meetings are held to decide *what* to buy. These are usually attended by representatives from Engineering and/or other specialists, but such meetings are generally chaired by production managers. Where some representative of Purchasing attends, this, in the author's experience, is because he has done some of the 'legwork' (checking delivery times and prices) not because he is expected to influence the decision. Such meetings are run very much by the production manager with support from his subordinates.

Other examples could be given but the general point will be clear. Whatever is depicted on the organisational chart, and these formal prescriptions tend in any case to extend the authority of the production manager, it is a reasonable assumption that the production manager will be expanding 'sideways' into staff functions and sometimes 'backwards' and 'forwards' into Design and Sales as well.

Termintreue

In discussing the German manager's vocabulary in Chapter 5 it was noted that the word *Termin* (deadline, delivery date) figures largely, as do a plethora of *Termin* related words, including *Termintreue* (faithfulness to deadlines). This general observation is especially true of German production managers. To say that a German production manager takes *Termintreue* seriously is a magnificent piece of understatement. German managers are obsessed with delivery punctuality.

But *Termintreue* is more than a figment of the German production manager's consciousness: it is also a reality. German industry does have a good reputation for delivery punctuality and German companies are at pains to sustain this reputation. If one seeks to explain the impressive average performance of German companies two considerations are relevant. The first of these, which has been explored in some detail earlier in this chapter, is that the context is more favourable in a multiplicity of ways: the possibility that anything will go wrong is much less. The second factor is simply that delivery punctuality is regarded as being of great importance. Completion dates are emphasised and anything which facilitates their attainment is given priority.

The *Termingespräch* (production scheduling meeting, delivery dates discussion) is both instructive and entertaining for a foreigner. This institution is at its best in, for instance, general engineering companies where there are a lot of different products, with modifications, being manufactured in a miscellany of long runs, short runs and single units, all going through the shop at the same time. Where it is really complicated, it is possible for a *Termingespräch* to last all day. The *Termingespräch* is invariably chaired by a production manager (or occasionally a subordinate production control manager). Participants work their way through seemingly endless lists of jobs muttering to themselves *'erledigt'* (done, ready, finished) with manifest satisfaction. Any job which is not *erledigt*, and with a comfortable margin, becomes the object of investigation and emergency action. The author has heard on such occasions subordinates give very rational and persuasive explanations as to why a job is not *erledigt* yet, only to be told: 'This could have been foreseen.' Representatives of other functions − Purchasing, Design, Engineering − who attend these meetings can also expect a fair amount of flak if their particular contribution has caused delay.

Another element in the German concern with *Termintreue* is that there is a lot of forward planning. German production managers are not especially keen to demonstrate their prowess as crisis handlers and would rather avoid such occasions. One finds them worrying in September about whether there will be enough volunteers for the second shift at Christmas; a German manager drawing up a holiday chart in August is thinking about next year's holidays.

German Production Management: Status

At the beginning of this chapter we reviewed some recent studies of British production management. A *leitmotif* of these studies is that Production is a low status management function: under-paid, under-privileged, with little glamour, poor promotion prospects and a fair amount of 'aggro'. Does all or any of this hold true for Germany?

In view of the many advantages enjoyed by the German production manager, from the positive impulse of a *Technik* culture to a better strike record, one might expect that Production in Germany would be free from these debilitating self-doubts. It is not, though it is fair to say that there is a difference of degree between Britain and Germany in this respect and there are some subtle differences of emphasis and presentation.

The British studies are consistent on this status question. The author himself has also found a rough consensus among British production managers on these status, promotion and privilege questions. In Germany there is no such rough consensus. On the first occasion on which the author questioned a group of German managers about these status relativities he was told Production undoubtedly was a 'Cinderella' function and that this fact was universally recognised. On putting the same group of questions at another company the following day the response was that there was no respect in which production managers were disadvantaged, the questions were silly and the managing director intervened to say that he would scarcely promote anyone who did *not* have experience in Production.

If one tries to 'average out' the very disparate replies and responses then two things emerge. There is certainly a substantial body of opinion among German production managers to the effect that Production is a neglected and underprivileged function. This view does not, however, seem to be as widespread, or as deeply felt, among them as among their British colleagues. This is the difference of degree.

But Germany is not just a paler version of Britain in this respect: there are other differences. If we break down the global indictment it runs like this.

1. Production is a low status management function.
2. Promotion prospects are poor.
3. It is underpaid.

In Britain all three are generally affirmed with probably the third objection as favourite. In Germany the first is affirmed much more often than the other two propositions. In Britain there is evidence that production managers are underpaid[17] but the author has not encountered similar evidence for Germany. Indeed, on several occasions German production managers have volunteered the fact that they are the best paid executives in their company, all functions combined, at a particular level. That German production managers should not feel themselves relatively disadvantaged in the promotion stakes is, again, consistent with our hypotheses concerning the greater relative strength of the line in German companies and the effects of the *Unternehmer* tradition (see Chapters 4 and 5).

Another difference is that where it is felt in Germany that Production is low status, there is no agreement as to what executive functions enjoy high status. In Britain the informal status map is quite clear: Sales and Finance are at the top, Design and Production at the bottom. In Germany it is much less clear. There is general agreement that Sales is a high status function and well remunerated. Incidentally, there is a body of opinion in Germany which holds that Sales is the best remunerated function and compared with it *all* other functions are 'second class citizens', Production not being in any way distinguished. There is no general agreement about the status of Finance in Germany and if one invites German managers to designate *prima donna* functions they also, quite often, name Design or Development (*Technik* again).

Furthermore, the Germans quite often give the impression that they have not thought about these issues very much. One often receives answers along the lines of: 'Now you come to mention it I suppose that . . .' To put it another way, a question like 'Do you regard executives in Finance as enjoying more esteem than those in Production?' is a perfectly meaningful question in Britain and will get a straight answer. It is rather less universally acceptable in Germany, where status issues are not so readily discussed. Questions of this kind may in fact evoke a rather puritanical reaction in Germany.

In discussing the British studies earlier in this chapter it was suggested that one does not have to treat these status issues as an absolute. Even, that is, if innumerable studies show Production, in any country, to be a low status function, this does not necessarily mean that production managers are demoralised or ineffective. They are not in Germany. If one has spent time in German companies and observed the robust self-confidence of the production managers in their dealings with other departments, their expansionism and their olympian pursuit of *Termintreue*, the whole attitudinal complex of relative status becomes rather secondary.

Conclusions

There is a lot of recent research evidence to suggest that in Britain production management is an unpopular, low status area of executive work. This point of view is not unknown in Germany, though it is less widespread; there is less consensus concerning these status issues in Germany and sometimes less willingness to discuss them.

Whatever the balance in such attitudinal questions there are reasons for believing that the German production manager operates in a much more favourable context. He benefits, *inter alia*, from the higher standing of industry, the *Unternehmer* tradition and the influence of the concept of *Technik* which leads to a very positive attitude to products — their design and manufacture. At a more tangible level the German production manager benefits, both directly and cumulatively, from the relative absence of strikes, has greater freedom in the deployment of workers and, probably, a more versatile workforce less circumscribed by imposed division of labour or demarcation considerations.

German production managers tend to be well qualified, invariably in engineering; they are less critical of other technical functions than their British colleagues and have a greater breadth of functional experience. They attach a very high value indeed to *Termintreue* — delivery punctuality.

The organisational arrangements in German companies tend to strengthen Production, integrating related functions such as Maintenance and Production Control at a lower level than in Britain. German production managers have a noticeable tendency to successfully expand their influence and activities beyond the formal organisational system. Their dealings with representatives of other functions are not marked by an excess of hesitation or humility.

Notes

1. It has been argued that the temporal sequence of Research and Development, Production and Marketing co-varies, or is a function of, the type of technology. See Joan Woodward, *Industrial Organisation: Theory and Practice* (Oxford University Press, Oxford, 1965).

2. For a summary of some of these British studies see S. P. Hutton and P. A. Lawrence, 'Production Managers in Britain and Germany', Interim Report to the Department of Industry, London, 1978.
3. C. C. New, 'Managing Manufacturing Operations', British Institute of Management Survey Report no. 35, 1976.
4. Ibid.
5. 'Higher Management Education and the Production Function', A Report by the Business Graduates Association, November 1977.
6. R. W. T. Gill and K. G. Lockyer, *The Career Development of the Production Manager in British Industry* (BIM, London, 1979).
7. M. K. McQuillan, *Graduate Engineers in Production* (Cranfield Institute of Technology, August 1978).
8. Ibid., p. 2.
9. Ibid., p. 2.
10. Ibid., p. 15.
11. V. B. Prabhu, J. W. Russell and M. G. Scott, 'Senior Executives' Perceptions of Factors Influencing Production Management Policy in the North East', unpublished paper, Newcastle Polytechnic, 1979.
12. N. A. Dudley, 'Industrial Productivity – Scope for Improvement', West Midlands Economic Planning Paper no. 8, 1975.
13. S. P. Hutton and P. A. Lawrence, 'Production Managers in Britain and Germany', 1978.
14. R. W. T. Gill and K. G. Lockyer, *The Career Development of the Production Manager in British Industry*, 1979.
15. Ibid.
16. Ibid.
17. Ibid.

7 THE FOREMAN

As in the discussion of the work and work context of the production manager, a discussion of the German foreman can usefully start outside Germany. This time we will begin in Cambridge, Massachusetts and work our way towards Germany via Birmingham, England.

The Problem of the First Line Supervisor

In 1945 the American sociologist Fritz Roethlisberger published what was to become a classic article in the history of the first line supervisor.[1] This article, poignantly entitled 'The Foreman: Master and Victim of Double Talk' was destined for frequent reprintings. As its author commented on one of these (reprint) occasions: 'It is one of the most popular articles I ever wrote. The *Review* (i.e. *Harvard Business Review* where it was first published) has sold thousands of reprints and the piece has been included in several books of readings'.[2]

In what sense is the foreman a victim? Roethlisberger's answer, in a much quoted sentence, is this:

> Thus the foreman, like each individual in the modern industrial structure, is in effect painfully tutored to focus his attention upward to his immediate superiors and the logics of evaluation they represent, rather than downward to his subordinates and the feelings they have.[3]

In other words there are two worlds in the factory. There are the workers, who cannot be expected to care all that much, who do not identify strongly with the company, which has bought some of their time but not their souls. And then there is management, which does care and identify, which is expected to 'act rational', to internalise the purpose of the work not just go through the motions. There has to be an interface between these two worlds: it is in the person of the foreman. Or to put it another way, the foreman is close enough to the workforce − physically, socially, organisationally − to know what is going on and 'the way things are'. But he is also 'part of management', or at least reports to management and has to tell management what it wants to hear or have a good reason why not. In these senses he is the classic 'man in the middle'.

There are ramifications to the foreman's plight. Once upon a time he knew, if not everything, at any rate more than anyone else. But that was before experts were invented:

> Under modern conditions of operation, for example, there seems to be always somebody in the organisation in a staff capacity who is supposed to know more than he (the foreman) does, and generally has more to say, about almost every matter that comes up; somebody, in addition to his boss, with whom he is supposed to consult and sometimes to share responsibility; somebody by whom he is constantly advised and often even ordered.[4]

Not only 'outgunned' on the specialist knowledge front, the foreman has also suffered a loss of direct authority, but without a corresponding reduction of responsibility:

> To the foreman it seems as if he is being held responsible for functions over which he has no longer any real authority. For some time he has not been able to hire and fire and set production standards. And now he cannot even transfer employees, adjust the wage inequalities of his men, promote deserving men, develop better machines, methods, and processes, or plan the work of his department, with anything approaching complete freedom of action. All these matters for which he is completely or partially responsible have now become involved with other persons and groups, or they have become matters of company policy and union agreement.[5]

This is the foreman's problem, or to use what has become the set phrase, the problem of the first line supervisor, as formulated by an American academic in 1945. In 1975 a British sociologist from the University of Aston, Birmingham, published a paper on the industrial supervisor.[6] The opening paragraph leaves us in no doubt; there has not been a change for the better:

> This paper first describes the significant diminution in the industrial supervisor's role that has taken place over the last sixty years or so. Nowadays, industrial supervisors (typically foremen) find themselves held responsible for the management of their sections in circumstances where they have little control over the organisation of work and little authority over their employees. It is not surprising that many foremen have come to feel a sense of great insecurity in recent years and have sought the protection of union membership.[7]

In the thirty-five years between the American and British analyses referred to here, the world managed to eliminate smallpox, men landed on the moon and the value of the Deutschmark changed from £1 DM 40 to £1 DM 3.7 but the world did not find it possible to solve the problem of the first line supervisor. Throughout the period just about every serious book on industrial psychology and management included some discussion of the problem. Nor is this line of analysis the prerogative of professional academics. The view is shared by industry itself. For instance, a Working Party of the British Institute of Management put the case just as bluntly in a recent report[8] claiming that:

> The evidence is clear that the front line manager generally has little authority to act independently. Our findings also show that though achieving output targets is undoubtedly the front line manager's ultimate aim, it seems he is rarely consulted about target setting, costs, budgets, and quality specifications. In some key areas of man-management the front line manager's role is limited, particularly where recruitment of workers is concerned, while his vital role of motivating the work group is given insufficient emphasis. In industrial relations, the typical front line manager is either not involved at all or he is restricted to the initial stages of procedure. A major cause of frustration is that the front-line manager's freedom of action has declined as a result of the growth and influence of shop floor trade unions.

There seem to the present writer to be four dimensions to the foreman's predicament as described in the Anglo-American literature. It may be helpful to itemise these. First, the foreman is, in terms of the organisational structure, 'the man in the middle'; this is the essential *point de départ* for Roethlisberger's critique, which to a large extent works out the moral and political implications of this organisational fact. This aspect of the foreman's predicament can be appreciated by means of organisational comparisons. The foreman, like the parish priest in the organisation of the Church or the corporal in the army, is close to 'where the action is'; junior authority figures in formal organisations have a problem reconciling reality and hierarchy — it is not so acute for managing directors, bishops and colonels.

Secondly, this organisational fact is reinforced by socio-cultural considerations. Although the foreman is 'part of management', in the words of the BIM report its 'front-line',[9] in social terms he has more in common with the workers. In the British context the foreman will probably, like the men he supervises, have attended a non-selective secondary school; he will live in the same kind of area as they do, have a similar life style and before he became a foreman he almost certainly was a shop-floor worker. Furthermore, he is not likely to become a manager (above the foreman level) and the foreman's chance of advancing up the management hierarchy is continually worsening. In terms of both general education and technical qualifications the British foreman does not appear to be clearly differentiated from those he supervises. Out of the 63 foremen in the BIM sample, 45 had no technical qualifications of any kind and 51 out of the 63 had no general educational qualifications.[10]

Thirdly, the foreman's technical and work-related knowledge has been eclipsed by that of others, a range of clerks, technicians, inspectors and engineers manning Production Control, Engineering, Quality Control and Maintenance. The area in which the foreman 'knows more than anyone else' is getting smaller as technicians and staff-specialists proliferate. The foreman has not just suffered a blow to his sapiential standing; this development also implies a loss of authority since the foreman is now faced with more people to whom he has to defer, more people who can challenge his decisions, circumscribe his freedom of action and overrule him.

Fourthly, and it is this aspect which receives most current emphasis, the foreman's authority over personnel has been very markedly reduced, both as a result of the development of specialised Personnel Departments and by the increase in the influence of trade unions and their local representatives.

The Problem in Germany?

This then is 'the case for the prosecution', espoused by managers and academics alike on both sides of the Atlantic. The first question this analysis provokes is: does Germany have a foreman problem? If we assume anything, we should assume that it does. Germany, after all, is not an industrial island.

It is a beguiling question. The phrase 'the problem of the first line supervisor' is such a standard expression in English that the author has tended to use it in the original in pursuing this theme in discussions with German managers. One would first ask the manager in question if he understood some English. The manager would invariably say yes. One then asks: what does the expression 'the problem of the first line supervisor' mean to you? The blank expression indicates that it does not mean anything at all. This is immediately interesting: a lot of

American and English expressions *are* used in German. In conversations with German managers the author has already encountered 'downtown', 'in the pipeline', 'general quality audit', 'top management', 'fishing for compliments', 'gentleman's agreement', 'tea break', 'know how', and 'inverted snobbery'. 'The problem of the first line supervisor', however, is not one of these domiciled expressions. One then translates it into German – still no reaction. The next stage is to offer a more elaborate paraphrase in German and then in desperation a fairly detailed summary of the Anglo-American analysis as presented in the last few pages. This more detailed account tends to be listened to with real interest and some approval. The typical German manager will in fact confirm parts of this analysis as relevant to Germany: the development of personnel departments, staff specialists, ancillary technical functions, union power (and remember the German company has a Works Council whose legal powers are far more extensive than those of a shop stewards' committee in Britain) all tending to diminish the foreman's traditional functions.

This does not mean, however, that German managers recognise the existence of an explicitly articulated foreman problem. Although they concede these points of organisational change within the factory they do not see these as constituting a 'problem of the first line supervisor'. The author has pursued this theme in Germany with a variety of personnel executives, training officers, production managers and even some chief executives. Almost to a man they claim that the German foreman has high standing in the company, has not experienced a loss of status and that there is no shortage of candidates for foreman posts – all of which represents a contrast with Britain. The author has also spent enough time in German companies and seen enough of the German foreman in action, to be convinced that these claims are substantially justified.

The Standing of the German Foreman

So the next question is, why is there no foreman problem in Germany, especially in view of the fact that German companies have on the whole experienced the same organisational change as British and American companies?[11] The question is not only of intellectual interest, intriguing as the contrast may be; answering it extends down to the grass-roots of the characteristics of production management which were the subject of the previous chapter and tends to substantiate in miniature some of the generalisations which have been offered about the nature of the German manufacturing company.

Some of the reasons for the higher standing and greater security of the German foreman will already be clear from earlier statements about the nature of German management. As was noted in Chapter 2 the trend towards increasing functional specialisation, the setting up of new specialist departments and entities, outside the line production hierarchy, is less marked in Germany (compared with both Britain and France). So one of the principal threats to the foreman's position, the curtailment of his authority by specialists, is less acute in Germany anyway.

Since the German tendency is to practise less division of labour and to incorporate specialisms and specialist knowledge into the line, if it is possible, everyone is expected to be more versatile. This applies to the foreman as well and his presumed, and usually demonstrable, versatility adds to his standing.

Furthermore, although there is no black and white contrast, there are reasons for believing that Production in general, where most foremen are located, has more standing in a German company than in a British one. Many of these relevant arguments were canvassed in the previous chapter. If we take these two points together – the line is stronger in Germany and Production has more standing – both redound to the advantage of the foreman. He is a key figure in Production and he is part of the line, in fact, he is where the line starts!

In discussions of the foreman's role and standing, German managers tend to thump the table and proclaim the foreman's importance and centrality in the company's operations. So do British managers. But there are two differences. First, the German claim is consistent with some other features of the German business enterprise – the *Unternehmer* tradition, the rejection of abstraction and corresponding emphasis on getting things done, identification with the products and so on. And secondly, although British managers make similar claims they tend to do so more guardedly, suggesting they know the way things ought to be ('We like to think of our foreman as . . .') but reality does not quite square with the *grand dessin*.

These are all considerations of background and context and they play their part. But a further question must be asked: how does one become a foreman in Germany? The answer is important for understanding the relatively high prestige enjoyed by the German foreman. It is also possible to give a more systematic answer for Germany than is possible for Britain.

The German word for foreman is *Meister* (literally, Master). The idea is that the *Meister* can exercise his craft in a *meisterlich* (masterly) way.

This skill connotation is important in the genesis of the *Meister*. The future German foreman will begin by doing a formal apprenticeship usually lasting three-and-a-half years. Most of the apprenticeship is spent in the factory, technical college attendance being on a day release basis – not 'first year off at college' as in the British system. At the end of the apprenticeship it is necessary to take an examination; if the apprentice passes this he becomes a *Facharbeiter* (skilled worker). As was mentioned earlier *Facharbeiter* is a legally protected status: a German is only entitled to call himself a skilled worker if he has done an apprenticeship and passed the final examination.

Several year's experience as a skilled worker will follow. In fact there is a minimum age limit of 25 for becoming a foreman in Germany. Then the worker who has aspirations will, on his own initiative, enrol for a foreman's course. These courses are offered by the *Industrie- und Handelskammer* (chambers of industry and commerce) and may be either full-time or part-time. In fact few workers undertake the full-time course (one would need considerable savings or secondary income) but the part-time course, lasting some two-and-a-half years, is generally reckoned to be substantial and demanding. At the end of the course there is, as with the apprenticeship, a final examination. The candidate who is successful in this obtains the *Meisterbrief* (literally, foreman's letter), a certificate of his qualificational readiness to become a foreman. Then he may actually be appointed to a foreman's post by his company, as and when a vacancy arises. Companies sometimes superimpose their own training course for newly appointed *Meister*, this usually being managerial rather than technical in content, in contrast to the foreman's course leading to the *Meisterbrief* which is primarily technical but with business economics input.

What we have described is the standard, majority route to the foreman's position. There are two variations on the above. First, companies sometimes appoint as foremen candidates who do not have the *Meisterbrief* if they are thought to be suitable on other grounds. Since *Meister* is also a legally protected status in Germany these *Meister* without *Meisterbrief* are officially designated as *Industrie-Meister* or *ernannte Werksleiter* ('company nominated' is the implication in both cases). The second variation is that one sometimes encounters foremen who are not ex-apprentice skilled workers – usually in mass production industries or transport where the skill content is relatively small. This category is not, in the author's experience, very numerous.

So the position of the typical German foreman is rather strong. In becoming a foreman he has completed an apprenticeship and a foreman's course, passed two terminal examinations, acquired two legally protected statuses (*Facharbeiter* and *Meister*) and had several years' experience as a skilled worker. He has acquired and demonstrated both craft skill and technical knowledge. All these things are attributes of his person, not his location in the hierarchy and as such they cannot be taken away from him. That is to say, however omnicompetent the Personnel Department becomes, however many staff specialists the company chooses to employ, however strong the unions are, the *Meister* is still going to be respected for his demonstrated skill, knowledge and experience. This is the German secret. Personal skill and know-how, put to the test, and in the favourable context of higher management's support, the strength of the line, the relative standing of Production and the influence of the idea of *Technik*. For these reasons there is no 'problem of the first line supervisor' in West Germany.

The Meister at Work

It is quite clear that in practice the *Meister* does enjoy a certain standing in the German company. His title, in fact, is one which is much used. The foreman is distinguishable by dress, the *Kittel* (three-quarter length overall coat, usually green) often with a lapel label bearing his name preceded by the *Meister* title. Foremen are often addressed by their bosses as *Meister* and sometimes address each other in this way, after the manner of senior NCOs exchanging compliments in front of enlisted men. Their behaviour, however, is not noticeably authoritarian. If they display a swashbuckling attitude this is more likely to be in their dealings with managers. The basic demeanour is one of quiet confidence.

Production managers, all over the world, lead rather full and busy lives. German production managers, however, do not seem to be under quite the same pressure as their British colleagues. This is not a polite way of saying that the Germans are idle. But they appear to face fewer crises, interruptions and demands on their time and attention originated by others. A lot of factors serve to explain this difference and in the previous chapter many of the cultural and situational advantages of the German production manager were discussed. In this connection the quality and morale of the German foreman is also a relevant factor.

Naturally the personal qualities of German foremen are variable: one occasionally encounters foremen with little initiative and drive. But the average performance is quite impressive. If one spends time in German manufacturing companies it becomes clear that the foremen are doing quite a lot for their superiors: they are able to do it, in terms of skill and knowledge, they are allowed to do so and they are expected to do so. One indication of this is the sort of thing the foreman does bring to his superior's attention. Sometimes these are disappointingly routine, but frequently foremen bring to their bosses issues that they have already had a go at solving themselves, problems where the first moves have already been made. A foreman, for instance, may notice some quality defect, perhaps before anyone in inspection spots it. The foreman will look at it *in situ*, talk to the relevant operators, think about causes, maybe do one or two tests on his own initiative to try to isolate a particular cause and then bring the matter to his superior's attention. Or there will be a serious breakdown, but by the time the foreman reports it he will have tried and failed to repair it himself, summoned on his own initiative an outside repair-man and come in to see his boss loaded with suggestions and cost information for replacement equipment.

German foremen often attend meetings alongside managers of higher rank; this is particularly the case with the *Termingespräch* (meeting to discuss work progress and deliveries, see Chapter 6) and meetings to discuss investment plans and machinery purchase. Indeed in a small company, employing, say, less than 1,000 people, the foremen may have the first responsibility for drawing up a section investment plan; an itemised account, that is, of desired future expenditure on plant and machinery. We noted in the previous chapter that decisions to buy plant and machinery are made by line production managers in Germany, not by staff specialists. It is also the case that these decisions start at the bottom of the line with foremen participating.

Another interesting thing about the German foreman is that he often travels. This fact should be put in context. German companies are fairly rational/not very particular (depending on one's point of view) about who they send into the outside world to represent them. More precisely, German firms are not influenced very much by status considerations in this connection, but do like to send someone who knows what he is talking about — this someone may well be a foreman. They get sent on occasion to trade fairs to inspect equipment, they visit (potential) suppliers to look at machines their company may purchase, they visit other firms in the group to have 'informal exchanges' with other foremen and sort out operating problems at other branches and even foreign subsidiaries. On one occasion the author witnessed what might count as a symbolic exchange between a foreman and his superior. The manager of a company in the Ruhr was planning a business trip with a colleague to Stuttgart. He had asked his secretary to check out the relative cost of the journey by car, first class rail and by plane. The secretary reported back, in the presence of the foreman, that for two people the journey was cheapest by car. The manager was pleased: with a bit of forethought he would be saving the company some DM 400. The foreman was unimpressed: 'I wouldn't waste my time driving down there; when I go some place for the company it's by air.'

Conclusion

For over thirty years the relevant literature in the USA and Britain has proclaimed the existence of 'the problem of the first line supervisor'. In this literature it is argued that the foreman's position is insecure and ambiguous; that his technical competence has been eroded by a proliferation of ancillary specialisms and his authority in personnel matters reduced alike by the emergence of Personnel as a departmental specialism and the growth of trade union influence.

Surprisingly we find no evidence that this problem of the foreman's authority and status is common in West Germany. A sample of German managers consistently deny that there is any problem of the first line supervisor in German companies. This interesting finding has been explained, partly with reference to certain contextual factors and partly in terms of the training and qualification system for foremen in Germany. This system guarantees that the foreman holds qualifications which differentiate him from those he supervises. It also implies that the German foreman amasses skill, experience and legally protected statuses — these are attributes of his person rather than his organisational role. As such they cannot be 'taken away' by an increase in the structural differentiation of the firm or the claims of trade unions.

Finally it has been argued that what is involved is more than a question of the foreman's *amour propre*. The security and effectiveness of the German foreman is a significant factor in the overall performance in Production. German foremen clearly exercise real initiative not just in the traditional matters of section manning and work allocation, but also in matters of quality, maintenance, equipment purchase and budgeting.

Notes

1. F. J. Roethlisberger, 'The Foreman: Master and Victim of Double Talk', *Harvard Business Review* (1945).

2. F. J. Roethlisberger, *Man in Organisation* (The Belknap Press of Harvard University Press, Cambridge, Mass., 1968).
3. F. J. Roethlisberger, 'The Foreman: Master and Victim of Double Talk', 1945.
4. Ibid.
5. Ibid.
6. John Child, 'The Industrial Supervisor', University of Aston Management Centre, Working Paper Series no. 33, 1975.
7. Ibid.
8. *Front-line management* (British Institute of Management, London, 1976).
9. Ibid.
10. Ibid. A similar picture emerges from an earlier study: David Jenkins, *Supervisory Selection and Training in Manufacturing Industry* (Staples Press Ltd, London, 1966).
11. This issue is also discussed in Michael Fores, Peter Lawrence and Arndt Sorge, 'Germany's Front Line Force', *Management Today* (March 1978).

8 THE STANDING OF INDUSTRY

The intention here is to say something about the relationship between industry and society in Germany and to describe some features of German society which are relevant to industry. This may also serve to bring together several themes which have been discussed previously.

Business firms are discrete units. They have physical, economic and organisational boundaries. But they do not exist in a vacuum: in these three senses they are located in a society and a national context. The values of the environing society are relevant for the firms located in it. In this connection we have already noted, at various points, some aspects and dispositions of German society — the overwhelming desire for material improvement in the early post-war years, strong achievement orientation, work as a central life interest, an emphasis on the practical and 'getting it done' — which are positive for the morale and operational effectiveness of German firms. These points already suggest that the attitude of German society towards industry is favourable. We would go further and say that German society positively esteems industry. Or, in the phrase which has become common parlance in the last few years, the status of industry is high in West Germany.

This statement is a meaningful one, but of course it gives rise to various questions. What is the evidence for the claim? What does it mean to say that the status of industry is high? What does it amount to in practice? What are the implications? The difficulty is not so much in answering these questions but in answering them discretely. To put it another way, it is difficult to distinguish between causes and consequences. For instance, it was suggested earlier (Chapter 3) that the educational level of German managers is high: is this one of the many factors which 'causes' industry to have high status, or is it a 'consequence' of that high standing whereby a prestigious occupational sector attracts highly educated recruits? This complication does not mean that there will be no attempt to come to terms with the questions posed above; only that there will be a tendency to answer them all at the same time.

A Note on Salaries

Salaries are an indication of occupational standing and we used salary data earlier to support the claim that engineers enjoy higher standing in

Germany than in Britain (Chapter 3). Indeed salary comparisons have become rather fashionable. In Britain, for instance, salary data have been used to support the contention that production management is a low status management function[1] and to show that British engineers are poorly remunerated compared with other middle-class job holders.[2] In a similar way one can use salary material to compare the public and private sectors in Germany. With one exception (see later in this chapter) this is not a precise exercise since there are no rules about who should be compared with whom on either side of the public-private divide. It is a question of arguing that, say, an army colonel ought to be the status equal of a chief executive of a medium sized company and then seeing who wins in salary terms. With this qualification, the exercise is quite an entertaining one and does tend to suggest the primacy of the private sector in Germany.

Taking salary data for early 1977 we may reasonably start at the top and argue that the highest job in the public sector is that of Federal Chancellor. At this time Helmut Schmidt was earning some DM 298,978 p.a. whereas a member of the *Vorstand* of the Volkswagen company earned DM 525,000 p.a.[3] Not all the contrasts one can make are as sharp as this but they all tend in the same direction. If one takes, for instance, the university professor as a person of some prestige and occupying a terminal career position in the public sector, it emerges that in salary terms he is about level pegging with the middle manager at DM 50,000. The professor is outranked by the personnel chief and by the 55-year-old graduate engineer in industry. A major general in the *Bundeswehr* is on a similar footing to the head of sales at around DM 58,000. The *Geschäftsführer* of a small GmbH type of company with 1,000 employees outranks the major general, the Inspector-General of the *Bundeswehr* (armed forces) and the head of the *Bundesanstalt für Arbeit* (Federal Labour Office). The only people in the public sector, apart from the Chancellor himself, who outearn the average *Vorstand* member are the cabinet ministers and here one is talking of a 1977 income of around DM 200,000 (about £50,000). Salary data do on the whole suggest that in Germany, an American rather than a British evaluation of the worth of the manager prevails.

Skill, Training and Needs of Industry

This book is about managers, but for every manager there are a lot of workers — especially in a German company. When a company hires workers it is buying not only their time but also their skill and knowledge or their capacity to acquire these. Our contention is that in a society in which the standing of industry is high, a lot of importance will be attached to the skill acquiring process. More precisely, the principal institution for acquiring industrial skills, namely apprenticeship, will first be an institution endowed with much respect and secondly be closely oriented to the needs of industry. Apprenticeship in Germany does satisfy both these criteria — reverence and relevance. In some respects this claim can be pointed up by comparison with Britain.

Some idea of the significance of apprenticeship has already been given (Chapter 7) in discussing the background of German foremen. Apprenticeship is both more widespread and more highly regarded in Germany than in Britain. In Germany apprenticeship is the way, and the only way, to become a skilled worker. The term *Facharbeiter* (skilled worker), and it is a legally protected status, means having successfully completed an apprenticeship, passed the final exam and obtained the *Facharbeiterbrif* (skilled worker's certificate). An apprenticeship is not only the *sine qua non* for the status of skilled worker, it is also invariably a prerequisite for the post of foreman, and until a few years ago it was a prerequisite for attending the *Ingenieurschule* and becoming an Ing Grad (see Chapter 3). Furthermore, a recent survey of an all-age sample of Dipl Ings (graduate engineers) revealed that a substantial minority of these had also completed an apprenticeship at an earlier stage in their career.[4] Indeed the author is acquainted with several PhD's, all managers in German companies, who began their working life with an apprenticeship.

Thus it is hardly surprising that, as was mentioned earlier, there are 467 *Lernberufe* (occupations for which a recognised apprenticeship exists) in Germany. Not all of these are for industrial occupations: the list includes such trades as car mechanic and hairdresser, as well as the much sought after *Banklehre* (Bank apprenticeship) which has become an alternative to University for some candidates with *Abitur* (German equivalent of 'A' level). But most of these apprenticeships do serve industry and included is the *Kaufmännische Lehre* (commercial apprenticeship) which again is increasingly sought after. As was argued earlier (Chapter 3) some surveys of managerial qualifications suggest that the proportion of managers with degrees and other higher qualifications is lower on the commercial side of the company than on the technical side. What these otherwise unqualified managers on the commercial side do often have, however, is a *Kaufmännische Lehre*: it is not unusual, in the author's experience to come across quite senior people in Personnel, Administration and Sales who started as commercial apprentices, and in some cases have not added any further qualification.

It would appear that the mid 1970s recession has added further to the lustre of the German apprenticeship and pushed up admission standards. The author has been told repeatedly by Personnel and Training Officers at German companies that applicants for apprenticeships vastly exceed available places. There is also some evidence that *Abitur* ('A' level) is becoming a prerequisite for the *Kaufmännische Lehre* (commercial apprenticeship) and on one occasion the author was told by the *Meister* (foreman) in charge of the apprentice workshop at a car factory, 'The lad from a non-selective secondary school with no formal qualifications does not stand much chance these days'. Another variation on this theme is that the author has also been told several times in the course of a factory tour that the company concerned has taken on more apprentices than it needed but had done so intentionally as a contribution towards fighting the recession and unemployment problem. Even if such claims were exaggerated, and they may not have been, the phenomenon is still of interest. The thinking is clear: the way to keep the kids out of the dole queues is to give them something worth having – a German apprenticeship.

A comparison with Britain is instructive.[5] Apprenticeship is quite simply rarer in Britain and apprenticeships are found less frequently in the Production trades as opposed to the Maintenance trades. In Germany one finds apprenticeships everywhere. Again: In Britain, apprenticeships have more of a traditional medieval flair because they have not been developed in emerging new trades to the same extent as in Germany'.[6] The German chemical industry with its trained process operator is a case in point. The German thinking is clear: the apprenticeship is 'a good thing', so it should be widely available, not restricted to old established crafts.

In the same context it is noticeable that in Germany apprenticeship is less restricted to a certain age than in Britain and in Germany it is quite common to serve one apprenticeship after another. In both countries the apprenticeship training is mainly conducted in the company but with some attendance at technical college. There are, however, differences in the way the firm and technical college are linked in the apprenticeship system. In Britain the pattern is 'first year off at college' and day release attendance at technical college thereafter. In Germany it is day release to the *Berufsschule* (technical college) throughout. It is only a small point but a symptomatic one: in the German scheme of things *Praxis* comes first. The German apprenticeship has a final examination (c.f. module based continuous assessment in Britain) and this exam has both a theoretical and a practical component. Finally, the apprenticeship is a little shorter in Germany, three-and-a-half as opposed to four years and in Germany the possibility exists of shortening the apprenticeship where entrants have the equivalent of 'O' and 'A' level.

Not only have the Germans managed to make a national institution out of the apprenticeship, they have also turned their attention to training for semi-skilled jobs in industry. While in Britain there are no recognised rules for semi-skilled training, this end is served in Germany by semi-apprenticeships, factory based but involving day release to the *Berufsschule*, lasting up to two years:

> Similar to apprenticeships, semi-apprenticeships are specified by chambers of industry and commerce, government, and educationalists together, at the national level. The specification is in the shape of a 'professional activity description' (*Berufsbild*) containing all the various activities the job-holder has to perform, and thus be trained in. During the two years of training, the trainee (*Anlernling*) is rotated around all the jobs in the factory area relevant to his trade, picking it up from the workers and sometimes being attended to by foremen. Therefore the semi-skilled workers in Germany are given a wider horizon within the factory from the start, due to their training by systematic rotation.'[7]

There are two points at issue here. First, what is being described is, on the whole, a set of desirable practices with regard to effectiveness of work. And secondly, the systematic importance with which even the training of the semi-skilled industrial worker is vested in Germany is also a manifestation of the standing of industry in national life. We have focussed here on the skilled and semi-skilled worker but the same industry related vocationalism can be observed in the dynamics of the higher education system.

What Students Choose

One of the articles of the *Grundgesetz*, the Basic Law of the German constitution passed in 1949, states that anyone who passes *Abitur*, the German equivalent of 'A' level, has the right to study at university — study anything at any university. More recently this freedom has been restricted somewhat in practice by the introduction of the *numerus clausus*, or restricted entry, for some over popular subjects, of which medicine is the most important, usually where equipment-laboratories-practical work requirements set a *de facto* limit to numbers anyway.

Even with these restrictions, however, the German *Abiturient* ('A' level holder) has more freedom of choice than his opposite number in Britain. In Britain passing 'A' level does not confer the right to go to university, only the right to be an applicant. Furthermore, one's choice of university subject is more heavily determined by the 'A' level subjects in Britain than in Germany. This is partly because the British 'A' level is more specialised anyway (smaller number of subjects taken in the examination, more dropping of subjects), though the German *Abitur* is moving in this direction too and partly because the intending British undergraduate has to be chosen (accepted) by a particular faculty at a particular university. Except for subjects where the *numerus clausus* operates, the German *Abiturient* does not have to be so chosen; he may do a set of *Abitur* subjects entirely suitable for the undergraduate study of business economics and in fact enrol in civil engineering.

So what subjects do German students choose to study at university? Or, since the answer would be a little vacuous without some comparison, do German students study the same subjects in the same proportion as British students? There is no point in comparing absolute numbers, since the student population is much larger in Germany, but one can compare proportions, along the lines of: what proportion do history undergraduates constitute of the whole undergraduate population in the two countries? It should be added that in Britain one is measuring a higher incidence of decisions taken at an earlier age and the effect of school influence (dropping of subjects at 14, 15, and 16; choosing 'A' level subjects) than is the case in Germany, because of the differences in the system. With this qualification, the exercise is worth conducting; there are interesting differences, and they are relevant to the present theme of the standing of industry.

The author tried comparing the student population for the 1972-3 period, taking the data from the Statistical Supplements to the UCCA annual reports for Britain and from the appropriate *Statistisches Jahrbuch* for West Germany.[8] The first thing to emerge is that Britain is much stronger, proportionally, on the humanities. The proportion of students in Britain studying English, French and German is getting on for treble that in Germany. The proportion in Britain studying geography is more than double that in Germany and Britain has proportionally six times as many students of history. A similar pattern emerges for the natural sciences, these again being more popular in Britain. In Britain natural science students, as a proportion of all students, have a 16 per cent lead over their opposite numbers in German universities. So if in this sense German universities are 'weak' on the humanities and natural sciences, where are they 'strong'?

As might be expected the Germans have more engineers absolutely and relatively, though the difference is not enormous. They have, proportionally, two-and-a-half times as many lawyers as the British — a fact which requires some explanatory comment. It is not that the Germans are particularly litigious but rather that law studies have a triple vocational significance in West Germany. First, law studies naturally lead to the practice of law; secondly, law is *the* subject for entry to the higher civil service; and thirdly, law is a subject for prospective industrial managers. This last point was discussed earlier in some detail (Chapter 3). Law, after engineering and economics, is an important subject in the graduate manager league; law graduates tend to be more numerous in commerce, banking and finance than in heavy industry and they are, relative to their numbers, favoured for positions on the *Aufsichtsrat* (supervisory board). It is also the case that many personnel managers are qualified in law, indeed the most typical qualification for the Chief Personnel Manager, in the author's experience, is a PhD in law. A third German strength is in economics. Here the Anglo-German comparison is difficult to make since German universities offer both economics and business economics but do not, like many British universities, offer business studies or management. If, however, we add together British students of both business studies and economics, they are still, as a proportion of the student total, outnumbered three to one by the German students of economics and business economics. There are a few other minor differences but these are the main points of divergence.

The pattern is clear.[9] The British students tend to favour traditional and main line academic subjects and exhibit in their collective choice an anti-vocational bias, except with regard to law and medicine (old established and academic). The Germans show less collective enthusiasm for the main line academic subjects as represented by the humanities and natural sciences, but are somewhat stronger on engineering, much stronger on law and overwhelming on economics. In other words the German student choices exhibit a strong, across the board vocationalism. And all these major comparative 'strengths' — engineering, law and economics — relate, *inter alia*, to industrial management. Our contention is that this pattern of student choice is a reflection of the high standing of industry in German society and a practical concomitant of this standing.

Industry and the Public Service: a Precise Comparison

One way to try to fix the relative standing of industry and the public service is to examine the attributes of an occupational group, homogeneous in terms of training and qualification, who may choose to work in either industry or the public sector. A group which fits the bill admirably is the engineers and especially mechanical engineers who are ubiquitous throughout the public and private sector. The key question then is how do engineers working in industry differ from those working in the public sector and what may we infer from any differences? A recent research study of German engineers is at hand, in which all the attributes were cross tabulated with working in industry or working in the public sector.[10] The comparison is enlightening.

To clear the deck a little it may be worth mentioning some of the ways in which the two groups do not differ. They are alike in their marital status, religious convictions and low membership of voluntary organisations (except for the VDI — the German Engineers' Association). There is no patterned difference in the educational standards attained by the fathers of the two groups of engineers and they themselves cannot be differentiated according to the age at which they decided to become engineers, their school grades, degree class, or the likelihood that they have published books and articles or presented technical papers at conferences (these technical-scholarly activities are very much commoner among German engineers than among their British colleagues).

The first difference to emerge is that those working in industry are on average more highly paid and the difference is appreciable. This is in line with the brief observations on salary differences at the start of this chapter. Another recent survey of German engineers, with an enormous sample of over 27,000, also showed that engineers working in industry were consistently better paid than those working in the public sector, that this held for all age groups and for all qualificational levels.[11] Again in analysing the results of the main survey[12] we set up a financial criterion of occupational success, namely, being in the top salary quartile for a given age group (age groups in five year spans). Along the lines of this criterion those engineers whose first job was in industry (whether or not they stayed there or 'migrated' to the public sector) and those engineers who were working in industry at the time of the survey, were both over-represented among the ranks of the successful. Also in this connection, those engineers working in industry were significantly more likely to benefit from non-contributory pension schemes than their colleagues in the public sector.

Secondly, if the industry group enjoys higher rewards there is also evidence of greater sacrifices, responsibilities and achievements. The industry group worked longer hours, actual not prescribed and spent less time working on their cars, doing jobs around the house and gardening. It was more likely to travel in connection with work, more likely to travel abroad, more likely to mention learning languages as a hobby and more likely to be able to speak English and also French. It had more decision-making authority, larger average numbers of subordinates and was more likely to be empowered to appoint other qualified engineers. The members were more likely to have done an apprenticeship and much more likely to have produced patented inventions. The industry group was also more likely to claim that they had recently rendered 'work beyond the call of duty'.

There are also some interesting attitudinal differences. Looking back, the industry group was more inclined to describe its university training as 'very good' and the *Praktikum* (period spent in industry by undergraduate engineers) as 'very necessary'. The members exhibited more respect for executive career success than for pure engineering achievements. But they were also more likely than their public sector colleagues to affirm that if they were starting out in life again they would still choose to study engineering at college. The industry group exhibited a higher level of job-satisfaction and a higher level of satisfaction with the engineer's status in German society. The industry group was also more committed to the view that non-technical work colleagues held favourable views of them. It was also noticeable that the children of the industry group were over-represented at the specialist economics and technical grammar schools, tending to imply an eventual career in industry, while the children of the public sector group were over-represented at the traditional grammar schools. And again with reference to the children a higher proportion of the sons of the industry group also wanted to become engineers than was the case with the sons of the public sector group (though in any case the top career choice for the sons of German engineers is engineering).

The emergent picture is quite striking. We have located in the engineers a strategic group for the comparison of industry and the public sector. In this way we hold training and qualifications constant and compare both self-selection traits and differences in work experience. The industry group emerges as the hardest worked and most highly rewarded, having more extensive responsibilities, more achievements especially of a practical kind to their credit and robust confident attitudes on everything associated with their work and its status –

attitudes they seem already as fathers to have transmitted to the next generation. All this does tend to support in a tangible and immediate way our central contention that the status of industry is high in West Germany. Again engineers are a particularly suitable qualificational group for this exercise since they are, in terms of training, the most representative group of German managers. More German managers are qualified in engineering than anything else.

Implications

We have tried by examining some aspects of the higher education system, industrial training practices, salaries and the characteristics of engineers employed in the public and private sectors, to give some substance and meaning to the claim that industry enjoys high status in West Germany. Readers who regard the claim as being reasonable may still, however, want to ask: 'So what? Does it really matter that much?'

It is argued here that the status of industry is more than a nebulous generality and that it is a significant determinant of managerial performance. Some ingredients for an answer to the 'So what?' question have already been proposed. It suits industry, for example, for apprenticeship to be regarded as a national institution of high standing. It suits industry that so many students choose subjects compatible with a subsequent career in industry to such an extent that the student body in Germany has a wildly different subject profile from that in Britain. It suits industry that 'everyone knows' that industry pays more than the public sector even if you do not have so much time for gardening! Incidentally, the pay relativities for engineers as between the public and private sectors are reversed in Britain: here every type of public sector employment for engineers is on average more highly remunerated than employment in industry.[13]

More is involved, and it is the general things which are important. The higher the standing of industry the more likely it is that industry can hire the people it wants and have some choice in so doing. German companies appear to benefit in this way. If they want craft apprentices from the A stream, or commercial apprentices with a knowledge of Asian languages (a real example casually proffered to the author by a personnel manager at a steel plant), PhD's who have done an apprenticeship or Ing Grads who can speak English – they can find them, and keep them.

Secondly, the higher the standing of industry, the higher, *ceteris paribus*, is morale. Some of the attitudes of those engineers employed in industry, described above, are a fair example of good morale. Morale is difficult to measure and more difficult to assign cash value to. Yet it is important both positively and negatively. High morale means purposeful concentration on what is central; low morale means dissipating psychological energy and looking over one's shoulder. It is remarkable how few 'hang ups' German managers have (see Chapter 5). They probably resent left wing student criticism; they regard higher civil servants as pampered under-achievers who have not grasped the work ethic and they tend to tell one that there was a time (the *Wirtschaftswunder*, in the sixties, before the oil crisis) when things were better than they are now; but that is really all. They have a positive attitude to the higher education system; they do not agonise over 'the purpose of the organisation' or 'the goals of the company'; they do not dissipate their energies on debates about whether management is 'a profession' or not; do not feel obliged to justify industry or management and do not seem to be jealous of anyone.

Thirdly, morale is important in another way. Management work is beset by uncertainty. No matter how good the staff work there are imponderables and unknowables and developments beyond the company's control. Decisions are taken, must be taken, on the basis of inadequate information. This is not a covert plea for irrationality. Of course the company will strive to increase its mastery of knowledge and events, but this will frequently be imperfect. It takes some courage to face all this and act with a sense of purpose. And morale and courage are interlinked.

Finally, German managers reading this will conceivably feel that the author has exaggerated in the claim he has made concerning the status of industry in West Germany. One has to admit that this claim is less valid now than it would have been five, ten, or fifteen years ago. The student movement of the late 1960s and the critique of industry and capitalism it enunciated has clearly not done anything for the standing of industry in Germany (though such views have little to do with those held by the general public). The 1973 oil crisis and ensuing world recession have lessened public confidence in Germany's economic prowess, although Germany survived the recession much better than most of her neighbours. And it so happens that the last few years have seen salaries rise faster in the public sector than in industry, at a time when other factors — higher unemployment, greater competition for all starting-a-career type jobs because of a formerly high birth rate — are making public sector employment more attractive with regard to security. The balance of attractions is still in industry's favour, but the gap is being closed. The second possible reply is to say that German managers are entitled to feel that the status of industry in their society is not as high as it used to be, but if they were confronted with a society in which industry does not enjoy high standing and has never done so, they would rapidly appreciate in both senses, the benefits described here.

Conclusions

It has been argued here that the status of industry in German society is high. This claim was supported with some brief reference to salaries in the public and private sectors. The nature of the apprentice training system, as a manifestation of German industry's integration in society, was examined in some detail. It is clear that society and industry converge in their positive evaluation of the system. Similarly the pattern of undergraduate subjects was examined and compared with that in Britian, to reveal another manifestation of pro-industry vocationalism in German life. Engineers working in industry were compared in some detail with those employed in the public sector as a means of identifying the relative rewards and demands. The industry group emerged with higher pay, morale and job satisfaction; with longer hours, more numerous subordinates and more extensive responsibilities and with a range of especially practical achievements to their credit.

It was further argued that the higher standing of industry in Germany has some important general effects. It enhances industry's ability to choose the managers it wants and retain their loyalty, it raises morale and this is particularly salient in work as beset with uncertainty as management work is. Finally, it was conceded that present trends in Germany tend to make public sector employment relatively more attractive in terms of remuneration and security: the attractiveness of industry is not as marked now as it was a few years ago.

Notes

1. By Keith Lockyer especially in his paper to the conference on Production Management, organised by the Business Graduates Association, London, June 1977.

2. M. J. Fores, 'Engineering and the British Economic Problem', *Quest*, no. 22 (Autumn 1972).

3. This and data for other public and private sector comparisons are taken from *Wirtschafts Woche*, Sondernummer Berufe (1 Quartal 1977).

4. S. P. Hutton, P. A. Lawrence and J. H. Smith, 'The Recruitment, Deployment, and Status of the Mechanical Engineer in the German Federal Republic', 2 vols., Report to the Department of Industry, London, 1977.

5. A perceptive and thoughtful account of Anglo-German differences in the institution of apprenticeship may be found in: Arndt Sorge and Malcolm Warner, 'Manpower Training, Manufacturing Organisation and Work Roles in Great Britain and West Germany', Discussion Paper 78-96 published by the Internationales Institut für Management und Verwaltung, West Berlin, December 1978.

6. Ibid., p. 4.

7. Ibid., p. 6.

8. The results are described in more detail in Hermann Bayer and Peter Lawrence, 'Engineering, Education and the Status of Industry', *European Journal of Engineering Education*, no. 2 (1977).

9. These and similar data are also interpreted in Hermann Bayer and Peter Lawrence, 'An Emphasis on the Practical in the Land of Idealism', *Times Higher Education Supplement*, 14 January 1977.

10. S. P. Hutton, P. A. Lawrence and J. H. Smith, 'The Recruitment, Deployment, and Status of the Mechanical Engineer in The German Federal Republic', 1977.

11. E. Kogon, *Die Stunde der Ingenieure* (VDI Verlag, Düsseldorf, 1976).

12. S. P. Hutton, P. A. Lawrence, and J. H. Smith, 'The Recruitment, Deployment, and Status of the Mechanical Engineer in The German Federal Republic', 1977.

13. See on this point Bayer and Lawrence, 'Engineering, Education and the Status of Industry', 1977.

9 EXPORT POTENTIAL?

> 'You are wise.'
> 'No, that is the great fallacy; the wisdom of old men.
> They do not grow wise. They grow careful.'
> 'Perhaps that is wisdom.'
> 'It is a very unattractive wisdom. What do you value most?'
>
> Ernest Hemingway, *A Farewell to Arms*

According to the hero of a great American war novel[1] there is a certain township on the approach road to which a signboard reads: 'Madisonville Kentucky, the greatest town on earth'. If this dubious claim is valid then across the state line in West Virginia they are probably asking what one has to do to get into this world league. More to the point, if one examines the institutions of a foreign country, it is reasonable to ask if one can learn from these and this is the purpose here. In the case of German management the question is obviously justified in principle by the overall success of the West German economy. The question is given further salience by the fact that there are a variety of differences between German management and American management, and attention has been drawn to many of these differences in the previous chapters.

It has to be admitted that this whole operation is fraught with intimidating difficulties. To learn from another country one has to evaluate its practices and institutions, and one will evaluate them in terms of what is familiar; in terms that is, of one's own country. We have already seen how this operation can backfire in the discussion (Chapter 4) of the American consultancy report on German management. This report has a latent structure along the lines: American management is good; it has certain features which German management does not exhibit and therefore German management must be bad. The objection is that the American way may well be a good way but it is not necessarily the only way. Indeed with an objective as complex as 'well-managed companies', if not well-managed economies and growing prosperity, it would be surprising if there were not different ways of attaining the objectives.

So the first difficulty about deciding whether in this context one can learn from another country is that we are not in the one cause-one effect business but dealing with a multi-cause complex effect entity.

This is just the tip of the iceberg. There are a set of logical problems about learning from other countries. The gist is this: even when one has identified the ideal country to learn from, one that has a sustained record of economic achievement in this case, there is no way of identifying with certainty the causes of this happy state of affairs in the country under consideration and therefore no way of knowing what practices and institutions are candidates for adoption.

Part of the difficulty is that one cannot know for sure that apparently laudable features of industrial organisation in West Germany really are contributing to national economic success. It may be that economic success occurs in spite of, not because of, such features. Consider, for instance, the German concern with *Termintreue* (the punctual delivery of orders), which was discussed at an earlier stage (Chapter 6). Now since German managers do take delivery punctuality seriously and German companies have a good record in this respect which is generally recognised, it seems reasonable to suppose that this is at least a relevant factor helping to explain the success of West Germany in export markets. But, of course, it can be argued the other way. One could posit, that is, an antithesis between punctuality and quality and argue that if the Germans stopped worrying about delivering on time they would produce goods of (even) higher quality and be (yet) more successful in export markets.

Another logical objection to the possibility of international learning, especially where the weight of common sense perception precludes the 'in spite of not because of' interpretation, is to argue that there is really no relationship between the alleged cause and effect. Instead they are both effects of some other cause, perhaps an unidentified 'master cause'. Consider as an example the claim that German foremen are well-trained and well qualified and have several years' experience as skilled workers so they demand high quality work from those they supervise. The quality of the foremen determines in part the quality of output on the shop floor. It sounds reasonable, but it might be objected that a 'master cause' is at work, in the form of German perfectionism. This innate perfectionism causes companies to appoint well qualified people to supervisory grades and workers to produce products of exemplary quality and there is no causal relationship between the two effects. So if the German foreman system were adoped in a country which did not have strong perfectionist drives, this would have no effect on the quality of work. Indeed the quality of work might even decline: in a society with no perfectionist impulses the workers might be alienated by the appointment of manifestly meretricious foremen and respond with a psychological go slow. This 'master cause' objection is particularly damaging, since it is not necessary for an objector to actually identify a tangible master cause; to identify the logical possibility of its existence is enough to cast doubt on any cause and effect proposition.

Just as troublesome as the master cause is the medial cause. Where it appears that A leads to B, but it can in fact be demonstrated that A leads to X (something else) and in turn X leads to B, then X is the medial cause (and an inscrutable nuisance). Take as an example industrial trade unions and demarcation disputes. West Germany does have industrial trade unions (see Chapter 1) and does not have demarcaton disputes. An industrial union is one which is open to *all* employees in a given industry, irrespective of skill level and specialism. The labourers and the craftsmen, the tool room workers and the lads from the paint shop, the assembly line worker and the repair man, are all in the same union. So of course there cannot be any demarcation disputes, the proposition is true by definition. Is it? These various workers are doing different jobs and receiving different rates of pay for them. Why should not the tool room strike if they are being diluted by semi-skilled entrants transferred from the paint shop on medical grounds? So if there are no demarcation disputes something else must be involved. Maybe industrial unions promote solidarity, industrial brotherhood, a reciprocal awareness of hopes and aspirations with commensurate tolerance; or an intra-organisational juxtaposition of varied interests produces a fine spirit of reasonableness. The answer is obviously something like this, even if there is no way of pinning it down exactly. Here is the medial cause.

The medial cause is not as devastating as the master cause since it does not invalidate some kind of connection between the originally posited cause and effect, but it shifts the causal emphasis and makes it less certain that A will produce B in a different context. To project our industrial relations example, suppose that industrial unions of the West German kind were introduced in Britain in the hope of eliminating demarcation disputes. It might happen that the industrial union would not, in this changed cultural milieu, produce the same fine spirit of reasonableness. Or maybe the greater solidarity would find expression in multi-lateral support for the preservation of job boundaries (when management try to dilute the tool room the dispatch clerks strike as well). As with the master cause argument, it is not necessary to actually identify a medial cause to throw doubt on some cause and effect proposition. Knowing that it is a logical and empirical possibility is again enough.

The operational impasse, which leads to a situation in which most cause and effect propositions can be undermined by logical objections, is the fact that it is difficult or impossible to test conclusively the propositions whose truth we would like to be assured of. Consider, for instance, the German foreman again. German companies for the most part have foremen who are well-qualified and who do not have a morale or status problem. One would really like to know exactly what difference this makes to the effectiveness of a manufacturing company, yet there is no way one can take a company as a test case, subtract the foremen, check out the loss in effectiveness while holding everything else constant and quantify it.

The substance of these logical-experimental difficulties is that they prevent the unequivocal recognition of just causes of desirable end states. So there is no way of knowing whether some feature of the foreign country's system is worth imitating: maybe it does not lead to success, it just looks that way. If these difficulties could be overcome, however, one is faced with the question of cultural compatibility. To be sure of what makes for economic success in West Germany is one thing; to make it work in Great Britain is another. After all they are different societies, with a different history and culture.

It may be felt that this last argument is a little *pro forma*. One can always say that two countries are 'completely different in history and culture' but does it really amount to much in practice and are Britain and West Germany really so different? Gratifying as it would be to dismiss this cultural compatibility argument as so much anthropological temporising, it has to be admitted that there are some manifest differences between British and German society. If we exclude for the moment strictly managerial considerations there are still a miscellany of social-cultural differences some of which have been noted in previous chapters. West Germany, to resuscitate a few examples, has the highest murder rate in Europe. On the other hand it is marked by an industrial peace beyond the sweetest dreams of those who frame social contracts. It is more openly materialistic, more obsessed with work, more committed to *Leistung*, less class conscious, and unable to distinguish between Arts and Sciences. As to institutions, they have no monarchy, no comprehensive schools, no Eton and no Oxbridge; they have apprenticeship, *Fachhochschulen*, technical universities and state parliaments and something called *Technik*.

Yet these differences are nothing compared with the difference in historical experience. Germany is the *verspätete Nation* (belated nation) of Europe, only achieving political unity in 1871 and then divided again in 1945. For what happened in Germany during the twelve years of Nazi rule there is no comparison anywhere in the world and no foreigner can expect to understand 'the way it was'.[2] Other distinctive experiences include an acquaintanceship with rampant inflation in the early 1920s, defeat in two World Wars (Italy and Japan, Germany's principal allies in the Second World War had been on the winning side in the First World War), and material destruction and military occupation in the 1940s. When Burkhardt wrote: 'We wish experience to make us, not shrewder (for next time), but wiser (for ever)' Germany must have been his inspiration![3]

These sufferings are more acute when one makes the comparison with Britain. Germany did not pioneer parliamentary democracy, have the first industrial revolution, or possess a vast empire (just some belated landholdings in Africa which were confiscated at the end of the First World War). This dynamic bifurcation of historical experience reaches its apotheosis in 1945. Britain has behaved magnificently and can rest on her laurels: Germany has lost everything — the war, self-respect, moral credibility, political sovereignty, territory, control over the material apparatus of modern life, personal liberty, shelter and food. Britons at this time may well have felt that what they had to offer the world was moral leadership and steadfastness of purpose: Germans were tutored to think they should offer the world an apology and sought for themselves only the satisfaction of basic needs.

So these two countries really are different; the differences are especially marked with regard to the recent past and we have already discussed the implications of this fact for economic activity (Chapter 1). Neither can these differences be conjured out of existence by applying to Britain and West Germany (and their neighbours) general labels — modern societies, parliamentary democracies, advanced industrial societies and so on.

None of this is to say that one cannot in practice learn useful lessons from other countries with respect to a complex socio-culturally embedded entity such as industrial management. The situation is really more tantalisingly uncertain than this. One can try, it may work or it may not and there is no way of knowing in advance.

The difficulties and imponderables involved in attempts at international borrowing have been made clear because they are real, important and incalculable. It is also only fair to give readers a choice. The choice is between the academic and managerial models. In the first case one is opting for logical rectitude and experimental validation; they are unattainable so one must be cautious. In the second case one is opting for the best decision and course of action one can get in an imperfect world with half the facts missing and none of the outcomes clear. If the question we confront is, can Britain learn something from German management? the academic model leads to highly perceptive inaction. So perhaps the managerial model is also worth a try. There can be no appeal to logic or history, sociology or economics, only to common sense. After all the Germans have made this transition from rubble to riches. Thirty-five years ago they were living on bread-crumb soup in unheated cellars. They must have got something right. What is it?

They have learned to think about running business enterprises without appeal to a lot of debilitating stereotypes. Germans do not counterpose thought and action, intellectual ability and practical prowess, engineering knowledge and commercial aptitude, inventiveness and profits, professions and non-professions, detailed knowledge and 'the overall view', line and staff, production and maintenance, or work and style. That they do not is important for the people they recruit and the use they make of them. It enables German industry to recruit and 'domesticate' a lot of university graduates and PhD's. Not, or not only, those with poorish degrees who are 'not really very academic' but reckoned to 'have personality'. The ranks include some chosen precisely on account of their very good degrees, even chosen for being clever. And when these recruits reach the shop floor there is not a lot of agonising about whether they are going to act uppiry, patronise the chargehands, or come to terms with the 'real world'. One just does not hear in German companies the 'graduate atrocity stories' so common in Britain. An anecdote may capture the essence of the difference. The author was once told at a medium sized British company that 'once' they appointed an engineering graduate fresh from college. On the first day he was asked to sweep the floor; he refused, and was damned from then on for acting high and mighty. Now this just would not happen in a German company: the young graduate would have no novelty appeal, no one would particularly want to check him out for humility and the floor would have been swept at 7 o'clock by the labourer anyway. But if we could imagine the incident occurring in a German company, the graduate's response would probably be to sweep the floor with exemplary dispatch to show *Leistung*.

The philosophy works the other way as well. Not only are PhD's not stigmatised as 'highly educated but . . .'; one also hears less of the 'Of course he does a good job of work but if we promoted him would he have authority?' or 'He's a magnificent craftsman but could he give orders?' Knowledge and cleverness are valued, but without being put on a pedestal. And as they are not counterposed to anything, nothing else gets devalued. So respect for skill and craftsmanship and experience and non-codifiable practical knowledge is strong too.

This freedom from a lot of phoney antitheses has implications for the way manpower is used. Since the Germans do not see any antithesis between the enjoyment of specialised knowledge (or skill) and an aptitude for the exercise of authority they are able, to an appreciable extent, to build the staff into the line. This keeps the line strong. At the same time it takes some of the sting out of the traditional staff *versus* line conflict, since one of the lines of cleavage, the conspicuous cleverness of the staff *vis à vis* the line, is relatively absent.

Talent and activity anomalies flourish in this ethos. One sees junior managers without a university education having telephone discussions in English with their opposite numbers at subsidiaries in South America. There are line managers with patented inventions and technical articles to their credit and general managers personally involved in research. The engineers illustrate very well this coming together in the German scheme of things of theory and practice. They are *par excellence* the practical men of industry yet this does not preclude a kind of mature academic participation. A recent survey of German engineers showed that a quarter of the Ing Grads (non-graduates) and half the Dipl Ings (graduates) had published technical books and articles.[4] The number who had given papers at technical and scientific conferences was higher still, for graduates and non-graduates alike. Furthermore, something like a quarter of both graduates and non-graduates had patented technical inventions and it was interesting to note that having patented inventions correlated with career success measured by age-related salary.[5]

To sum up this issue, the relative absence of stereotyping described here is advantageous in two ways. First, it enables a better utilisation of talent. People's plus points are not cancelled out by a ritualistic ascription of corresponding weaknesses. And as there are less presumed incompatibilities more people are seen as capable of more tasks. Secondly, the kind of straight thinking for which we are praising German managers here means that there is more scope for more relevant criteria of recruitment and advancement. To put it another way, if there is evidence that German managers are not thinking in terms of such antitheses and presumptions their claim to advance individuals on the basis of *Leistung* (performance) is that much more credible.

A second cognitive achievement of the Germans is that they have kept their distance from the idea of management *per se* and certainly from management rhetoric. Now this is not an unambiguous gain, but it implies some advantages. Earlier on (Chapter 4) we discussed informed American criticism of German managerial practice and made the negative aspect clear. It is arguable, that is, that German companies lose something by being less accomplished than American ones in the areas of corporate planning and control, business manoeuvres and the utilisation of more managerially specialised staff advisers. But we would also like to argue that there are corresponding strengths.

Paradoxically, although the status of industry and thus that of its principal employees, is high in West Germany, there is not a great deal of concern about 'the status of management'.[6] Consequently there is not much investment of time and attention in measures presumed to raise the status of management and no energy is wasted on the 'is management professional?' debate, a proposition which is largely meaningless when not formulated in English. All this is gain: it leaves more time for work.

There is also a gain in the realism of expectations. The relatively slight engagement of Germans in the management movement means that they are less likely to expect that their problems will be solved, or the uncertainty taken out of executive life, by mastering the precepts of classical management, by exposure to 'management science', by Operations Research, or recourse to ever more sophisticated models of planning and decision-making. It is also noticeable that one hears less of the purely managerial formulations in Germany, such as Management by Objectives, Career Development, or Executive Job Evaluation.

The management idea is also a force for generalism and generalisation. If one abstracts management work, analyses it, treats it as a discrete entity and assigns to it its own laws and dynamics, then all this implies some depreciation of what it is that is being managed. So the pure manager does not care whether it is motor cars or mortgages, grapefruit or forklift trucks. But what it is that is managed *does* matter in the German scheme of things, because what they choose to emphasise is the product, its quality and knowledge and experience of it.

Finally, in connection with the management idea, German managers have avoided another pitfall. This management concept emphasises what is generalisable and systemic; it points away from daily operations and in the direction of planning and control. It represents the 'civilising influence' of head office not the hurly-burly of the plant. It is a kind of academic rationale for arms-length management. But this tendency runs counter to the German *Unternehmer* tradition (see Chapter 5). German managers have gained by rejecting the arms-length approach.

The direct involvement of senior managers in the here and now, the problem of Tuesday afternoon and the deadlines for Wednesday morning, is exactly what they are good at. And they will carry on being good at it so long as no one turns their heads with too much talk of Career Development.

Moving now to a new concern, it is noticeable that there is no particular mystique of authority in Geman companies. There is no fetish about having it, being fit for it, or in positions of it. It is not that positions of authority do not exist in German companies, but that there is more emphasis on the rational and less on the hierarchical element. Some forty years ago a one time President of the Bell Telephone Company, Chester Barnard, made the distinction between structural and sapiental authority.[7] By structural authority is meant the authority which attaches to positions in the hierarchy of formally constituted organisations, like the position of company president. Structural authority is thus an attribute of the position; it is independent of the personal qualities of particular incumbents. Sapiential authority is that which is based on knowledge (experience or skill). In his discussion of the bases of authority Barnard spoke of the desirability that the two should overlap; that structural authority should go hand in hand with sapiential authority.[8]

Now obviously this proposition is not to be treated as any kind of an absolute, but there are some reasons for thinking that German industry practises what Chester Barnard preached. One piece of evidence is linguistic. The word *Fach* in German denotes subject, specialism, or craft. It is used in a variety of compounds and the connotations are entirely favourable. Apart from *Facharbeiter* (ex-apprentice skilled worker) which has come up several times, there is *Fachkompetenz* (job proficiency), *Fachwissen* (specialist knowledge) and *Fachkenntnisse* (know-how in one's specialism). Like *Technik* (see Chapter 4) these are terms which are frequently used. Ask a German manager what are the requirements for such and such a post and one will be bombarded with *fachspezifisch* statements.

Another manifestation which has come up before is the practice of German companies to exploit the practical and experiential knowledge of workers and lower supervisors in what might be thought of as decision areas which were management's prerogative. The most obvious example is machinery purchase; not whether to buy, but what to buy. It is standard practice for someone with practical experience of working the relevant machine types — a skilled worker, charge hand, or foreman — to attend machinery purchase meetings, hold forth to the 'higher-ups' and critically examine the technical specifications sheets prepared by Engineering. It is also not uncommon for the same people to receive representatives from potential suppliers, or go on trips to examine machinery at trade fairs, manufacturers' premises, or *in situ* at some other firm.

'Going on trips' in the German context is another minor example of the best utilisation of relevant knowledge. When someone has to do something outside, or represent the company in some way, there is very little interest in the status of the emissary. Quite humble people, organisationally and socially, get sent so long as they are deemed to know enough about the matter in hand. This works the other way round as well. The author has on several occasions heard managers decline what sounded like quite enjoyable trips on the grounds that they did not know enough to deal with the issue concerned.

Another example of this concern with relevant knowledge and skill which has already been discussed in some detail (Chapter 7) is the German foreman. Indeed in the German system the *Meister* (foreman) is a perfect example of Barnard's sapiential authority. Selected on the basis of skill, experience and success in completing courses and passing the relevant exams, the *Meister* is in a strong position. If his authority were structural, or primarily so, he would have lost standing like his Anglo-American colleagues as a result of organisational and other change. As it is, the Germans, by operating a recruitment system for the first line supervisor with a strong sapiential base, have largely avoided 'the problem of the first line supervisor' much celebrated on both sides of the Atlantic.

And finally on this subject of the German penchant for sapiential authority the generally high level of formal qualifications among German managers should be cited, a topic dealt with in some detail in Chapters 3 and 6. With reference to any kind of constructive imitation by Britain, this particular lesson need not be learned particularly from West Germany; Japan or Belgium, Switzerland or Canada would do just as well as exemplars. Though the German management qualification profile fits very well the sapiential authority argument developed here. That is to say, the most manifestly relevant skill and knowledge in industry is technical and this is precisely where the qualifications of managers in West Germany are strongest.

Turning to another aspect of German industrial practice there is some suggestion that companies in West Germany have been practising what those who wish to improve the quality of the work experience call job enlargement. Or rather it is not so much that German companies have been enlarging jobs; it would appear that they did not practise such stringent division of labour in the first place. Now this is clearly a difficult proposition to document decisively, but some evidence for this has already been canvassed. The comparative study of French and German companies, with a parallel British study conducted later, which was discussed in Chapter 2, is very relevant here. The key finding is that in the German factories in the study the direct production workers constituted a higher proportion of the total company personnel. This means that there were proportionally less maintenance workers, less ancillary and ancillary technical employees and less staff specialists. This in turn means that production workers and line managers between them have done this work as well to a higher degree than was the case in the French and British companies in the study. And if we concentrate for a moment on the production workers in the German companies it is clear that they have larger jobs whether or not their jobs have actually been enlarged.

This claim is also entirely consistent with what we know about the German emphasis on training extensively both skilled and semi-skilled workers (see Chapter 8). The importance attached to the apprenticeship in Germany and even to the semi-apprenticeship for semi-skilled workers, is more meaningful when it is clear that these workers are expected, like their immediate supervisors (see Chapter 7), to take on more. They are more likely to do their own marking out, job setting, preventive maintenance, minor repairs and so on; more likely to be moved around (see Chapter 6) to suit the short-term exigencies of shop loading and more likely to be encouraged to develop *Einsatzbreite* (versatility) and be rewarded for it.[9]

If our diagnosis in this last matter is correct, namely that blue collar jobs in production in West Germany are larger — involve more work components, more skill, more versatility and more autonomy, or any combination of these factors — than the equivalent jobs in Britain and France, then this is pure gain for Germany. It is gain in the sense of the humanisation of work; in the sense of, *ceteris paribus*, enhanced worker involvement and gain in the sense of calling forth more skill and competence.

This leads us to another consideration. The German concept of *Technik* (see Chapter 4 for a detailed discussion and Chapter 5 for some practical illustrations) has a variety of implications for the operation of German industry and they are all positive. It tends to stress skill and technical knowledge and any courses and qualifications which demonstrate that people have acquired these. It tends to differentiate engineering from natural science and is a factor in the standing of the engineer in West Germany. It provides a kind of cultural underpinning to the prevalence of engineers in the management of German companies, a phenomenon explored in some detail earlier (Chapter 3 and Chapter 6). The role of engineers in German management, and it would scarcely be an exaggeration to speak of their dominance of German management, is again decisive for the corporate *modus operandi* in West Germany. This dominance of engineers, that is to say, is a standing, prestigious, articulate lobby for design, development, production and quality; for those things, in short, for which German industry is internationally rated. A side effect of this *Technik* culture cum engineers' dominance has also been explored at an earlier stage (Chapter 6). It has a homogenising influence on the technical side of the firm as a whole, tending to reduce functional rivalries and inter-departmental friction.

Now it will be clear that these German emphases are not the only way to make an economy work. But they do constitute *a* path to industrial success and one which has given West Germany one of the highest standards of living in the world. Perhaps paradoxically, German ideas of *Technik* have conditioned the approach to profits, this approach being both less overt and more successful. German companies show an implicit grasp of the fact that profits are not to be pursued directly. To use a grammatical metaphor, profit is never the direct object of the verb to make. Companies do not make money, only the mint does that; they make goods and services and if people want to buy them, profits ensue. In the author's experience there is far less obsession with the various indices of performance and profitability in German companies. But then they have a different obsession.

The German corporate obsession is products. Their design, construction and quality. This product orientation has already been discussed in some detail (Chapter 5). The tendency to enthuse endlessly about the firm's products is perhaps most marked with owner-managers. But the surprising thing is how widespread the tendency is. It is by no means confined to design engineers and production managers. A visitor to a German company will always be told about the product range whatever the purpose of his visit. And it is similarly taken for granted that he will want to see how and where they are made (not talk about management principles in the front office). One senses a generalised identification with the workplace among German managers, irrespective of their actual function. Symptomatic expressions of the type 'You *must* come and see final assembly' and 'We'll come back in half an hour and you can see them test this machine' seem to fall as naturally from the lips of personnel managers as production bosses.

A final issue we would like to urge concerns the idea of the status of industry. It is generally agreed that the status of industry in Britain is not high. This is not, as has been argued earlier, any kind of absolute determinant of performance, but its implications for recruitment and morale can only be negative. The status of industry in West Germany, on the other hand, is substantially higher, and the case for this claim, and its implications, have been discussed (Chapter 8). It follows that any measures to raise the standing of industry in Britain are to be welcomed and such a change could have only a positive effect. We wish to add both a word of warning and a supplement.

If the status of industry in Britain were to become as high as we believe it to be in West Germany this would mean that British managers would enjoy higher standing in the community and higher income than they do at present, both absolutely and relative to other middle-class occupational groups. The potential gains of this state of affairs are obvious (and it is probably true that the situation is already changing for the better). The word of warning is that this may well be a necessary condition for improvement, but it is unlikely to be a sufficient condition of greater industrial success. It is not likely, that is, to bring about a great change on its own. If one wished to play devil's advocate one could argue that if the status of industry in Britain were very high, such that to be an industrial manager accorded the same prestige as to be say an Ambassador, this could even have a de-motivating effect. What else would there be to aim for?

The supplement is to suggest that what has been claimed for the status of industry in West Germany stands, but is more cogent when considered in conjunction with another feature. One is aware of a strong sense of purpose among German managers. It is this, plus the quality of recruits, functioning in a thoroughly favourable environment of which the status of industry aspect is a major part, which yields an unbeatable combination. Indeed a major achievement of German industry has been to sustain the conviction that *Leistung* (performance) will be rewarded; and that this, and not some secondary criteria, will condition the individual's advancement.

Conclusion

This final chapter has confronted the question: is there anything that Britain can profitably learn from German management? It was argued that this whole question of learning from other countries is very uncertain. First, it may well be that there are a variety of ways of achieving the desired end — in this case good management as a contribution to national economic success. So if alternatives exist, why borrow? Maybe the potential borrower has a good way already. Secondly, it is difficult to know what should be borrowed because there are a range of logical and experimental barriers to ever being sure of the causes of success in the other country whose performance appears to be exemplary. And thirdly, there is again no way of knowing in advance that the 'methods' of one country will work in another country if they are adopted: there is, that is, the incalculable question of cultural compatibility.

At this point it was suggested that there is nevertheless another option. It is possible to ignore the difficulties and press on, being guided by common sense rather than formal logic. And to follow this option would at any rate be a *managerial* decision. We then discussed some of the strengths of German management, in its own context, but in the hope that something can be learned from these.

In deciding to emphasise certain aspects of German management to this end some choices have been made. First, we have tended to leave out the obvious things which 'everyone knows' (the exemplary strike record, the pattern of industrial relations, the effects of the War and so on) especially where these have been discussed in earlier chapters anyway. Instead we have pursued some of these aspects where more than a superficial acquaintance with Germany is needed for their appreciation. Secondly, we have also adopted a cost conscious policy, stressing not the purchase of the most expensive equipment but the development, *inter alia*, of some helpful states of mind. Scrapping debilitating stereotypes does not cost anything, can be regarded as a pleasure and entails no health risk.

Here it has been argued that Germans benefit from not setting up antitheses between practical and theoretical exigencies and by not stereotyping the human resources as to aptitude and limitation. Similarly German managers' relatively slight involvement in the management movement frees them from certain non-debates (for instance that concerning management's professional standing), from excessive management generalism and from the inanity of arms-length management. We then developed the idea that German companies are stronger for the fact that they emphasise the sapiential (knowledge and experience based) dimensions of authority and some manifestations of this phenomenon were discussed including the high overall level of educational attainment among German managers.

Some comparative research data were recalled to indicate that

German industry has probably practised less shop floor division of labour so that blue collar jobs tend to be larger. In so far as this is the case it represents a gain in terms of humanisation, commitment and the elucidation of skill.

Some of the implications of the German concept of *Technik* were then discussed. It tends to value skill and technical knowledge and to underpin the important role of the engineer in German industrial management. The dominance of the engineers in turn guarantees an emphasis on design, production, and quality. German companies tend to be alike in the considerable emphasis they place on product quality and this appears to take priority over an overt concern with profits. Finally the status of industry argument was again briefly reviewed and it was argued that this consideration is important especially when accompanied by a strong sense of purpose and a meritocratic climate.

Notes

1. Private Prewitt in James Jones' novel *From Here to Eternity*.
2. This phrase is in fact the title of a recent autobiographical account of life in the Third Reich by a left wing German novelist: Max von der Grün, *Wie war das eigentlich?* (Luchterhand Verlag, Darmstadt, 1979).
3. Jacob Burkhardt, *Reflexions on History* (George Allen & Unwin, London, 1943).
4. S. P. Hutton, P. A. Lawrence and J. H. Smith, 'The Recruitment, Deployment, and Status of the Mechanical Engineer in the German Federal Republic', 2 vols., Report to the Department of Industry, London, 1977.
5. Ibid.
6. An arguable exception to this claim is that the mid-seventies debate about the extension of the co-determination system gave rise to some soul searching and grievance articulation on the part of middle-management on the subject of what should be their share in the new system. See Heinz Hartmann, Erika Bock-Rosenthal and Elvira Helmer, *Leitende Angestellte: Selbstverständnis und Kollektive Forderungen* (Luchterhand Verlag, Neuwied, 1973).
7. Chester I. Barnard, *The Functions of the Executive* (Harvard University Press, Cambridge, Mass., 1938).
8. Ibid., Chapter 12.
9. This line of argument is also developed in Michael Fores, Peter Lawrence and Arndt Sorge, 'Why Germany Produces Better', *Management Today* (November 1978).

BIBLIOGRAPHY*

Arbeitsgemeinschaft Selbständiger Unternehmer e.V 'Selbständiger Unternehmer', 1967
Arndt, Hans Joachim, *West Germany: Politics of Non-planning* (Syracuse University Press, New York, 1966)
Barford, Edward, 'Reminiscences of a Lance-corporal of Industry' (Hamish Hamilton, London, 1972)
Barnett, Correlli, 'Technology, Education and Industrial and Economic Strength', Cantor Lecture delivered to Royal Society of Arts, London, November 1978
Bayer, Hermann and Lawrence, Peter, 'Engineering, Education and the Status of Industry', *European Journal of Engineering Education*, no. 2 (1977)
— 'An Emphasis on the Practical in the Land of Idealism', *Times Higher Education Supplement*, 14 January 1977
Beaud, Michel, *La Croissance de l'Allemagne de l'Ouest (1949-62)* (Editions Cujas, Paris, 1965)
Böll, Heinrich, *Children are Civilians Too* (Penguin Books, Harmondsworth, 1976)
— *Gruppenbild mit Dame* (Kiepenheuer u. Witsch, Köln, 1971)
Booz, Allen and Hamilton Report, English translation, in 'German Management', *International Studies of Management and Organisation*, Arts and Science Press Inc. (Spring/Summer 1973)
Borsdorf, Ulrich and Niethammmer, Lutz (eds.), *Zwischen Befreiung und Besatzung* (Peter Hammer Verlag, Wuppertal, 1977)
Brett-Smith, Richard, *Berlin '45: The Grey City* (Macmillan, London, 1966)
Bridgemans, Tessa and Fox, Irene, 'Why People Choose Private Schools', *New Society*, 29 June 1978
Brinkmann, G., *Die Ausbildung von Führungskräften für die Wirtschaft* (Universitätsverlag Michael Wienand, Köln, 1967)
British Institute of Management, *Front Line Management* (London, 1976)
Brockway, Fenner, *German Diary* (Victor Gollancz, London, 1946)
Brossard, Michel and Maurice, Marc, 'Existe-il un Modèle Universel des Structures d'Organisation?', *Sociologie du Travail* (1974)

* A few works of fiction, evocative of the German mood or experience, have been included.

Business Graduates Association, 'Higher Management Education and the Production Function' (London, 1977)
Capital, no. 4, 'Jeder dritte Manager hat nicht studiert' (1964)
Carlson, Sune, *Executive Behaviour* (Strömbergs, Stockholm, 1951)
Catt, Ivor, *The Catt Concept* (Rupert Hart-Davis, London, 1972)
— 'Management against Innovation', *The Business Graduate*, vol. VI, no. 2 (Summer 1976)
Child, John, 'The Industrial Supervisor', The University of Aston Management Centre Working Paper Series, no. 33, 1975
Child, John and Kieser, Alfred, 'Organisation and Managerial Roles in British & West German Companies — an Examination of the Culture Free Thesis', University of Aston Management Centre, Working Paper Series, no. 39, April 1975
Clark, D. G., *The Industrial Manager: His Background and Career Patterns* (Business Publications Ltd., London, 1966)
Clay, L. D., *Decision in Germany* (Heinemann, London, 1950)
Cleverley, Graham, 'Managers and Magic' (Penguin Books, Harmondsworth, 1971)
Cohen, L. and Derrick, T., 'Occupational Values and Stereotypes in a Group of Engineers', *British Journal of Industrial Relations*, vol. 8 (1970) pp. 100-4
Cooper, Matthew, *The German Army 1933-45* (Macdonald & Janes, London, 1978)
Cotgrove, Stephen and Box, Steven, *Science, Industry and Society* (Allen & Unwin, London, 1970)
Crawley, A. M., *The Rise of Western Germany, 1945-72* (Bobbs-Merrill, Indianapolis, 1973)
Cullingford, E. C. M., *Trade Unions in Western Germany* (Wilton House Publications, London, 1976)
Department of Industry (discussion paper), 'Industry, Education and Management', London, July 1977
Drucker, Peter F., *The Effective Executive* (Harper & Row, New York, 1966)
— *The Age of Discontinuity* (William Heinemann, London, 1969)
Dubin, Robert, Homans, George C., Mann, Floyd C. and Miller, Debert C., *Leadership and Productivity* (Chandler Publishing Company, California, 1965)
Dudley, N. A., 'Industrial Productivity — Scope for Improvement', West Midlands Economic Planning Paper no. 8, 1975
Dunlop, J. K., *A Short History of Germany* (Oswald Wolff, London, 1968)

Dyas, Gareth P. and Thanheiser, Hanz T., *The Emerging European Enterprise* (Macmillan, London, 1976)
Ebsworth, Raymond, *Restoring Democracy in Germany: the British Contribution* (Stevens & Son Ltd, London, 1960)
Engelmann, Bernt, *Meine Freunde die Manager* (Deutscher Taschenbuch Verlag, Munich, 1969)
Fallada, Hans, *Ein Mann will nach oben* (Rowohlt, Reinbek bei Hamburg, 1970)
Fassbender, Siegfried, 'Management and its Environment in Germany' in Joseph L. Massie and Jan Luytens (eds.), *Management in an International Context* (Harper & Row, New York, 1972)
Flenley, Ralph and Spencer, Robert, *Modern German History* 4th edn (Dent, London, 1968)
Fletcher, Colin, 'The End of Management' in John Child (ed.), *Man and Organisation* (Allen & Unwin, London, 1973)
Fores, Michael, 'Engineering and the British Economic Problem', *Quest*, no. 22 (Autumn 1972)
— 'Science of Science: a Substantial Fraud', *Higher Education Review* (Summer, 1977)
Fores, Michael and Glover, Ian 'The British Disease: Professionalism', *Times Higher Education Supplement*, 24 February 1978
Fores, Michael and Glover, Ian, *Manufacturing and Management* (HMSO, London, 1978)
Fores, Michael, Lawrence, Peter and Sorge, Arndt, 'Germany's Front Line Force', *Management Today* (March 1978)
— 'Why Germany Produces Better', *Management Today* (November 1978)
Fores, Michael and Sorge, Arndt, 'The Rational Fallacy', Discussion Paper of the Internationales Institut für Management, Berlin, 1978
Galtung, Johan, *The European Community: A Superpower in the Making* (Allen & Unwin, London, 1973)
Gerstl, J. E. and Hutton, S. P., *Engineers: the Anatomy of a Profession* (Tavistock Press, London, 1966)
Gill, Roger, 'Why we need a Personnel Policy for Production Management', *Personnel Management* (February 1978)
— 'The Production Hang Up', *Management Today* (January 1979)
Gill, R. W. T. and Lockyer, K. G., *The Career Development of the Production Manager in British Industry*, (British Institute of Management, London, 1979)
Gimbel, John, *A German Community under American Occupation: Marburg 1945-52* (University Press, Stanford, California, 1961)

Bibliography

Glover, Ian A., 'The Backgrounds of British Managers: A Review of the Evidence', Report presented to the Department of Industry, London, 1974
— 'Executive Career Patterns: Britain, France, Germany and Sweden', *Energy World* (December 1976)
— 'Managerial Work: A Review of the Evidence', Report to the Department of Industry, London 1977
Gollancz Victor, *In Darkest Germany* (Victor Gollancz, London, 1947)
Granick, David, *The European Executive* (Doubleday, New York, 1962)
Grosser, Alfred, *Germany in Our Time* (Pelican Books, Harmondsworth, 1970)
Grün, Max von der, *Am Tresen gehen die Lichter aus* (Rowohlt, Reinbek bei Hamburg, 1974)
— *Wie war das eigentlich?* (Luchterhand Verlag GmbH & Ko KG, Darmstadt u. Neuwied, 1979)
Hall, David, de Bettignies, H. Cl. and Fischgrund, G. Amado, 'The European Business Elite', *European Business* (October 1969)
Hartmann, Heinz, 'Der zahlenmässige Beitrag der deutschen Hochschulen zur Gruppe der industriellen Führungskräfte', *Zeitschrift für die gesamte Staatswissenschaft*, vol. 112, no. 1 (1956)
— *Authority and Organisation in German Management* (Princeton University Press, 1959)
— 'Managers and Entrepreneurs: A Useful Distinction', *Administrative Science Quarterly* (1959)
Hartmann, Heinz, Bock-Rosenthal, Erika and Helmer, Elvira, *Leitende Angestellte: Selbstverständnis und Kollektive Forderungen* (Luchterhand Verlag, Neuwied, 1973)
Hartmann, Heinz and Wienold, Hans, *Universität und Unternehmer* (Bertelsmann, Gutersloh, 1967)
Hazelgrove, H. L. (Chairman), 'Report of the Committee on Technician Courses and Examinations' (HMSO, London, 1969)
Heller, Frank and Wilpert, Bernhard, 'Limits to Participative Leadership: Task, Structure and Skill as Contingencies – a German British Comparison', *European Journal of Social Psychology*, vol. 7, no. 1 pp. 661-84
Hissocks, Richard, *Germany Revived: An Appraisal of the Adenauer Era* (Victor Gollancz, London, 1968)
Hopper, Kenneth, 'The Growing Use of College Graduates as Foremen', *Management of Personnel Quarterly*, vol. 6, no. 2 (Summer 1967)

Hudson Report, 'The United Kingdom in 1980' (Hudson Institute, 1974)

Hutton, S. P., Lawrence, P. A. and Smith, J. H., 'The Recruitment, Deployment and Status of the Mechanical Engineer in the German Federal Republic', 2 vols., Report to the Department of Industry, London, 1977

Hutton, S. P. and Lawrence, P. A., 'Production Managers in Britain and Germany', Interim Report to the Department of Industry, 1978

Jenkins, David, *Supervisory Selection and Training in Manufacturing Industry* (Staples Press Ltd, London, 1966)

Jones, Robert and Marriott, Oliver, *Anatomy of a Merger* (Jonathan Cape, London, 1970)

Kahn, Hermann, *The Next 200 Years* (Associated Business Programmes Ltd, London, 1976)

Kemper, John Dustin, *The Engineer and His Profession* (Holt, Rinehart and Winston, New York, 1967)

Kogon, Eugon, *Die Stunde der Ingenieure* (VDI Verlag, Düsseldorf, 1976)

Körber, Kurt A., *Gespräch mit sowjetischen Wirtschaftspraktikern* (Hauni Werke Körber, Hamburg, 1962)

— *Ein Unternehmer reist durch die Sowjetunion* (Hauni Werke Körber, Hamburg, 1967)

Krause-Burger, Sibylle, 'Allein die Leistung zählt', *Die Zeit*, 23 April 1976

Kruk, Max, *Die oberen 30,000* (Wiesbaden, Betriebswirtschaflicher Verlag Gabler, Frankfurt, 1972)

— *Die Grossen Unternehmer* (Societätsverlag, Frankfurt, 1972)

Laboratoire d'Economie et de Sociologie du Travail, *Production de la Hiérarchie dans l'Entreprise: Recherche d'un Effet Social Allemagne –France*, 2 vols. (Aix-en-Provence, October 1977)

Lawrence, Peter, 'German lessons for Non-graduate Engineers', *The International Journal of Mechanical Engineering Education*, vol. 5, no. 2 (April 1977)

— 'It's the Product that Counts', *CBI Review* (Winter 1977/8)

— 'The Engineer and Society', *Energy World* (May 1978)

— 'Executive Head Hunting', *New Society* (May 1978)

Lehndorf, Hans von, *East Prussian Diary* (Oswald Wolff, London, 1963)

Lutz, B. and Kammerer G., *Das Ende des graduierten Ingenieurs* (Europäische Verlagsanstalt, Frankfurt a.m.-Koln, 1975)

McGregor, Peter, 'One Board or Two', *The Business Graduate*, vol. VIII, no. 3 (Autumn 1978)

MacInnes, Colin, *To the Victor the Spoils* (Penguin Books, Harmondsworth, Middlesex, 1966)
McQuillan, M. K., *Graduate Engineers in Production* (Cranfield Institute of Technology, August 1978)
Malik, Rex, *What's Wrong with British Industry* (Penguin Books, Harmondsworth, 1964)
Mansfield, Katherine, *In a German Pension* (Penguin Books, Harmondsworth, 1964)
Mant, Alistair, *The Rise and Fall of the British Manager* (Macmillan, London, 1977)
Maurice, Rita, *National Accounts and Statistics: Sources and Methods* (HMSO, London, 1968)
May, Brigitte, 'Social, Educational and Professional Background of German Management', Report to the Department of Industry, London, Autumn 1974)
Melen, Brigitte, 'Un Patron Allemand Face á ses Cadres', *La Vie des Cadres*, no. 5 (December 1972)
Melrose-Woodman, J., 'Profile of the British Manager', Management Survey Report no. 38, British Institute of Management, 1978
Miller, Gordon W., 'Some Aspects of the Interface between Higher Education and Industry in the United Kingdom', Paper given to the European Association for Research and Development in Higher Education, University of Klagenfurt, Austria, January 1979
Mintzberg, H., *The Nature of Managerial Work* (Harper & Row, New York, 1973)
— 'The Manager's Job: Folklore and Fact', *Harvard Business Review* (July-August 1973)
New, C. C., 'Managing Manufacturing Operations', Management Survey Report no. 35, British Institute of Management, 1976
Nichols, Theo, *Ownership Control and Ideology* (Allen & Unwin, London, 1969)
Nimmergut, Jorg, *Deutschland in Zahlen* (Wilhelm Heyne Verlag, München, 1974)
Oppelt, Claus, 'Ingenieure im Beruf', Max-Planck-Institut für Bildungsforschung, Berlin, 1976
Panic, M., *The UK and West German Manufacturing Industry 1954-72* (NEDO, London, 1976)
Payne, J. P. (ed.), *Germany Today: Introductory Studies* (Methuen, London, 1971)
Penguin Survey of Business and Industry (Penguin Books, Harmondsworth, 1965)

Piettre, André, *L'Economie Allemande Contemporaire (Allemagne Occidentale) 1945-52* (Librairie de Medicis, Paris, 1952)
Political and Economic Planning Ltd, *Attitudes in British Management: A PEP Report* (Pelican Books, Harmondsworth, 1966)
Prabhu, Vas and Russell, John, 'The Man with his Head on the Block', *The Production Engineer* (May 1979)
Prandy, Kenneth, *Professional Employees: A Study of Scientists and Engineers* (Faber and Faber, London, 1965)
Pross, Helga and Boetticher, Karl, *Manager des Kapitalismus* (Suhrkamp, Frankfurt, 1971)
Radford, J. D. and Richardson, D. B., *The Management of Production* (Macmillan, London, 1963)
Read, Piers Paul, *The Junkers* (Secker and Warburg, London, 1968)
Revell, Jack and Roe, Alan, 'National Balance Sheets and National Accounting – a Progress Report', *Economic Trends* (May 1971)
Roethlisberger, F. J., 'The Foreman: Master and Victim of Double Talk', *Harvard Business Review* (1945)
— 'Training Supervisors in Human Relations', *Harvard Business Review* (1951)
Rothwell, Roy, 'Where Britain Lags Behind', *Management Today* (November 1978)
Sawistowski, H., 'Chemical Engineering Education in Germany', *The Chemical Engineer* (February 1978)
Schoenberg, Hans W., *Germans from the East* (Martinus Nijhoff, The Hague, 1970)
Servan-Schreiber, Jean-Jacques, *Le Défi Americain* (Editions Danöel, Paris, 1967)
Snow, C. P., 'The Two Cultures and the Scientific Revolution', The Rede Lecture, 1959
Sofer, Cyril, *Men in Mid-career: a Study of British Managers and Technical Specialists* (Cambridge University Press, Cambridge, 1970)
Sorge, Arndt and Warner, Malcolm, 'Variety and Determinants of Factory Organisation in Britain, France and Germany: The United Kingdom National Report', Social Science Research Council, Fall 1977
— 'Manufacturing Organisation and Work Roles in Great Britain and West Germany', Discussion Paper of the Internationales Institut für Management, Berlin, 1978
— 'The Societal and Organisational Context of Industrial Relations', Discussion Paper of the Internationales Institut für Management, Berlin, 1978

Spender, S., *The European Witness* (Hamish Hamilton, London, 1946)
Stewart, Rosemary, *Contrasts in Management* (McGraw Hill (UK) Limited, Maidenhead, 1976)
Sylvestre, J. J., 'Industrial Wage Differentials: a Two-way Comparison', *International Labour Review*, vol. 110, no. 6 (1971)
Thurley, Keith and Wirdenius, Hans, *Supervision: A Reappraisal* (Heinemann, London, 1973)
Toynbee, Polly, 'The Academic Sample', *The Guardian*, 24 July 1978
Tugendhat, Christopher, *The Multinationals* (Penguin Books, Harmondsworth, 1974)
Wallich, Henry C., *Mainsprings of the German Revival* (Yale University Press, New Haven, Conn., 1955)
Wallraff, Günter, *Industrie-Reportagen* (Rowohlt, Reinbek bei Hamburg, 1970)
Warner, W. Lloyd and Abegglen, James C., *Big Business Leaders in America* (Harper & Brothers, New York, 1965)
Weinshall, Theodore D., *Culture and Management* (Penguin Books, Harmondsworth, 1977)
Willatt, Norris, 'The Lesson Linde Learnt', *Management Today*, (April 1978)
Williams, Roger, *European Technology: The Politics of Collaboration* (Croom Helm, London, 1973)
Williams, Trevor, *The Chemical Industry* (Penguin Books, Harmondsworth, 1953)
Willis, F. R., *The French in Germany, 1945-9* (Stanford University Press, Stanford, California, 1962)
Witte, Eberhard u. Bronner, Rolf, *Die Leitenden Angestellten* 2 vols. (Verlag C. H. Beck, München, 1975)
Woodward, J., *Industrial Organisation: Theory and Practice* (Oxford University Press, Oxford, 1965)
Woodward, J. (ed.), *Industrial Organisation: Behaviour and Control* (Oxford University Press, Oxford, 1970)
Wormald, Avison, *International Business*, Pan Management Series (Pan, London, 1973)
Young, Gordon, *The Fall and Rise of Alfried Krupp* (Cassell, London, 1960)
Zapf, W., 'Die deutschen Manager — Sozial profil und Karrierweg' in W. Zapf (ed.), *Beiträge zur Analyse der deutschen Oberschicht*, 2nd ed. (Piper, München, 1965)

INDEX

Abitur 62, 63, 65, 70, 83, 110, 165-6, 167-8
Aix-en-Provence 51
Aktiengesellschaft (AG) 31, 39, 53, 112
Aktiengesetz 31, 43
American influence in Germany 85-8
American view of German Management 89-92
American Zone 20, 86
apprenticeship 115-16, 132, 158, 165-6, 172
Arbeitsdirektor 45, 47, 48
'arms-length' management 124, 183
Aufsichtsrat 36-7, 40, 44, 45, 46, 47, 49, 53, 56, 67, 69, 71, 72, 80, 104

Baden-Württemberg 115
Banklehre 165
Barnard, Chester 184-5
Berlin 10, 15, 31, 32, 59, 109, 137
Berlin Wall 18
Betriebsrat 47, 134, 135 *see also* Works Council
Betriebsverfassungsgesetz 45
black Market 10
Böckler, Hans 24
Bonn 31, 136
Bremen 61
British influence 86
British Occupation Zone 24
British Zone 10, 11, 20, 86
Bundeskanzler 23
Bundesverfassungsgericht 23
Bundeswirtschaftsministerium 88

co-determination 30, 42-9
Cologne 7, 9, 59
Common Market 90
concentration camp 22, 25
context of production management in West Germany: engineering qualifications 131; power cuts 136; punctuality 132-3; status of industry 131; weather 136-7; work ethic 131-3
cost reduction 91
Currency Reform 19-20, 25
Czechoslovakia 8, 12, 18, 59

delegation 90
Deutsche Arbeiter Front 25
Deutscher Gewerkschaftsbund (DGB) 24
Deutschmark 20
die Stunde 0 8, 27
Diploma in Management Studies 68, 76
discounted cash flow 89
dismantling 13-15
Düsseldorf 7, 32
Düsseldorf Industry Club 44

economic miracle 13, 26, 83
educational background of German managers: assessment of data 75-7; comparisons with Britain 67-8; examples of qualifications at the top 77-9; limitations of evidence 67; main subjects studied 67; owner-managers 74-5; particular surveys 68-77; standing of engineers 79-82
education system and qualifications in West Germany: apprenticeship 64-5; international management education 64; management education 63-4; no undergraduate courses in management 63; subjects studied and later career 62-3; vocational courses 65-7

Einzelfirma 30
Erhard, Ludwig 21
Essen 7
extermination camps 17

Facharbeiter 115, 118, 158, 159, 165, 184
Facharbeiterbrief 64, 70, 165
Fachhochschule 65-6, 75, 77, 81, 83, 88, 109, 111, 115, 179
Fachhochschulreife 65-6
First World War 25, 43, 180
Ford factory 9
foreman in West Germany: German foreman at work 159-61; standing 156-9; training 158-9
France 14, 16, 17, 31, 50
Franco-Prussian War 13

200 Index

Frankfurt 7, 9, 31, 32, 136
French influence 86
French Occupation Zone 13-14
French Zone 20, 86

German Democratic Republic 18, 23, 59
Germany 1945 plus: malnutrition 6, 9-11; material destruction 6-9
Geschäftsführer 69, 70, 78, 79, 139, 164
Geschäftsführung 39, 53, 68, 73, 77, 78, 80, 107, 112, 139
Gesellschaft mit beschränkter Haftung (GmbH) 31, 39, 78, 164
Government and Relief in Occupied Areas (GARIOA) 16
Great War 13
Gross National Product (GNP) of West Germany and other countries 1-2, 11
Grundgesetz 23
Gymnasium 59, 60, 62, 70, 71, 72, 75, 83

Habilitation 64
Hamburg 7, 31, 32
Handwerkslehre 64
Hanover 32
Hauptschule 61
Hauptversammlung 36
Hitler 21, 44
Hungary 18

IG Farben 9
industrial concentration 32-5
industrial democracy; a summary 42-9; assessment 48-9; the formal system 42-6
industrial unions 24, 134, 178
Industrie-Kaufmann 65
Industrielehre 64
Industrie und Handelskammer 158
inflation, West Germany and other countries 3-4
Informationsrecht 45

Kassel 7, 8
Kommandit Gesellschaft (KG) 30, 31, 53, 78
Königsberg 17, 18
kaufmännische Lehre 65, 165

learning from Germany: debilitating stereotypes 181-3; inherent difficulties 176-81; *Leistung* and the status of industry 188; management concept 182-3; product obsession 187-8; rejections of 'arms-length' management 183-4; sapiental authority 184-5; job enlargement 185-6; *Technik* 186-7
legal status of German firms 30-1
Leistung 61, 101, 111, 113, 122, 179, 181, 182
leitende Angestellten 40, 46, 47, 48, 93, 95

Management Information Systems 91
manufacturing company as bureaucracy 50-3
Marburg 60, 87
Marshall Aid (European Recovery Programme) 11, 13, 15-17, 19, 21, 49
Meister 138, 157, 158, 159, 185
Meisterbrief 65, 158
Mitbestimmung 42-9
Mitbestimmungsgesetz 45
Mitbestimmungsrecht 45
Mittlere Reife 62, 110
Mitwirkungsrecht 46
Montanindustrie 44, 45, 46, 47, 48, 70
Munich 31, 32

National Socialist 25, 27, 44
nature of German management: collegial aspect 93; concept of management 93; diversification 95; German view of marketing 94; goals of the company 93; management techniques 93; non-American 92; non-doctrinaire 92-3; self-sufficient 93; *unternehmer* tradition 94-5
Nazism 12; nazi party 25; nazi period 21; nazi propaganda 86; nazi regime 17; nazi rule 25, 180; nazis 19, 24, 25; nazi seizure of power 44; nazi takeover 22; victims 13
new machines 12-13

Occupation 11, 21, 44
Occupation period 11, 19, 21, 27
Occupaying Powers 12, 13, 14, 16, 18, 25, 26
Oder-Neisse 9, 18

offene Handelsgesellschaft 30
Opel 32
Operations Research 90-1, 183

Poland 9, 17, 18, 19, 59
political stability 22-4
Praktiker 73, 74
Praktikum 110, 115, 171
problem of the first line supervisor 152-5; in Germany 155-6
Procter and Gamble 32
production management: British research on production management 125-9; German production management and strikes 135; organisational dimension 144-7; production and relations with other functions 140-4; qualifications of production managers and those in other functions 137-40; relativising the British findings 129-30; status of production 148-50; worker deployment in German firms 134-5
Prokurist 69, 71

Realschule 62
Reichsmark 19, 20
refugees 17-19, 27
Royal Air Force (RAF) 13
Ruhr 15, 44, 107, 115, 160
Russia 13, 17, 18, 23, 104
Russian occupation 17
Russian Occupation Zone 18, 23, 59
Russian Zone 15, 19, 59

Saarbrücken 7
Schleswig-Holstein 136
Schmidt, Helmut 47, 164
Schumacher, Kurt 22
Second World War 1, 11, 17, 26, 27, 180
Siemens 31
social background of German managers: *Beamtenschaft* origins 58; class origins 56-8; elitist school background 59-60; geographical 58-9; religious 58; university background 60-1
Social Market Economy 20, 21, 27, 28
Soziale Marktwirtschaft 20
standing of industry in Germany: British and German apprenticeship 166-7; engineers in industry and the public sector 170-2; implications of industry's standing 172-4; in salary terms 163-4; subject choices of students 167-9; training of employees 164-6
strike record of West Germany and other countries 5-6
Stuttgart 32, 160

Technik 38, 82, 96-9, 100, 119-20, 122, 124, 141, 142, 145, 150, 159, 179, 184, 190
Techniker 81, 139
Technikerprüfung 65
technische Hochschule 63, 79
Termin (and derivatives) 101, 147-8, 150, 160, 177
trade surplus 2-3
trade union structure 24-5
tuberculosis 10
Two Cultures 96
two-tier board 30, 36-42
typhus 8

unemployment-West Germany and other countries 4-5
United States Army Air Force (USAAF) 13
Unternehmer/Unternehmer tradition 94-5, 99, 111, 117, 122, 124, 149, 150, 157, 183

views of German managers: abstraction 102; authoritariansim 114-15; capitalism and competition 104; civil service 105; classless society 106-7; defensiveness 103; firm as de-economised 105; human relations 102; on Britain 120-1; personal career 108-11; practicality 115-16; professionalism 103; problems 117-19; punctuality 117; stereotyping 111-14; team work 116-17; work and punctuality 101
vocabulary of German managers 101-3
Volkswagen 31, 32, 104, 164
Vorstand, powers and composition 37-42, 45, 47, 48, 49, 53, 56, 67, 68, 70, 71, 72, 73, 74, 77, 80, 90, 93, 95, 104, 107, 110, 112, 139, 140, 164
Vorstand Technik 37, 39

202   *Index*

Weimar 22, 23, 24
Wiesbaden 7
Wirtschaftsausschuss 46.
Works Council 43, 46, 47, 49, 54,
   93, 134-5, 156

Zusammenbruch 8, 19